IRONCLAD

PAUL CLANCY

IRONCLAD

THE EPIC BATTLE,
CALAMITOUS LOSS, AND
HISTORIC RECOVERY OF
THE USS *MONITOR*

International Marine / McGraw-Hill

Camden, Maine • New York • Chicago • San Francisco
Lisbon • London • Madrid • Mexico City • Milan • New Delhi
San Juan • Seoul • Singapore • Sydney • Toronto

The **McGraw·Hill** Companies

Visit us at: www.internationalmarine.com

1 2 3 4 5 6 7 8 9 DOC DOC 9 8 7 6

Library of Congress Cataloging-in-Publication Data
Clancy, Paul R., 1939-
Ironclad : The epic battle, calamitous loss, and historic recovery
of the USS *Monitor* / Paul Clancy.
p. cm.
Includes bibliographical references and index.
ISBN 0-07-143132-2
1. *Monitor* (Ironclad) 2. Hampton Roads, Battle of, Va., 1862.
3. Shipwrecks—North Carolina—Hatteras, Cape.
4. Underwater archaeology—North Carolina—Hatteras, Cape.
5. Excavations (Archaeology)—North Carolina—Hatteras, Cape.
6. Hatteras, Cape (N.C.)—Antiquities.
7. United States—History—Civil War, 1861-1865—Naval operations.
I. Title.
E595.M7C55 2005
973.7'52—dc22
2005008643

Image on title page: Wreck of the *Monitor*, print from a wood engraving
in *Harper's Weekly*, January 24, 1863. (Mariners' Museum)

For my grandfather Jim
As ever aye.

CONTENTS

Photos may be found following page 182.

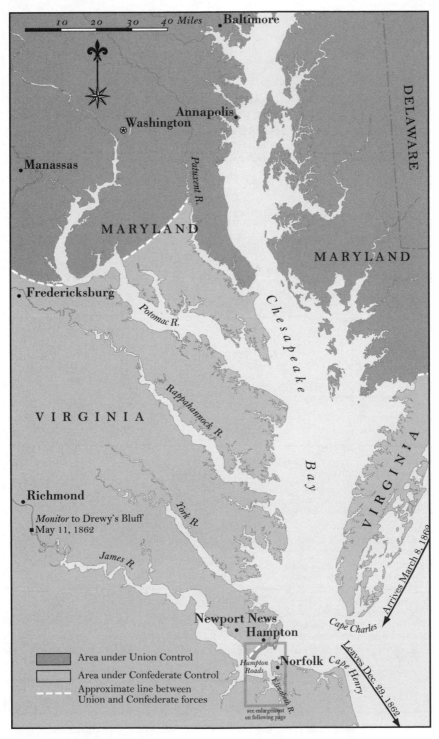

The Naval Theater, 1862. (Map by International Mapping)

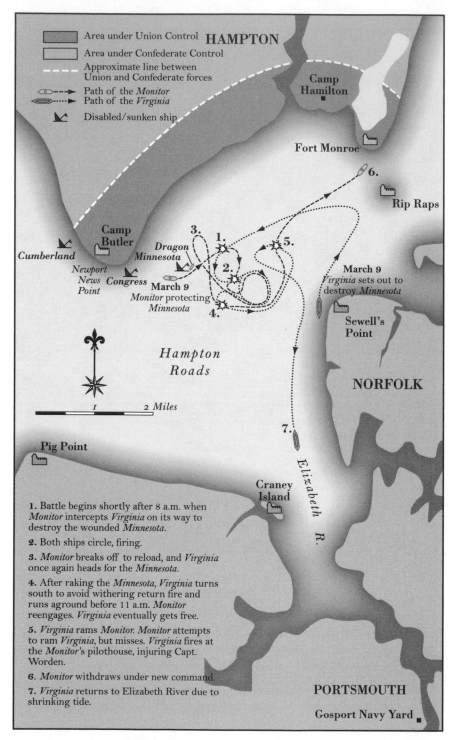

Battle of the Ironclads at Hampton Roads. (Illustration by International Mapping, based on a map by Robert E. Pratt)

PROLOGUE

OWN THROUGH the deep ocean we dive, silver fish pulsing around us, cobalt blue sliding toward gray as the light fades. It is surprisingly serene here in the cockpit of a bubble-faced submersible, with soft, confident voices burbling in my earphones—except that my heart is racing. We are about to drop in on one of the most intriguing shipwrecks of all time, the plucky, improbable ironclad that on a cool dawn 140 years ago saved the day and, just possibly, the United States of America.

Lights from the sub illuminate yellowtails and amberjacks as we plunge through the depths: 150, 180, 200 feet, white letters superimposed on a small monitor inform us. It feels as though we're falling through limitless space, but suddenly the flat, sandy bottom zooms up at us like the view through a camera lens. The sub's captain eases our vessel forward with toggle-switch commands and we lope across a desert-like bottom. Slowly, out of the gloom, a dark shape creeps into focus.

"We've got the wreck in sight," the captain purrs into his headset to the mother ship above. "We're at the stern, coming right up on the turret."

"Beautiful, absolutely beautiful," exclaims the historian from his aft observation chamber, an edge of excitement in his voice. "This is something you've heard about all your life," he says, "and here it is, right before your eyes, the USS *Monitor*."

The historic Civil War ironclad with revolving turret is lying where she came to rest almost ten months after her fierce battle with the CSS

1

Virginia, the menacing metamorphosis of the once-proud Union ship *Merrimack.*

The souls entombed in the *Monitor*—those few who were not swept overboard into the tumultuous Atlantic but went down with the ship— have made the wreck hallowed ground. They could not have imagined in the last seconds of their lives that divers from another century, breathing mixed gases, wearing video cameras on their helmets, sustained by warm water coursing through their dive suits—not to mention scientists and writers in battery-powered submersible vehicles equipped with carbon dioxide scrubbers—would one day pay them a visit and perhaps carry their bones to a final resting place.

We've crept directly up to the turret, that signature feature of the ship that allowed Yankee gunners to bedevil their Confederate counterparts, firing at will from almost any angle. It looks even stranger now than it must have in 1862; it lies upside down, with only a segment of it jutting out from under a massive armor belt. The tough iron shield that protected the ship from enemy fire landed on top of the turret as both crashed to the bottom. Because our vision is distorted by the sub's five-inch-thick acrylic sphere, the wreck looks smaller than it is. Thousands of small fish, deep vermilion in the sub's xenon arc lights, flow in and out of the crevice formed by belt and turret. A coral fan, waving in the current, clings to the side of the turret.

We hover within feet of the iron cylinder, almost touching it. A laser beam that aims a sonar pulse plays on the hoary surface, gauging its distance. The turret is heavily encrusted with sea life, but in a couple of places red splotches have bled through. Could they be dents where cannonballs clanged against its armor and sent sailors reeling?

Gauges on the little screen read the water temperature as 17.5 degrees Celsius, salinity as 36.24 parts per thousand. The current is half a knot from the southwest, nudging us slightly off course. Reoxygenated air whooshes into the cockpit. A sonar pinger sounds. The sub skipper toggles the joystick, the thrusters hum, and we begin a slow tour of the rest of the hulking wreck, flying over it as though in a spaceship.

The *Monitor* and this buglike intruder are old acquaintances, going back to 1977 when observers paid their first visits in person. Aside from the turret, the *Monitor* looks every bit as disintegrated as fourteen decades under the deep ocean could make her, with powerful currents and salt constantly tearing at her and corroding her once-thick iron skin. Much of the hull near the bow is gone; encrustations make her look more like a reef than a warship. "The wreck is falling apart before our very eyes," says the historian.

At the stern is a gaping crater where the steam engine used to be; forward of that is the berth deck—the strange, and eventually terrifying, quarters below the waterline where the crew lived—and then the wardroom, or what's left of it. Someday, underwater archaeologists will sift through these spaces for belongings that the sailors left behind in their rush to save themselves. We glide right over the bow and swing around to the port side, noting the hole that was once the anchor well, and move on to the captain's stateroom with private head. "That's where the important decisions were made," says my droll tour guide.

Another burst of our thrusters and we're back near the turret. All the while, the sub's video camera records the scene. This is important, because tomorrow divers will descend on this sprawling piece of history and change it forever. Some 160 U.S. Navy divers will undertake one of the most extensive underwater excavations in history. Day and night, they'll drop down to the wreck, removing tons of coal and iron rubble, expecting to recover precious artifacts and perhaps human remains. Saturation divers, living under high pressure for weeks at a time, will saw and blast through pieces of the ship's armor. If they can succeed—and it's not certain they will, given the constraints of time and funding and the unpredictability of the sea—they'll retrieve one of the great icons of United States naval history: the *Monitor*'s revolving gun turret.

There are those in the archaeological community who would prefer to leave the wreck as it is, granting it whatever dignity nature accords. But there is a selfish side to that argument, because only the experts, only the scientists and deepwater specialists, would be able to see it. If the turret can be recovered, perhaps millions of visitors will have that chance. The big question is, Can they do it?

It's hard to believe that vital parts of this celebrated ship could be saved from the ravages of the sea. By now it is a massive lump of collapsing iron, and the turret, the biggest prize of all, is a potentially lethal 200-ton wrecking ball. In the back of every project participant's mind is the prospect of calamity. And then there is this: one day, on the gas plasma screens of their computers, relayed from a weather satellite, they may see images that sailors of another century could only imagine—the telltale signs of a storm gathering strength and heading this way.

Slowly, slowly, we rise to the surface. Tomorrow the dives begin.

ONE

NOTHING IN THE HEAVENS ABOVE

Few believed that the peculiar vessel slipping down the ways would float, much less take on the Confederacy's dreaded new warship. Perhaps that was why hundreds of spectators, including ships' captains and naval officials and their wives, braved the cold, stormy weather to be at Continental Ironworks in Greenpoint in Brooklyn, New York, on January 30, 1862: they thought the preposterous flatiron of a ship would surely "dive into the depths of the river altogether," as one publication put it.

There was no such doubt about the competition, at least not in Union minds. The former Union frigate *Merrimack*, now raised from the deep and cloaked in iron, struck terror into Northern hearts. So ominous was the ship's rebirth on the banks of the Elizabeth River— near Norfolk, Virginia—that President Lincoln's appointees feared she would not only rip through the Union blockade at Hampton Roads, Virginia, but lay waste to Northern cities.

Could this squat, top-heavy steam battery, so studded with bolts and rivets that she looked like a barnacle-encrusted whale, possibly be the North's champion? Why, she was no ship at all, her critics scoffed—not a fitting command for an officer, nor a stable platform for guns. And so low in the water, how could she acquit herself in battle? Or even get to the battle in the first place?

The spectators could not have guessed that they stood at a turning point in naval history.

Only the previous August the Navy Department had invited plans
and proposals for building armored vessels. Seventeen were submitted
and three approved, among them this most unorthodox "sub-aquatic
system of naval warfare." The vessel was an unlikely marriage of technology and necessity, the serendipitous creation of a brilliantly ec-
centric engineer. John Ericsson, born in Sweden in 1803, dreamed
about "caloric" engines driven by superheated air. He had invented
dozens of marvels, among them an evaporator, a depth finder, and
an improved steam locomotive. The locomotive, *Novelty*, had set a land
speed record in 1829, covering a mile in fifty-three seconds. His *Flying Devil*, a propeller-driven tug, had been impressive but deemed
too radical, and so were his ideas for propeller-driven warships.

John Ericsson, inventor. (Mariners' Museum)

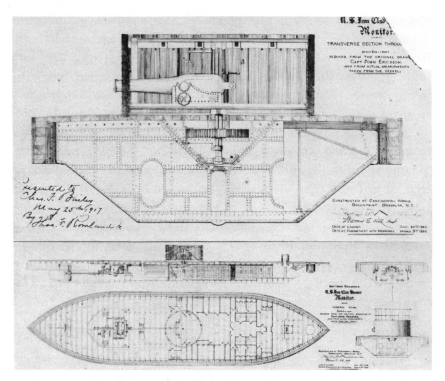

Monitor blueprints. (Mariners' Museum)

After being persuaded to emigrate to America, Ericsson was awarded a contract to build a steam-powered, screw-propelled ship for the navy. Launched in 1843, the USS *Princeton* was the first such warship in American naval history, but it also marred Ericsson's reputation. In a demonstration cruise with President John Tyler, members of his cabinet, and congressional leaders on board, one of its guns exploded, killing the secretaries of state and navy. Even though the inventor had nothing to do with the guns, his career with the government seemed over. Undaunted, he turned to the French with an audacious plan. "Ericsson's Impregnable Battery and Revolving Cupola," an ironclad warship with living quarters below the waterline and a turret on deck, was considered but ultimately rejected by Napoleon III.

But as Lincoln's woefully thin navy struggled to find an answer to the South's ironclad, New York industrialist Cornelius Bushnell took

a liking to Ericsson. When he asked Ericsson's advice on plans for
other ironclads, the inventor said they were fine as far as they went.
Even though he wanted no further dealings with the navy, Ericsson
could not resist showing Bushnell his model for a radical, half-submerged vessel. Bushnell was so impressed that he immediately lined
up investors. Secretary of the Navy Gideon Welles, desperate to
counter the South's menacing threat, was intrigued enough to
arrange a meeting with Lincoln.

The president gave an oblique endorsement: "All I have to say is
what the girl said when she put her foot in the stocking. 'It strikes me
there's something in it.'"

But the decision was not his to make. It belonged to the Navy Department's three-member Ironclad Board, which had a clear man-
date to find iron-armored alternatives but was composed of senior
naval officers who were steeped in, if not downright wedded to, traditional designs.

"We are somewhat apprehensive that her properties for sea are not
such as a seagoing vessel should possess," the board pronounced. One
member said the design resembled "nothing in the heavens above or
the earth below or the waters under the earth." Despite its reserva-
tions, however, the board left the door slightly ajar, and Bushnell deftly
led Ericsson through it. He told the inventor that the board had some
minor questions for him and squired him to Washington to meet with
the three members. The thin-skinned Ericsson, unaware of the
board's cool reception, made an inspired presentation that turned its
doubting members around. So full of misgivings were they, however,
that their $275,000 contract offer was contingent on performance. Full
payment would not be made until the ship had proved itself in battle.

Ericsson and his investors ignored the insult and plunged ahead
with the project even before the final contract was signed. Besides
Bushnell, the other investors were John Griswold, principal partner in
Rensselaer Iron Company, and John Winslow, co-owner of Albany Iron
Works. The four men, who called themselves "Battery Associates,"
put up $10,000 each. All their receipts, for items ranging from screw
bolts to iron sheets, referred to the "Ericsson Steam Floating Battery."
On October 4, 1861, Ericsson was given instructions to have the vessel "ready for sea in one hundred days." He promised to build it in

ninety, only a slight exaggeration. In a letter to James Gordon Bennett, editor of the *New York Herald*, he said that even as the navy was drawing up the contract, "the iron which now forms the keel plate of the *Monitor* was drawn through the rolling mill."

The keel was laid on October 25. In a dazzling feat of contracting and subcontracting—the turret, engines, and hull were built separately—the ship was in the water ninety-six days later.

The government wanted to test the ironclad, send it directly to Hampton Roads, and then, according to a memoir by Secretary Welles, "proceed up Elizabeth river to the Navy Yard at Norfolk, place herself opposite the dry-dock, and with her heavy guns destroy both the dock and the 'Merrimac.' "

But news from a Union spy changed everything. A Portsmouth slave passed through Confederate lines at great risk to her life to bring news that the Confederate ironclad was nearly complete. Welles said she "took from the bosom of her dress" a letter from a Navy Yard mechanic confirming the news. So much for destroying the enemy ship at the dock; she would have to be dealt with in open combat.

Ericsson dubbed his warship the *Monitor* so all would know that she was capable of taking charge. The "impregnable and aggressive character" of the vessel would "admonish" Southern leaders about their vulnerability. She would also admonish Great Britain, which at the time was sympathetic to the Confederacy, to mind its own business. But critics had quite another name, "Ericsson's Folly," and they proclaimed that she would not even float.

The *Monitor* was more submarine than ship, with only thirteen inches of heavily armored freeboard when trimmed for battle. Aside from the small forward pilothouse, the only prominent feature was a strange-looking cylinder that enemies would at their peril mistake for a water tower—its revolving gun turret. The Ironclad Board could not resist one caveat: Ericsson's contract called for a vessel that would not only proceed under steam but also be able to make six knots under sail. True to form, Ericsson ignored the requirement. After all, since the government was withholding payment until the vessel proved itself, he and his backers technically still owned it.

The turret, rising nine feet off the deck and wrapped with eight one-inch-thick iron plates, could pivot completely around, allowing the crew to aim and fire two eleven-inch Dahlgren smoothbore cannons almost at will. Never mind squaring off with another ship in broadside formation. Swivel the turret, raise the heavy iron port stoppers that covered the gun ports, run the guns out, and fire. If it worked, it would represent a huge tactical advantage. Doubters notwithstanding, it could make all other naval ships in the world obsolete. Perhaps that's what the navy men all privately feared.

The ship was built in two sections, with upper and lower hulls. The upper hull, with armored deck and sides, covered the lower hull like the top of a hatbox. The five-foot overlap, extending below the waterline, was oak and pine plated with five layers of iron to make a robust armor belt. The lower hull, protected by a much thinner iron skin but completely submerged, housed all the ship's vital spaces—its crew quarters, its stores, and its engines. It had all manner of clever machinery: a low-slung steam engine that drove a four-bladed propeller and smaller, separate donkey engines to revolve the turret. The engines pulled fresh air into the living quarters and created a draft for the furnaces. By one estimate, the strange-looking vessel housed forty patentable inventions. Ericsson seemed to have thought of everything, including what were apparently the world's first underwater flushing toilets.

She was small for a warship: 173 feet long and 41 feet, 6 inches in beam, with a draft of 10 feet, 6 inches and a weight of 987 tons. If that seems hefty, consider that the *Merrimack*, before being converted, had been more than four times as heavy and now was covered with at least one thousand tons of iron.

One thing the *Monitor* was not—and Ericsson never pretended otherwise—was seaworthy, and in this regard the Ironclad Board was right. She was designed for river and harbor defense. Her squared-off bottom, shallow draft, single-chine hull, and top-heavy deck with 120-ton turret made her exceptionally vulnerable to rough seas. The navy knew that if the vessel was to move about on the open sea she would have to be towed. But she was not, Ericsson knew, going to the bottom of the East River.

While rescue boats stood ready to pull survivors from the water if the ship sank, the imperious inventor, his chief engineer, and a few

The *Monitor* is launched at Greenpoint in Brooklyn, New York, January 30, 1862.
(Mariners' Museum)

associates stood defiantly at the bow for the ride down the rails. With
barely a splash, the iron ship entered the water and floated within
inches of the inventor's designed waterline.

For Union officials the launch could not have happened at a more
critical time. No sooner had navy officials congratulated the builder
on launching the radically original vessel than they attempted to push
him further. "Hurry her for sea," they pleaded in a telegram, "as the
Merrimack is nearly ready at Norfolk and we wish to send her there."

Hurrying a ship, especially an experimental one, is fraught with
peril. For one thing, the ship needed a crew of sailors who were willing
to face a previously untested kind of life at sea. The *Monitor* was no
sailing vessel but a floating factory whose sailors were to live and work
in a dark and gloomy underwater world, breathing air constantly
refreshed by pumps. Except for port lights on deck, gun slits in the

turret, and a grating on top, there was nothing to bring natural light into living or fighting spaces.

As if to compensate for its claustrophobic interior, Ericsson fitted out small staterooms at his own expense, with black walnut berths, drawers and closets, lace and damask curtains, and gilt-framed mirrors. William Keeler, the ship's paymaster, wrote to his wife that his stateroom came equipped with "slop jar, tumbler, water pitcher, soap dish &c &c, all of nice white ware with '*Monitor*' on each in gilt letters."

After seeing his "iron home" for the first time on February 12, Keeler assured his dear Anna, to whom he wrote nearly every day, that he would be in no more danger from rebel guns than if he were sitting with her at home. "There isn't even danger enough to give us any glory."

He was wrong, but Keeler was seeing a glimpse of the future. Sailors' lives were soon to change forever. Instead of scrambling to the yards to change sails, they'd heap coal onto the fire grates. Instead of facing an enemy along a gun line, they'd peer through vertical slits in thick armor. As one enlisted man would put it in a letter to his father, "There is not much sailorizing to do."

All of this was perhaps far from the minds of the crew in the early weeks of 1862 when they assembled at the Brooklyn Navy Yard, where the *Monitor* was transferred after twenty days of post-launch fitting out. They were advised of the peculiarities of the vessel and the dangers of their mission, but they volunteered. All of them. They were mostly new to navy ranks and likely to receive no more training than what they were soon to learn at sea; many of them, fresh off the streets of New York, were recent arrivals from Ireland, Wales, Scotland, Denmark, and Austria. The accents on board were thick enough to pierce with a marlinspike.

More than a few of the crew were tough and scrappy, ready for a fight or a drink or both. Life aboard would be cramped and monotonous, but a sight better than they had known in the city's slums. Some would become deserters, some brawlers and drunkards, but many, when the time came, would step forward in the face of death.

TWO

FLOATING CITY

IN THE spring of 2002, another ungainly vessel puts to sea and makes its way slowly from the Gulf of Mexico to Cape Hatteras, North Carolina, hauled by a seagoing tug. The *Wotan* is no Wagnerian Norse god but a huge derrick barge, 299 feet long and 90 feet wide, with living quarters for 117 people. Housing modules, each with eight bunks and connecting bath and showers, are stacked like condos, with a mess hall, workout rooms, several operations shacks, generators, water makers, a sewage treatment system, and a helicopter pad. Once on station, the great platform will stay put with the help of eight 20,000-pound anchors, two per corner, splayed out like a sunburst. The business part of the barge is a 275-foot crane that can lift and swing objects weighing as much as 500 tons, depending on the angle of the lift. The *Wotan*, owned by Manson Gulf LLC of Houma, Louisiana, usually installs and removes offshore oil platforms in the Gulf of Mexico, but this time the barge and its twelve-person crew have been pressed into service for *Monitor* recovery operations.

It is on this football field of a platform that Navy divers and archaeologists from the National Oceanic and Atmospheric Administration (NOAA) and the Mariners' Museum have loaded their equipment and supplies. Among the most important items are dozens of steel torpedo-like cylinders containing mixed helium and oxygen, a diving bell, double-lock decompression chambers, and enough gear for scores of divers.

In a monumental undertaking, the team shipped seven tractor-trailer loads of equipment from Norfolk to Houma. With only two trucks and drivers, it took seven trips to haul all 40,000 pounds of gear. On June 1, eight divers arrived and went to work. They cleared the barge of extraneous equipment in a single day, then loaded it with over a thousand tons of diving and salvage gear. The Navy divers worked twelve-hour days in hundred-degree heat and 95 percent humidity.

Together, the sailors and crew prepared their gear. They fabricated lift points, rollers, and piping systems for berthing, and they ran wiring for electrical systems, cameras, and communications. Though they had originally scheduled nine days for loading, they put to sea in six. The energy and spirit with which the load-on was accomplished has set the tone for the expedition.

The work was demanding and dangerous. At times, as many as five cranes were loading and unloading gear, the booms performing a futuristic mechanical ballet. The divers and civilian riggers developed a camaraderie that will last throughout the operation. Most important, no one got hurt. Chief warrant officer Rick Cavey, the dive officer for the expedition, will later say, "I have memories of the yard dogs—as they called themselves—cooling themselves in the canal until they saw a ten-foot alligator and cleared out fast."

Running around like a bare-chested halfback during the loading—chalk marker, tape measure, and walkie-talkie at the ready—was Jim Mariano, the project's master diver. Ever so carefully, he directed the load-on of the racks of mixed gases the divers will breathe.

The gas was stored in sixteen-foot-long steel flasks, with eight flasks lashed together in racks four feet high and eight feet wide. Mariano ordered eight racks holding three gas combinations: bottom mix, decompression mix, and pure oxygen.

This is one of the largest Navy dive operations in history, involving over 160 divers from more than two dozen commands, including one from England. Mariano has calculated that the surface-supply divers—the ones who will drop down to the wreck from the barge, breathing gas from onboard pumps—will need 200,000 cubic feet of bottom mix: 15.5 percent oxygen and 84.5 percent helium. It is a precise calculation for an average depth of 230 feet of salt water. There's more: the surface-supplied divers will also need 100,000 cubic feet of 50-50 oxygen-helium and 47,000 cubic feet of pure oxygen—the final tonic for divers who, in their recompression chamber, will be gently brought back to sea-level pressure while the potentially deadly helium seeps from their bodies.

Navy divers—there are about a thousand of them—are assigned some of the toughest jobs in the world. Their mission, in peace or war, is salvage and recovery. When aircraft or boats go down, the dive teams are there on the bottom, recovering bodies and salvaging the downed aircraft or vessel. Ship husbandry units service and repair ships below the waterline, keeping them afloat and sparing them constant trips to shipyard drydocks. But on rare occasions like this they find themselves rescuing pieces of history. This is a plum assignment for most of them, considering the kind of work they normally do.

On this mission, much of the heavy lifting will be done by an elite corps of divers. Eighteen saturation divers from the Navy Experimental Dive Unit (NEDU) in Panama City, Florida, arrived on June 4. NEDU, the Navy's underwater equivalent of NASA, has been quietly testing divers and gear for more than fifty years.

Saturation diving allows divers to stay under pressure almost indefinitely—so long as they undergo a lengthy recovery period. The time required to off-gas is sixty-six hours, or nearly three days. But no matter how long divers stay pressurized, be it two hours or two weeks, the decompression period is the same because after a certain period, depending on depth, the tissues become saturated and the pressure of dissolved gases in the body is identical to that in the diver's surroundings. Whether divers remain at pressure for an additional hour or month, the tissues will absorb no more inert gas. What's more, saturation divers can work on the bottom in good weather or bad, as long as deep ocean currents are not too strong. The other divers, whether surface-supplied or self-contained, must never remain underwater longer than dive timetables allow or they will risk injury or death when they surface.

Navy diving is serious business. Only the most dedicated, motivated, and physically fit sailors make it past dive school. Swimming, bicycling, and weight lifting are important components of the course, but greater importance is given to running. In order to build lower-body strength and aerobic capacity, candidates at the Navy's dive school in Panama City, Florida, are expected to run six miles in forty-five minutes or less—clearly, not a jogger's pace. At the end of fifteen weeks, candidates should be doing this five times a week. Beyond running, the daily recommendations also include twenty sets of twenty push-ups, twenty sets of twenty-five sit-ups, five sets of twelve chin-ups, and twenty sets of fifteen dips, plus swimming continuously for seventy-five minutes with fins. Almost as an afterthought, the manual recommends that students stretch, that they eat well, pack in lots of carbohydrates and protein, and drink about a gallon of water every day.

If the atmosphere on the *Wotan* is any indication, the need for rigorous physical conditioning extends well beyond dive school. Tucked away under the iron stairway at the aft end of the barge is a fully equipped exercise area, with weights and benches, stationary bikes, and rowing machines. Some of the divers on the barge are already working up to five hundred push-ups a day. That may sound excessive, but their jobs demand strength and stamina. Out at the *Monitor* site they'll be racing around the bottom, forty fathoms down, often against swift currents and always under the pressure of six or seven atmospheres, putting demands on their bodies that few can withstand—or would want to. Round-the-clock diving is the norm. Two twelve-hour shifts mean that divers will nearly always be in the water, both the surface-supply or "sprint" divers, who spend thirty to forty minutes on the bottom, and the saturation divers, who virtually live there.

DURING THE ten-day trip, from Houma to Cape Hatteras, Jeff Johnston, the NOAA historian, reminds the divers about the care and handling of artifacts. The interaction between salvage divers and archaeologists inevitably ranges somewhere between urgency and caution. They've been working together on this project for several years, recovering other parts of the historic ship, and Johnston feels good about the relationship. "The first year, working with these guys in 1998, they quit using the word 'salvage' around us and started talking about 're-covery,' " he says.

In all of their minds, too, is the likelihood that somewhere in the wreck, probably in the turret, they will find human remains. The protocol for this eventuality is the ultimate in careful, respectful—and time-consuming—steps. If they find skeletal remains, the divers say, those long-lost sailors will be accorded the highest respect, just as if they'd died in the line of duty only yesterday.

Near Jacksonville, on the east coast of Florida, Commander Bobbie Scholley hitches a ride on a launch and joins the barge crew. An accomplished diver and leader, and one of the top female diving officers in the Navy, Scholley has moved up to the most important post of her career: tactical commander of the expedition and head of the Mobile Diving and Salvage Unit Two (MDSU TWO, or "mudsu two," as it's pronounced), the primary East Coast Navy diving operation. She has plunged into a world dominated by strong-muscled and strong-willed males who give no quarter to weakness or indecision, and so far she has been equal to the job. In 2001 she was in charge of the massive effort that freed the *Monitor*'s steam engine from the belly of the ship and raised it from the deep. She has been in the presence of the brooding wreck more than most divers and knows it as well as anyone. But lifting over 200 tons of turret and cannon and setting them down on the barge without serious damage or injury is something else entirely.

Scholley takes in the sheer size of the *Wotan*, the vast layout of deck and living spaces, and then, as the barge continues its journey along the coast, she launches a series of meetings. Her journal for that day includes the following: "Meeting with Capt Chris Murray, CWO2 Cavey, Jeff Johnston (NOAA), to discuss basic Four Phase Salvage Plan: 1) Clear Aft Deck and Armor Belt, 2) Excavate inside turret, 3) Install lifting Spider mechanism, 4) Lift Turret to barge."

Those are the goals, all right, but no one imagines it will be that simple.

She's grateful for the presence of Captain Murray. He was her mentor and the previous commander of MDSU TWO and is hands-down the most knowledgeable figure associated with the *Monitor* recovery. The recovery itself was his brainchild, his scheme for training divers in hazardous conditions while retrieving a storied part of naval history.

But the command structure is unconventional, if not awkward. Murray outranks Scholley, but she's in charge. She'll have to rely on the qualities that earned her the job in the first place: intelligence, ability, and competence.

Also on the barge is a heavy-duty mechanism that resembles a giant claw. The Spider, as it has been dubbed, has eight steel legs designed to wrap the turret in a clawlike embrace and then, after it is joined to a lifting platform, bring the turret to the surface. The twenty-five-ton claw has hydraulic devices that will permit divers to spread the legs as it drops to the bottom, then close them around the turret, locking its feet in place. Synthetic slings will then be shackled to the tops of the legs, and the captured turret will be lifted from the bottom, lowered to the lifting platform, and locked onto it. Hopefully—and a lot of breaths will be held—this will preserve the contents intact as the precious cargo, some 210 to 220 tons, rises through the long water column.

ON JUNE 17, off Morehead City, North Carolina, the Manson crew begins rigging the mooring anchors, but during the operation a steel shaft on the swing motor for the big crane shears. No one is hurt, but it forces the barge, with expedition crew on board, to travel all the way to Norfolk for repairs. The delay costs the recovery effort a week. This is not good news. There is not much give in the schedule for getting that turret on the barge. About forty-five days is all the time they will get; after that the funding runs out, and in all likelihood so does the weather. Repairs done at last, the *Wotan* is towed around Cape Hatteras, retracing the course the *Monitor* followed 140 years before. Finally, after moving into position and setting mooring anchors, dives begin on the crystal clear morning of June 26. The first to splash is Rick Cavey, a quintessential can-do Navy diver upon whose shoulders much of the operation rests. As dive officer, he is in charge of everything pertaining to the lift, from scheduling to problem solving. This often means walking a fine line between the archaeologists and the two Navy officers, or "oh-sixes" (Cavey's expression for the numerical ranking of Captain Murray and Captain-designate Scholley). And, somehow, he's got to get everyone to agree.

Cavey has one other slight problem: he's never seen the *Monitor* in person.

The twenty-year veteran diver has spent eight months studying pictures and drawings and reading reports, but huge questions loom in his mind. How fragile is the turret? How much digging will they have to do to get the Spider's legs around it? How much work will it take to remove the forty-five-foot, forty-ton armor belt section that rests on the turret? And how dangerous will it be for those who will have to get the job done?

Cavey is thirty-eight years old, a backyard mechanic who learned about machinery working on his truck and his vintage Volkswagen. He couldn't even swim before joining the Navy and had to learn in boot camp. Yet he seems to have no lack of self-confidence. As he descends, tethered to life-support machines on deck, the wreck goes from fuzzy to clear. The visibility is incredible, he realizes as he nears the stern; he can see almost the entire ship. He has a mental checklist that he's trying to stay focused on: the height of the armor belt over the turret, the stability of the hull, the place in the belt where the cutting is to be done. The stage stops about ten feet over the belt, and Cavey simply steps off and glides slowly down. He lands squarely on the *Monitor,* just above its turret.

That's when it hits him: Back in sixth grade, it was a big deal—the *Monitor* and the *Merrimack* and the great battle of the ironclads. He remembers his history teacher describing this plucky Union warrior, the one with the revolving turret that changed everything about naval ships, and he's standing on it, at the bottom of the ocean! It's pretty much colorless down here. Most of the light spectrum, except for blues and grays, has been filtered out, but the light from his helmet picks out burnished red rust splotches and pink coral. But these are fleeting impressions. He'll be making most of the recommendations about what needs to be done, so he needs to focus on his job. He's got to get it right, take the mental pictures he needs, and haul himself back up to the stage before he exhausts all 35 minutes of allowable bottom time.

Later, when he's finished with his checks and the stage ascends, pausing at prescribed decompression stops, he tells himself, "Take a minute and feel this. What an incredible scene this is—what an amazing opportunity."

Among the next to dive is Commander Scholley herself. At 240 feet, she makes a survey of the wreck and begins clearing the area around the ship's stern, moving debris out of the way by hand. She's been in the presence of the *Monitor* many times, but it always gets to her. Those who served and fought and died on this ship were fellow sailors. To be part of this recovery operation is thrilling.

But pressure has already begun to build. There was the delay of the crane mechanism, and now the weather begins to behave as it always does off Cape Hatteras. The barge is equipped with a satellite dish that gives the team access to NOAA weather forecasts, but the immediate warnings come from the pilothouse of the tug, *Delta Force,* where approaching storms can be seen on radar. Shortly before sunset on June 28, a severe thunderstorm arrives, packing winds of over fifty knots. Ten-foot seas with breaking tops wallop the barge, straining its anchors and throwing towers of water and foam onto its deck. Suddenly this supposedly stable platform seems vulnerable. It doesn't take long for those on board to begin thinking about what it must have been like for those sailors 140 years before as they fought to subdue their worst fears.

THREE

STANDING OUT TO SEA

I T HAD been a brutal week for shipping all along the East Coast. Tuesday morning, February 25, 1862, a schooner bound for New York with lumber from New Bedford, Massachusetts, went aground near the tip of Long Island during a heavy gale, with a total loss of crew, vessel, and cargo. That day in New London, Connecticut, nearly all vessels in the harbor dragged anchor, and several ended up ashore. A day later, the Union warship USS *Cumberland* dragged anchor off Newport News, Virginia, and several schooners went adrift, causing collisions in the harbor and, surely, gnashing of teeth on shore. Out in the Chesapeake Bay, a steamer laying telegraph cable from Fort Monroe to the Eastern Shore of Virginia—from where it would run overland to Washington—was struck by a severe gale and driven across the bay to Cape Henry, where it broke in two.

Well before dawn on Thursday morning, February 27, Lieutenant John L. Worden, the new captain of the *Monitor*, woke to find snow falling at the Brooklyn Navy Yard. His entry in the ship's log is matter-of-fact, disguising what he must have felt about his extraordinary new assignment: "February 27 comes in cloudy weather, light wind from NE. 2 A.M. commenced snowing."

There is no hint that he was on board an unproved, experimental vessel, expected to sail that day for Hampton Roads and do what he could to help save the Union.

Worden had grown up on a modest farm in Westchester County, New York, and joined the navy at age sixteen. After his promotion to

John Worden, first captain of the *Monitor*. (Mariners' Museum)

lieutenant in 1846 he saw unexceptional duty in the Pacific, supporting vessels involved in the Mexican War, but he had never fought in a
battle. His career seemed to be passing. Then, on April 6, 1861, he was
summoned to the office of Secretary of the Navy Gideon Welles and
assigned a secret mission. He was to travel from Washington to Pensacola, Florida, with orders for the commander of the fleet standing in
the harbor to reinforce Union troops at Fort Pickens.

The war had not yet commenced, and there was an understanding with Confederate leaders that the fort would not be reinforced; any action to the contrary would be considered an act of war. The secrecy of the mission was so critical that Worden was instructed to commit his orders to memory and swallow the message if caught. Stopped in Atlanta, he indeed ingested the message before he could be searched. He arrived safely in Pensacola on April 12, the day Confederate forces opened fire on Fort Sumter in Charleston Harbor. Fort Pickens did not suffer the same fate, perhaps because the troops had been landed. Worden took a train back north, however, and was apprehended in Montgomery, Alabama. He became the Confederacy's first prisoner of war.

He languished in prison until November 20, when he was taken to Norfolk and exchanged for a Confederate naval officer who had been captured at Hatteras, North Carolina. Seven months of confinement had left him pale and sickly. But when he was offered command of the *Monitor*, even though he was warned that she was an experimental vessel and even though his wife and doctor pleaded with him not to, he replied that it was an honor to accept the challenge.

He would soon have good reason to question his decision.

On February 19, just days before Worden arrived for his assignment, the *Monitor* had been turned over to the navy for testing, departing from its Continental Ironworks berth at Greenport. But she barely made it to the nearby Navy Yard because, due to a faulty valve setting, the engine ran backward instead of forward, and one of the blowers malfunctioned. The much-awaited ship anchored out for the night and was towed to the yard in the morning. Nevertheless, six days later she was commissioned, and a day after that the crew was mustered on board and told to prepare the vessel for sea. They would have left on February 26 had the ammunition arrived on time. Instead, they prepared to depart at dawn the next day.

After rising long before first light, Worden ordered the engine room to get up steam. A pilot came on board at 7:00 A.M., and soon the ironclad ventured out into the East River. But her maiden voyage was almost an immediate disaster. She careened back and forth between the New York and Brooklyn sides of the river and slammed into a gasworks before being towed back to the Navy Yard. She performed, Paymaster

William Keeler said, "like a drunken man on a sidewalk." Her rudder was so overbalanced that the helmsman could not hold the wheel once it was put over. Back to the Navy Yard she went, with a call to Ericsson to fix the problem. He rejected suggestions to replace the rudder, saying it would cost another month. In three days he figured out how to multiply the mechanical advantage of the wheel over the rudder. Worden demanded a twenty-four-hour shakedown cruise before taking to sea again.

Some accounts assume that the February 27 excursion had been a test run, but official records prove that the *Monitor* left the Navy Yard that February morning intending to go directly to Hampton Roads. That is to say, the ship was to depart without a successful sea trial, without even testing her guns, and having barely exercised her crew. It illustrates chillingly how desperate the Union was to protect its helpless wooden fleet.

George Geer, a twenty-five-year-old first-class fireman from New York's Lower East Side, was beginning to wonder about the wisdom of having signed on with the *Monitor*. In one of dozens of letters he would write home to his wife, Martha, he expressed chagrin over the ship's first outing and a poignant regret about their separation. "When I go on deck today and look over towards home it makes the tears start to think I am so near you and cannot be with you. Oh, how I would like to see all of you."

The fireman's job epitomized the new navy and the burgeoning steam age. Geer, who had grown up in Troy, New York, and worked at his father's stove foundry, was no stranger to such machinery—and this was a better credential for the job than sea time. For a nonofficer bunking on the berth deck, though, life was anything but grand.

Working conditions below were atrocious. The *Monitor*'s boiler room was a closed-off, airless place, with only lanterns for light. Firemen in the engine room had to wrestle great chunks of anthracite coal, pushing themselves nearly to exhaustion. The *Monitor*'s engines called for a uniform bed of coal six inches thick, but with holes between the chunks to let air pass through. Somebody had to stand in front of the furnace doors, breaking coal into small pieces to add to the fire while at the same time removing clinkers, or cinders. The coal heaver and the engineer worked more or less back-to-back, with one toasting his nose and the other his hindquarters at the same fire.

The iron ship throbbed from stem to stern with the sound of the engine, a constant whump-whump-whump, slightly slower than once a second, accompanied by the hiss of steam, the roar of the furnace, and the whine of fan belts. Ericsson had designed a low-profile two-cylinder vibrating-lever steam engine that—along with its two boilers—sat completely below the waterline.

The boilers used salt water, and at cruising speed the engineers had to maintain pressure on the piston. Because of its salt content, the more water they boiled, the more concentrated the brine became, raising the water's boiling point. The higher the boiling point, the more coal they had to burn. They also had to constantly measure the density of the water, but every time they did the fire had to be banked, just the wrong thing to do when steaming into a headwind or approaching a dock, when they'd need all the power they could coax from the boilers. These were complex problems, requiring disciplined, competent men performing complicated tasks in the dark. And all the while they were building up coal dust in their lungs.

The food was uninspired, and the late-winter nights were freezing. Geer swallowed his discomfort with a kind of stoic eloquence. "Kiss both the Babys about 24 times apiece for me and don't get sick and as for you I have got no love for you, you have it all."

Like others of the crew, Geer was impatient to get underway, but his new-fangled ship seemed unable to leave the East River. Meanwhile, 300 nautical miles south, on the banks of the Elizabeth River near Norfolk, the newly rechristened CSS *Virginia* was almost ready. With big guns, a massive iron ram, and impenetrable armor, she was a terrifying prospect for the Union blockade's aging wooden ships and their crews in Hampton Roads.

Secretary Welles was becoming desperate. He had been told that the Confederate demon was ready to attack, and he was under tremendous pressure to counter the threat. Now, from his own navy, came news of more delays. A huge storm on March 3 nearly wrecked the blockading squadron at the entrance to Hampton Roads. On the same day, the *Monitor* held gun trials. The ship's logs mention only that the guns were successfully fired, first using blanks, then grape shot, but they do not mention what appears to have been a fiasco.

Alban Stimers, chief engineer during the *Monitor*'s construction, insisted on running the first gun trials out on the East River, but he did not seem to understand how the gun carriages worked, according to Charles McCord, Ericsson's draftsman. The guns, when fired, recoiled violently on their carriages and had to be stopped by brakes that were tightened by hand cranks. Because the big cannons were side by side, the cranks were placed on the outer sides of the carriages. This way the gunners did not have to stand between the weapons to make adjustments. The arrangement suggested that one would be turned one way and the other the opposite, but both were designed to be turned to the left. Just as the first gun was to be fired, Stimers turned the wheel to the right, relieving whatever braking power the carriage had.

"The great weapon gave a sullen roar, and, being entirely free, flew back until it was stopped by the cascabel striking against the interior of the turret," McCord reported. The gun's recoil could have killed anyone standing in the way, but fortunately no one was injured. He added that Stimers, thinking that what was wrong for one gun would be right for the other, turned the crank for the other gun to the right, and again a 17,000-pound gun jumped from its carriage and slammed into the turret wall. The inside wall of the turret would forever bear those indentations. There are no reports of further gun trials. There was no time. Pressure was mounting.

In what was surely a fit of panic, on March 5, the day before the *Monitor* was at last to weigh anchor from Brooklyn, Welles fired off a telegram to commanders in Hampton Roads, ordering them to instruct Worden, when the ironclad arrived, to immediately steam up the Potomac River to protect Washington. The next day he sent a similar telegram to the Navy Yard, but it failed to arrive until after the *Monitor*'s 10:30 A.M. departure. Five and a half hours later, unaware of the new orders, Worden sent a message to Welles by way of the pilot that he had cleared Sandy Hook and was standing out to sea.

FOUR

STRUCTURAL TIME BOMB

THE ROOTS of the massive salvage effort in summer 2002 go back more than half a century. In August 1949, the Navy chose an area south of the Cape Hatteras Light to test a new underwater locator to see if the long-lost ironclad could be found. In 310 feet of water the searchers found something suspicious—a 140-foot object with enough bulk to be a shipwreck. When divers attempted to investigate, however, they had to give up in the face of powerful currents, and the idea, without much steam behind it, was shelved. But the *Monitor* files were begun, and others, many others, took note.

The Navy was soon deluged by requests for assistance from groups hoping to salvage the famous shipwreck. Rather than honor all of them, almost as a defensive measure, the Navy decided to abandon the ship and let private interests find it—if they could. The *Monitor* became, briefly, a salvage prize.

The most notable attempt threw investigators off the trail for almost two decades. In 1955 Robert Marx, then a Marine Corps corporal, wreck diver, and prolific author, wrote a book suggesting that the *Monitor* had actually drifted into shallow water before sinking. The theory was based on an old ship captain's claim that a vessel like the *Monitor* had been seen in the surf north of Cape Hatteras Light, and then the theory was spiced up by legend. The story held that several bodies washed ashore near the lighthouse a few days after the sinking and that Union soldiers carted them off and buried them.

Marx claimed he had found the wreck, dived on it, and placed a Coke bottle with his name on it in the barrel of one of the cannons. It may have been a fanciful story (he could never back it up), but he managed to attract the interest of the press, the Coast Guard, the U.S. Coast and Geodetic Survey (a forerunner of NOAA), and *Life* magazine.

At this point, a pivotal figure entered the story. John Broadwater—a soft-spoken, blue-eyed Kentuckian—might as well have salt water in his veins, a pretty unlikely condition for someone who grew up in a played-out coal mining town near the Cumberland Gap. He escaped to the University of Kentucky and then, as a newly minted electrical engineer working in the defense industry in the Pacific, developed a passion for wreck diving. He dived on wrecks in the Marshall Islands and wrote a book about them, *Kwajalein: Legend of Found Ships.* The experience gave birth to a lifelong passion for solving shipwreck mysteries.

While still in his twenties, Broadwater was bitten hard by the *Monitor* bug. He started a company called Marine Archaeological Research Services in Southport, North Carolina—about as close as he could get to the Graveyard of the Atlantic without being in it—and offered his services for hire. One of his first investigations was the site where Marx was supposed to have found the wreck of the *Monitor.* In September 1971 he conducted an extensive search of the area and found "nothing so much as a beer can."

But the *Monitor* experience would keep cycling back into his life, almost as if he was destined to one day encounter the lost ship face-to-face.

One thing the Marx theory did accomplish was to stimulate interest in where the wreck actually lay. In the spring of 1973 a group of midshipmen at the U.S. Naval Academy in Annapolis, Maryland, began Project Cheesebox, a systematic search of ships' records, official reports, and survivors' accounts, along with researching what could be learned of the sinking properties of the ship and the likely set and drift characteristics of the sea in that treacherous part of the world.

The midshipmen made several attempts to find the wreck, at one point taking a boat and dive gear to Cape Hatteras with plans to coordinate with a P-3 antisubmarine aircraft that would search from the air. But severe weather chased them back to Annapolis. They built a scale model of the ship and did towing-tank tests to study how the *Monitor* would have performed in rough seas. Although Project Cheesebox fell short of finding the *Monitor*, it gave researchers clues to why and how she sank.

At almost the same time, John Newton, superintendent of the Duke University Marine Laboratory Oceanographic Program, and Gordon Watts, a marine archaeologist from the North Carolina Division of Archives and History, huddled over ships' logs, official reports, and offshore charts to zero in on where the lost ship might lie, and developed a pretty good idea where to look.

On August 27, 1973, the research vessel *Eastward* knifed through uncharacteristically calm seas south of Cape Hatteras. The search by the Duke team was supported in part by the National Geographic Society and the National Science Foundation. On board were Newton, Watts, and other scientists, who thought they had a chance of finding, down on a ridge of the Atlantic continental shelf, the remains of one of the most celebrated warships of all time. *Eastward* towed a torpedo-shaped sonar "fish" hundreds of feet behind that bounced sound pulses off the seabed. When the acoustic pulses struck something solid, the stronger return pulses painted a denser image on the chart recorders in the ship's control room. With this powerful new tool, the scientists initiated a tedious electronic survey of a five-by-fifteen-mile rectangle of featureless sea.

The *Eastward* was sixteen miles south-southeast of Cape Hatteras when, just after noon, a crew member passing one of the sonar recorders noticed an irregular blip, a dark "amorphous" mark in 240 feet of water that could have been a shipwreck. At this point another new tool, the ship's loran receiver, became critical. Loran is an acronym for LOng RAnge Navigation, and this precursor to satellite navigation—just a few years old in 1973—permitted a ship in a loran coverage area to triangulate its position from precisely timed pulses of radiowaves emitted by shore-based transmitters. The scientist on watch logged the loran coordinates of the blip, and the sonar signature was added to a growing list of possibilities.

The survey recorded twenty-two targets, all possible candidates. Watts, in a report on the search, wrote that, one by one, the size and shape of each target signature was compared with known characteristics of the *Monitor*, and all but two were eliminated. With building excitement, the scientists lowered a still camera and a television camera down through the water column over the first of the final two candidates. The 35-mm camera was attached to a cable with an acoustic pinger that tripped its shutter when a wreck was indicated. As the *Eastward* held its position, the low-light television camera sent back images that were recorded on videotape.

The first site they examined was nineteen miles southeast of Cape Hatteras, in 320 feet of water. It looked promising, with a semicircular feature that could have been a turret, but as the researchers examined the images further they noticed a well-defined superstructure and the modern deck machinery of a fishing trawler, immediately eliminating the candidate from the list. They were down to one, the blip they had recorded and logged sixteen miles southeast of Hatteras.

The site was puzzling at first. It was the size of the long-lost ship, but its details were all wrong. There was something resembling a turret, eight inches thick to be sure, but sticking out from *under* the hull. To add to the confusion, the camera images were fuzzy and inconclusive, and before they could complete the pictures, the camera designed by famed strobe inventor Harold Edgerton of the Massachusetts Institute of Technology snagged on the wreck and was lost.

Newton, Watts, and their colleagues spent six months examining the images. So obsessed was Watts that he decorated his refrigerator door with the grainy photos, and eventually had an idea. Over Christmas dinner with Broadwater, with whom he had become closely associated, the archaeologist tested his new theory. What if they looked at these images as though the ship had turned upside down when it sank? What if the *Monitor* had rolled over during the descent and the turret, either right away or when the stern struck the hard, sandy ocean floor, broke free and came to rest under the armor belt? Suddenly it all made sense, the turret resting under the ship's port quarter, the size of the hull, the flat bottom, the false keel, the shape of the rudder, and the geographic location. On March 8, 1974, the Duke team formally announced that the wreck of the USS *Monitor* had been found.

Still, further proof was needed, and a new expedition was launched, again with support from *National Geographic*. The *Alcoa Sea Probe*, an ultrasophisticated research vessel able to hover over a site on the ocean floor, was pressed into service in late March 1974. Video cameras whirred and still cameras clicked off a mosaic of pictures. This time the images were clear enough to count the eight layers of inch-thick iron plates that made up the turret. With a bit of geometry they could calculate from the arc of the exposed section of turret that it was twenty-two feet around, the exact dimension of Ericsson's design. There was no longer any doubt. This was the *Monitor*.

Now the challenge was how to preserve this storied hunk of American history. The researchers realized that the ship, though intact in a few places, was rapidly disintegrating. Some sections seemed to have been destroyed by explosions, perhaps by military depth charges during World War II. It might take decades of study before a plan could be implemented. Some interim step to minimize further damage was a must. The State of North Carolina was powerless to protect the wreck because it lay outside its three-mile territorial limit. And because the Navy had officially abandoned the wreck in 1953, it was now open season for wreck divers and private salvage companies.

A plan was hastily devised by all parties to the discovery. The recently passed National Marine Sanctuaries Act, designed to protect environmentally important areas of the continental shelf from offshore oil drilling, fit the situation perfectly. On January 30, 1975, the 113th anniversary of the *Monitor*'s launching, the wreck and everything within a half-nautical-mile radius, including the vertical column of water above it, was designated a national marine sanctuary—America's first. Not only did the sanctuary shield the wreck, it preserved it as the productive artificial reef it had become. The warm Gulf Stream waters that often bathe the wreck provide an abundance of food for the amberjacks, dolphins, sea bass, red porgies, toadfish, barracudas, and

tiger sharks that make it their home, as well as an ideal environment
for coral and sponges, barnacles, sea anemones, mussels, oysters,
shrimps, and crabs.

The sanctuary designation created a little breathing space to decide
what to do about the long-slumbering wreck, but not much, because
the corrosive effects of salt water and the dynamics of swift currents
were conspiring to do what rebel gunfire had failed to do—tear the
Monitor apart. Ambitious ideas about raising the entire ship were
quickly abandoned as far too costly and probably impossible. Selective
recovery was the only logical route.

In 1977, after studying the site remotely for four years, Watts
boarded the *Johnson Sea Link*—a four-person submersible owned by
Harbor Branch Oceanographic Institution—to become the first person since 1862 to see the *Monitor* up close. As he climbed into the
five-foot-diameter Plexiglas observation sphere and slid into one of
the two seats, surrounded by communications equipment, gas scrubbers, and a well-organized maze of plumbing, he found it hard to
contain his enthusiasm. And then, after plunging through the depths
and gliding across the ocean bottom, he realized that he and the sub's
pilot had made the first of many exciting discoveries. About thirty
feet from the wreck was what appeared to be a tin can half covered
by sand. Later, after closer inspection, the object turned out to be the
remains of a brass marine lantern. "Its unmistakable red lens led us
to the inescapable and perhaps ironic possibility that our first evidence of the wreck was the same lantern that provided rescuers their
last contact with the *Monitor* 115 years earlier," Watts wrote.

The Fresnel-type lens had suffered multiple cracks, but apparently
not from impact when the ship hit the bottom. Instead, the damage
pattern suggested thermal shock as the hot glass of the lighted lantern
plunged into the sea. Over the next month, Watts and his colleagues
made dozens of submersible dives on the wreck, even leaving their
bubble-encased world to visit in person. Watts wrote:

> Tapping on my leg, dive tender Richard Roesch signaled that pressur-
> ization in the lockout chamber had reached 200 feet. Before I had fin-
> ished pulling the KMB-10 mixed gas helmet over my face, I felt the
> hatch beneath my feet give way as the pressure inside and outside equal-

ized. The 68 degree water leaking into the holes of my wetsuit boots provided instant relief from the 100+ degree temperature created by pressurizing the chamber. With a last abridged review of the tasks at hand, I slipped through the manway and wiggled out on the port side of the *Johnson Sea Link*. Hundreds of large Jack crevalle swirling about the submersible almost obscured the *Monitor*.

Using a dredge powered by the submersible's pump, the archaeologists meticulously removed sediment inside the *Monitor's* hull and began retrieving artifacts: part of a leather book cover, pieces of a porcelain soap dish, a leather shoe, fragments of an ironstone pie plate, a glass storage jar, "Guaranteed Air Tight," containing excellently preserved relish. They were burrowing into a time capsule that, except for the punishments of time and a deep ocean environment, had been undisturbed for more than a century.

After the *Monitor's* discovery, John Broadwater established close ties with the investigators, and in September 1979 he and Watts descended to the wreck in the submersible. Broadwater was by then an accomplished deepwater diver, and the submersible method—being pressured down to depth in the lockout chamber and simply exiting and walking over to the wreck—seemed astonishingly easy. His job was to place a PVC marker near the turret. In the hazy gloom, no longer able to see the sub, he approached the turret nervously. And then he realized he was in the presence of the legendary Civil War ironclad. He couldn't resist the urge to walk over and touch it. "When I laid my hand on it, it was just a magical feeling," he said. "If that doesn't float your boat, you're in the wrong business."

Later that day he confessed to Watts that he had taken time out from his archaeological task to lay a hand on the turret. "Don't tell anyone, but I did the same thing," Watts replied.

"I think everyone felt very privileged to be there," Broadwater said. "We talked about it a lot in the evenings. The idea of leaving it on the bottom is always the archaeologist's first option—if it's on the bottom and really stable. But the *Monitor's* never been buried, and it's definitely not stable. Much of the ship's forward hull had collapsed, either from stress or from corrosion. Rapid deterioration was occurring as a result of the anode-cathode relationships created between the plates and the rivets securing them. Some of the plates were almost paper thin." Should we leave it there and watch it disintegrate, Broadwater asked, or try to bring it up?

This debate would go on for years. Meanwhile, Broadwater realized that marine archaeology wasn't taking him anywhere. He had married Sharon Thompson, his high school sweetheart from Middleboro, Kentucky, and started a family, and he needed to earn a living. So he packed away his underwater dreams and took an engineering job in Richmond. It afforded his family a nice lifestyle. He took clients to see Washington Redskins games. He drove a new company car. He got big Christmas bonuses. And he was bored.

What he couldn't forget was the tingling he felt every time he strapped on a scuba tank and dived on a shipwreck. "I can't explain it, even to myself," he would later say, "but it really is a special kind of thing." Again and again he volunteered for underwater projects, including one that was to change his career, an investigation of the ships that Lord Cornwallis had scuttled off Yorktown, Virginia, in 1781. That led to an offer to become Virginia's first underwater archaeologist, even though at the time he had no advanced degrees. What he did have was bottom time, hundreds of hours exploring wrecks and recovering artifacts that told stories about the people who had gone down with them.

It was an exciting opportunity, but financially it made no sense: a salary of $15,000 a year—about a third of what he had been making—and no security; each year he'd have to reapply for grants to keep his job. Nonetheless, he jumped on it.

Broadwater's decade as underwater archaeologist for the Virginia Historic Landmarks Commission turned out to be a frustrating exercise because the commission had almost no funds for research. Still, he and Sharon made the best of it. They moved to Williamsburg, Virginia, where she went back to school, earned a doctorate in biology at the College of William and Mary, and became a tenured professor there. He got a master's degree in American studies and later a doctorate in maritime archaeology from St. Andrews University in Scotland. Meanwhile he continued diving on wrecks. In 1988 he wrote an article for *National Geographic* on the Yorktown shipwrecks.

For all his polite, soft-spoken demeanor, John Broadwater was driven by his infatuation with the deep. Holding down a job, diving on wrecks, getting his Ph.D.—all that left him with little time for other interests. He wished he had time to ski and go sailing—he would eventually own a sailboat and let it sit unused at a marina on the York River. Instead he plugged away at what he knew best, establishing himself as Virginia's undisputed authority on underwater archaeology.

Then the bottom fell out of his career. Governor L. Douglas Wilder, looking for ways to trim the 1991 state budget, abolished Broadwater's department. This was a blessing in disguise, because in spite of the frustrations of running a department with virtually no money, Broadwater might have lived out his working days as a state bureaucrat, shuffling papers and filing reports. Broadwater would later thank Wilder for freeing him.

At the time, though, it was devastating. Broadwater spent more than a year unemployed. Then, in 1992, a job came along that seemed tailor-made for him, manager of the *Monitor* National Marine Sanctuary. The position was a bit cushy at first. There was little to do but conduct periodic investigations of the wreck and watch it deteriorate. It did not occur to him at the time that the *Monitor*'s fate would soon be in his hands.

As dozens of artifacts were recovered from the wreck, it became clear that something serious had to be done to care for them properly. Several institutions were interested, all with ties to the *Monitor*'s history. They included the South Street Seaport Museum of New York, just across the East River from where the ironclad was built; the City of Portsmouth, Virginia, right next to the former Gosport Ship Yard; a consortium made up of the State of North Carolina, the U.S. Navy, and the Smithsonian Institution; and the Mariners' Museum of Newport News, Virginia, which sits on land less than a cannonball's flight from the Hampton Roads battles.

It might have been stiff competition, but those close to the discussions say the Mariners' Museum seemed best able to house and care for large, sea-damaged artifacts. On March 9, 1987, the 125th anniversary of the battle between the *Monitor* and the *Virginia*, NOAA designated the Mariners' the principal repository for *Monitor* artifacts.

The red signal lantern, perhaps the last thing seen of the ship when it went down, went on display, along with a four-fluke, 1,500-pound anchor. Divers had located the anchor in 1983, with two of the flukes buried in the sand, almost five hundred feet from the starboard bow of the wreck. Other items, like condiment bottles and soap dishes, went into a temporary exhibition. But the ship itself, or at least the main components like the propeller, engine, and turret, lay waiting.

For the next decade, investigators photographed, mapped, and studied the wreck. Submersibles hovered over it, and divers inspected it again and again. What they could not do was agree on a course of preservation. In the meantime they could see the ship crumbling before their eyes, and the rate of collapse was alarming. Exposed to this high-current, high-temperature saltwater environment, the *Monitor* was finally succumbing. Galvanic and electrolytic corrosion were eating through her iron skin, and shipworms were gnawing at her wooden structures. The wreck was, as one Smithsonian curator put it, a "structural time bomb."

By 1997 it was obvious that what was left of the *Monitor*'s hull was about to collapse. The options were sixfold: first, leave it completely alone, except as a site for researchers and divers to visit and allow the wreck to continue on its path to oblivion; second, preserve the vessel on site by entombing it with sand or crushed stone and, again, allow it to collapse; third, shore it up with sandbags, grout bags, or jacks (this would cost an estimated $3.4 million, not counting annual maintenance, and still permit deterioration); fourth, preserve it by cathodic protection, which would reduce but not halt the corrosion; fifth, recover select, historically significant artifacts such as the propeller, engine, guns, and turret; or sixth, attempt a complete recovery—an almost impossible alternative because of the difficulty and the estimated $50 million price tag.

What NOAA recommended to Congress was a combination of two of the options—shoring up parts of the hull and armor belt and removing, over a period of five years, select artifacts, including the ship's propeller, her engine, and in the last phase, her signature component, John Ericsson's revolutionary revolving turret. More than $20 million would be needed, and the only deep pockets the agency could identify belonged to interested individuals and organizations within the private sector.

It would take millions to raise key parts of the wreck and millions more to restore them. It soon became clear that no one had that kind of money. Broadwater was able to scrape together a mere $30,000—enough for research, but nothing more.

But there was one other possibility. Although the Navy had abandoned the wreck almost fifty years before, it now viewed the *Monitor* as a valuable part of its history. And it had another motive that had to do with deep water and dangerous, challenging conditions.

IT WAS August 1995 when Navy divers first attempted to recover the driving mechanism that sent the *Monitor* into battle—its nine-foot, four-bladed propeller. It lay intact behind the ship's rudder, still attached to the shaft. With limited funding, the operation proceeded on a shoestring. From the deck of the USS *Edenton*, the divers descended to the wreck and chipped away the encrustations encasing the propeller. They attached a sling to the propeller and began cutting through the shaft. They had managed to cut halfway through it when a relentless series of big storms, including two hurricanes, sent the sailors and archaeologists running for cover. Before the season ended, it turned out to be the second stormiest ever recorded off Cape Hatteras. Beginning in August and running through most of October, the Navy and NOAA teams made five trips to the site, only to retreat each time in the face of the deteriorating weather. The treacherous seas off Cape Hatteras—and the lack of a proper salvage platform—had won round one. Round two would not begin for three years.

MEANWHILE, COMMANDER Chris Murray had just taken over at Norfolk's Mobile Diving and Salvage Unit Two (MDSU TWO) and was looking for challenging environments in which to test equipment and train divers. When one of his master divers brought the sunken wreck off the North Carolina coast to his attention, he knew that was the project for his team. They'd be working in deep water, in strong currents, and in midocean. If they could dive the *Monitor*, they could dive anywhere.

Murray has no trouble with self-confidence. The forty-eight-year-old career veteran grew up in Oxen Hill, Maryland, near the nation's capital. He was a competitive swimmer and a compulsive diver. As a young boy, he would visit his grandparents' home on the Patuxent River every weekend and conduct his own underwater experiments, going into the water with a bucket over his head and a hose poking above the surface. His parents finally had enough of that, and when their son turned ten they bought him an air tank. In high school he played football a couple of years, as offensive guard and linebacker, then fulfilled a long-held dream of playing for the Naval Academy. But he got banged up and decided to switch to rugby. A trip to Hawaii put him in touch with professional divers, and he realized he could get paid for diving. He was going to be a Navy diver.

Now, after a long career of living and breathing Navy diving, Murray knew how to work the Washington system.

The money, he explained to Broadwater, could come from the Department of Defense Legacy Resource Management Program. The Legacy program had been established to preserve natural and cultural resources on twenty-five million acres of military bases. It had funded preservation of petroglyphs in canyons on a California weapons base and satellite tracking of large soaring birds. The Legacy program was also funding the restoration of "Old Ironsides," the USS *Constitution*. The country's historic ironclad seemed like a worthy candidate.

Murray knew he had Broadwater's attention, but he could also sense Broadwater's reluctance to hand responsibility to Navy salvage divers, whose credo was getting tonnage off the bottom as fast as possible. Murray assured him that the divers would treat the wreck with utmost delicacy. He went further: he offered the senior archaeologist the final say every step of the way. Broadwater's suggestions would be regarded as military orders.

That was the reassurance Broadwater needed. Whereas in the past he had had no money and no effective partners, just hopes and dreams, he now had a new and resourceful ally. Besides, after several meetings with the impressive, enthusiastic Murray, Broadwater felt he could trust him with this archaeological treasure.

Murray worked out the budget with the archaeologists, fought for it among his colleagues, and pleaded his case on Capitol Hill. Among the key figures he approached was Senator John Warner, the powerful former secretary of the navy and chairman of the Senate Armed Services Committee. It did not hurt that MDSU TWO, the Mariners' Museum, and the site of the celebrated Civil War battle were all in Warner's state.

Murray put together a five-year plan for the mission, and he and Broadwater met with Navy and Senate staff. When Navy officials offered $2 million from the Legacy Fund for two years, Broadwater was thrilled, but Murray shook his head. "We'll need two more years and $10 million," he told them.

"Are you crazy?" Broadwater said during a break.

"Don't worry; I've got this worked out," Murray told him. And he did. "We presented it to Senator Warner and his staffers. They didn't blink. They just wanted to hear diving stories." The money was assured.

Murray understood the archaeologist's alarm. "For me," Murray recalled, "it was 'the adventure continues.' For John, this was his life and the blood and sweat he's put into this for years."

The total cost of the recovery efforts, over the full five years from 1998 through 2002, was projected to be $14.5 million, with some additional funding coming from NOAA. The 2002 project alone was budgeted at $6.5 million. But the money is enough for an estimated forty-five days on site only, and it is unlikely there will be more after that. Not a day more. Planning has to be precise, scheduling rigorous.

THE RECOVERY operations for pieces of the historic ironclad began in earnest in 1998. Led by Commander Murray, divers from MDSU TWO and NOAA staged an all-out assault on the propeller, this time from a commercial salvage vessel, the *Kellie Chouest*. But even careful planning and the lessons learned from 1995 couldn't prepare them for the conditions they encountered.

There were fewer than thirty divers on the mission, and it soon became clear that they were in for a struggle, fighting not only powerful currents but a work ethic that demanded the quickest results possible. It's easy to understand why. At depths over two hundred feet, the divers could stay down no more than a half hour each time they arrived at the work site, then they had to spend hours decompressing, both on the way back up and in a pressure chamber, releasing dangerous levels of helium that had built up in their systems. Tag teams of two divers each succeeded each other again and again, but the work was incremental. And for every team on the bottom, a dozen or more tenders, master divers, and dive officers had to support them—changing the breathing mix, feeding the heavy umbilical lines, suiting and unsuiting the divers. And still they had to abide by the archaeologists' demands for care of the fragile artifact.

Although the propeller recovery had not been planned as a round-the-clock operation, it nearly became one, with divers working well past dark, extending their normal day from five dives to eight and their bottom time from the normal thirty minutes to almost forty. Using a reciprocal saw with carbide teeth, they managed to slice through most of the remaining half of the nine-inch iron propeller shaft— but, cursedly, not all the way. Late in the day on June 8, the only divers available to complete the job were Murray himself and one of his master divers.

The lift was supposed to have been conducted in daytime, with plenty of photo opportunities, but the seas had finally calmed, and there was no telling what the days ahead would bring. They decided to go for it.

It was well after dark when Murray and the other diver used a thin wire to slice through encrustations that cemented one of the propeller's blades to the hull, and then, with a guillotine-like saw, severed the last inches of the shaft. As the propeller rose toward the surface, a school of amberjacks circled it for forty feet or more. The divers on their platform ascended beside their retrieved artifact, making sure it didn't swing or tilt in its harness. They turned on their lights in the darkened sea. Several hours later, as John Ericsson's four-bladed propeller broke the surface, it glistened in the spotlights of the recovery ship, cloaked with sea life and history. There were just a few seconds of awed silence before the divers and scientists broke into relieved and lusty cheers.

The propeller, carried back in a mist of spray, went directly into a conservation tank at the museum. Almost six years later, just in time for a new exhibition of *Monitor* and *Virginia* artifacts, the propeller, dents and gouges and all, would be freed from its chemical bath, slathered with preservatives, and put on display.

Divers returned to the *Monitor* in 1999, mostly to investigate. They studied the port-side deck and armor belt to see how these structures could be stabilized; they examined the lower hull in order to plan the removal of the engine; they did a test excavation at the base of the turret; and they continued to train in deep, mixed-gas conditions, making a total of twenty-nine dives.

The 2000 project was anything but glamorous. It involved pumping more than eight hundred cubic feet of grout into specially made bags at the bottom of the ocean. The grout bags shored up the port side of the vessel—where the turret rested—to prevent collapse. Divers also recovered the aft section of the propeller shaft and the skeg. There were 158 dives on the wreck in 2000, a major breakthrough in deepwater diving experience and a big morale booster for the Navy program.

After the 2000 season, Murray elected to take the project a step further. Even though the Navy had pioneered the use of saturation diving, and even though private industry now used it extensively, the military had completely dropped out of the saturation game. Now master diver Chuck Young urged him to consider sat diving for the last major recoveries, the engine and the turret. Murray went to bat for it and got it.

It would be an experiment; they'd contract for a private system and see how it worked. If it did, maybe the Navy would decide to purchase a system of its own. In 2001, it worked as hoped. There were more than twice as many dives that season as in 2000, and saturation divers, including Murray, spent 450 hours on the bottom. In 2001 MDSU TWO removed the engine and it joined the shaft, skeg, and a growing collection of artifacts at the Mariners' Museum. There, like the propeller, these components began years of conservation in chemical and electrolytic baths to remove more than a century's encrustations of salt, corrosion, and coralline algae.

Murray and NAVSEA not only got two bangs for the buck—recovering artifacts and training Navy divers in deep ocean conditions—but they improved safety as well. The divers had been experiencing unacceptable levels of toxicity when decompressing in 100 percent oxygen, and several had had convulsions. When the dive tables were adjusted to require 50 percent oxygen and 50 percent helium, the improvement was dramatic.

Meanwhile, in October 2000, Murray's career took a new turn. After many years of leading Navy dive teams, he moved from commander to captain and from MDSU TWO to a desk job in Washington, supervisor of diving for Naval Sea Systems Command (NAVSEA). It was perfect for him, because it gave him an excuse to keep diving. Enlisted men affectionately referred to him as "the highest-paid second-class diver in the Navy."

Like a player-coach, he could continue to work on site while also running most of the Navy's other dive operations. And because of his history with the *Monitor*, he also was put in charge of the funds earmarked for the project by the Legacy program. Though he didn't write all the checks, having Murray in that position could not have been a happier coincidence.

Now, in the summer of 2002, the salvage team aboard the giant barge is ready for the real deal, the recovery of the biggest and heaviest and by far the most symbolic part of the little warship: the turret. Out on the barge, Murray is asked if he's happy about the move to Washington. "Hell, no," he says. "But it's an important job. You can make a difference. This is really the biggest thing, diving-wise, in the Navy." The complexity of the mission, with surface-supply divers and saturation divers working side by side around the clock, is something the Navy has never done. It's a win-win situation, and Murray has never had a problem getting the funds he needed.

"I got everything I asked for, every dime." There is just one blemish. "Last year they shorted me a case of beer." What? "Twenty-four dollars," he explains. Out of more than $5 million requested for 2001, that was the only shortcoming.

Any way he looked at it, the *Monitor* recovery project is a bargain for the Navy. It offers both the high-profile distinction of recovering priceless artifacts and unprecedented deepwater training. "Every one of these guys is excited about coming down here," he says. It has quickly become the prestige dive training opportunity in the country. If politics makes for the strangest of bedfellows, the *Monitor* salvage operation is not far behind.

Despite all the paperwork Murray has to deal with, he has managed to dive on the *Monitor* as much as any of the others. A powerful man and an accomplished diver, he's been in on every phase of the recovery, from propeller to engine. He's dived on the wreck, tunneled under it with a hydroblaster, and studied it from every angle. There is no way he was *not* going to be present for the turret recovery. He knows, perhaps better than anyone, that it can be done.

FIVE

AS DEAD AS MEN EVER WERE

T HE *MONITOR*'s sendoff had been anything but rousing on that dreary morning of March 6, 1862. While passing alongside the *North Carolina,* the receiving ship from which most of the crew had transferred, first class fireman John Driscoll noted the grim faces of sailors watching the ironclad depart. "Those we passed," he said, "seemed to think it would be better to have played the funeral dirge than to give us the customary cheer."

There were no other accounts of how the sailors viewed their possible demise, but it is not difficult to imagine, after the near-calamities of their first outings, how vulnerable they must have felt.

The *Monitor* was taken in tow by the powerful oceangoing tug *Seth Low* and, along with a pair of gunships, the *Currituck* and *Sachem,* rounded Sandy Hook and headed south. A gentle westerly wind barely ruffled the sea. At night officers took the air on top of the turret and marveled at distant sails glowing white in the light of the crescent moon.

Down below was another matter. Sailors trying to sleep in hammocks in the berth deck were soaked by water that poured through ventilator stacks into the engine room and worked its way under the turret. Not trusting Ericsson's plan for the 120-ton turret to seal itself by resting on a bronze ring on the deck, engineers had raised the turret and stuffed the opening with oakum—a loose, stringy fiber usually treated with tar or pitch. Oakum was the time-tested substance for sealing cracks between the planks of wooden boats. What this accomplished was to allow waves breaking over the ship's deck and striking the base of the turret to open gaping holes in the seal and find its way down below. "When I awoke this morning," Paymaster William Keeler wrote to his wife, "I found much more motion to the vessel & could see the green water through my deck light as the waves rolled across the deck." The water was not all that was green. Several of the crew, including Captain Worden, were seasick.

Keeler, a forty-year-old jeweler and watchmaker, had left La Salle, Illinois, to join the navy. His prodigious and frequently eloquent letters home to Anna, usually written by candlelight late at night in his "little snuggery" of a room, would constitute the most informative record of the *Monitor*'s brief career. To him and others of the ship's company—nearly all raw recruits—the experience of having waves roll over the deck and slam against its pilothouse and turret, not to mention cascading down into the living spaces and engine room, must have been a troubling introduction to life at sea.

The officer in the pilothouse at the time, Ensign George Frederickson, a slightly built twenty-eight-year-old native of Denmark, was able to hold his pen steady enough to write legibly in the ship's log that conditions were "very rough, the sea making a clean breach over the vessel."

Samuel Dana Greene, the ship's executive officer from Cumberland, Maryland, wrote to his parents that by noon the wind freshened and the sea became quite rough. He was twenty-two years old, dark-eyed, observant. "In the afternoon the sea was breaking over our decks at a great rate, and coming in our hawse pipe, forward, in perfect floods. Our berth deck hatch leaked in spite of all we could do, and the water came down under the tower like a water fall."

By 4:00 P.M., Greene added, "the water had gone down our smoke stacks and blowers to such an extent that the blowers gave out, and the Engine Room was filled with gas." The engineers struggled with the blowers until they were overcome by fumes and collapsed, "apparently as dead as men ever were." Greene and others dashed into the engine room, themselves nearly suffocating as they carried the engineers and firemen to the top of the turret. There the men were laid out until fresh air and brandy could bring them around.

"The water continued to pour through the hawser-hole," he wrote, "and over and down the smoke-stacks and blowerpipes, in such quantities that there was imminent danger that the ship would founder."

Keeler met one of the engineers coming up the stairs, pale, blackened, wet, and staggering, gasping for breath. "He asked me for brandy & I turned to go down & get him some & met the Sailors dragging up the fireman & other engineers, apparent[ly] lifeless."

The paymaster burst into the engine room, stumbling over coal and ashes, and found one of the engineers lying on the floor. He and another sailor carried the nearly dead man to the tower where he, like the others, was revived.

Fireman Driscoll, who had been asleep in his hammock, tied a handkerchief over his mouth, crawled into the engine room, and managed to reattach a belt on one of the blowers, but the fan box was full of water and the belt kept flying off. He took a hammer and chisel and punched a hole in the box. The water gushed out and drenched him, but he was then able to restart the blower. He climbed back to the turret, received a shot of brandy, and passed out for the rest of the night.

The *Monitor*, almost dead in the water, was towed close to shore where the sea was calmer. Toward evening the wind moderated briefly, long enough to restart the engines, and the crisis appeared to be over.

"But at midnight, in passing over a shoal," Greene recounted, "rough water was again encountered and our troubles were renewed, complicated this time by the jamming of the wheel-ropes, so that the safety of the ship depended entirely on the strength of the hawser, which connected her with the tug-boat. The hawser, being new, held fast; but during the greater part of the night we were constantly engaged in fighting the leaks, until we reached smooth water again, just before daylight."

Assuming that they were making between five and six knots, daylight on March 8 would have found them creeping along the Virginia coast somewhere near Assateague Island. Shortly after 8:00 A.M., they spotted Hog Island Light, bearing about six miles southwest. The lighthouse was erected in 1852 to guard the entrance to the Great Machipongo Inlet on Virginia's Eastern Shore. With the weather now turning fine, they were making good time. By 1:00 P.M., the light at Smith Island, near the southern end of the Eastern Shore, hove into view, and by 3:00 P.M. they rounded Cape Charles and entered the Chesapeake Bay. At that moment, watch officer Louis Stodder heard an ominous rumble in the distance, the sound of heavy gunfire.

The *Monitor* and her crew had just missed one of the bloodiest days in the history of American naval warfare. Had they arrived half a day sooner, the story might have been entirely different.

SIX

IF THE BUG AIN'T FLYIN'

Moments after the powerful squall moves out to sea on June 28, 2002, the weather turns clear and beautiful. Stars pack the sky as dive operations resume.

The next morning I join a group of Navy divers on board the *Emmanuel*, a crew boat from Grand Isle, Louisiana, and we set out from Hatteras. After ninety minutes of jouncing over the waves, we begin to see the outlines of the massive *Wotan*, squatting upon the sea. It looks like a small city, or at least a village. The skipper of the *Emmanuel* throttles back the boat's growling engines, and we sidle up to the barge. Then, four at a time, we throw our gear into the middle of a doughnut-shaped life ring, which the divers call a "Billy-pew," and grab support ropes. Up and over we go, courtesy of a small crane, and bang down on the aft deck of the barge.

Among the first to greet us is John Broadwater, chief archaeologist on board and manager of the *Monitor* National Marine Sanctuary. With his trim beard and "DeepArch" T-shirt, he's the picture of a dedicated underwater archaeologist. Beside him, with a warm greeting and smile, Commander Bobbie Scholley looks every bit the Navy diver, tanned and toned in a dark blue tank top. Although Broadwater is in charge of recovering the turret, there is no doubt who runs the Navy side of the operation. "I'm Bobbie Scholley," she says, with a strong handshake. "Welcome to the *Wotan*."

I get a quick tour of the football-field-sized barge. At the stern are most of the crew quarters, stacked like egg cartons, three stories high with a helicopter deck on top. I'm assigned the top bunk in a four-person room, but I'm certain to rarely see my roommates, who are constantly working in twelve-hour, round-the-clock shifts. In the middle level of the stacked units is a cramped galley that also runs day and night, in sync with the dietary rhythms of the floating city, serving up hot meals—heaping plates of pasta and meat and a never-ending supply of pies and cakes and soda, with ice cream cones available night and day. Action videos drone constantly on a nearby television monitor.

Down on the main deck is a corrugated metal box that serves as NOAA headquarters. TV monitors swim with images from the cameras on divers' helmets and from a remotely operated vehicle that provides an almost-constant, insomniac view of the work on the bottom.

As we walk the deck, I'm aware of the steady growl of generators. An 800-kilowatt main generator, backed up by two standby and emergency generators, powers everything on board, from the lights and toilets and watermaker to air compressors, winches, and communications equipment.

Amidships on the port side of the barge is the saturation dive complex. Outside, lounging on beach chairs under an awning and reading well-thumbed paperbacks, are saturation divers who are temporarily off-duty. They look like beach musclemen, soaking up the sun. But they're slowly recovering from exhausting shifts at the bottom of the ocean. Up one flight is the sat shack, the cramped room where master divers watch the constant operations and confer with divers working on the bottom. Beside it is a docking station where the diving bell, when hoisted from the deep every twelve hours, locks onto a recompression chamber, like a spaceship onto a space station.

The only thing visible right now is a taut cable, snaking into the water with breathing gas, power, hot water, and communication hoses attached. The bell is down. We will not see it again for several hours.

Next door to the saturation station are racks of cylinders containing the life-giving gasses that are pumped down to the divers through umbilical hoses. Also on the port side of the barge is the dive station for surface-supply divers, along with their own recompression chambers and communications shack. There's a constant hubbub as divers suit up for their plunge to the bottom. Master divers and tenders and a host of others cry out and echo commands.

"Both divers traveling!" the master diver barks, indicating the sailors have left the stage near the ocean bottom and are heading for their assigned jobs. We move on. There will be plenty of opportunities to watch this precision ballet in the days ahead.

Closer to the bow is a separate shack where an operator controls the "bug," the all-seeing ROV that constantly hovers around the wreck, twenty-four hours a day. Sometimes when the current is running strong and the ROV's motor has a hard time keeping it on station, the divers know that they too had better sit it out. If the bug ain't flyin', the saying goes, the divers ain't divin'.

Near the bow is the pedestal and machine house of the 500-ton derrick crane, with a red-painted boom that lies along the length of the deck like some great elephant's trunk. Next to it, on the starboard side, is the winch room for the crane, with a second-story tower where yet another set of monitors watches the winches that control all eight anchors. It's also a communications hub for the entire operation, with computer stations and satellite phones.

Shortly after our arrival, Broadwater huddles in the small main-deck control room with master divers who are directing the work of surface-supply divers on the bottom. Onscreen the helmeted sailors, trailing long umbilical cords, seem like astronauts bounding over the surface of the moon. Cameras on their helmets show exactly where they're looking as they paw through debris on the wreck of the ironclad warship.

Broadwater is a compact man, diminutive next to the huge divers, polite and courtly but seemingly ever-present and aware. "Oh, wait! What's that?" he exclaims as one of the two divers passes over an object on the deck aft of the engine room. "I don't know. Possible lantern base."

Chief warrant officer Cavey asks the diver, 240 feet below, to move back and check out the item, which turns out to be not a lantern base but part of a pulley, a small but still incalculably wonderful part of the most important treasure hunt in Broadwater's career. Later, at an improvised station amidships on the barge where likely artifacts are examined, the archaeologist lovingly examines a wheel the size of a dinner plate with a grooved rim and, in the middle, a circle of brass roller bearings.

"It looks like something from an old sailing ship," says Broadwater, cradling the bronze and wood object as though it were a newborn. He consults a book in the on-deck shack that serves as all-purpose headquarters. "Here it is, in a drawing," he exclaims. "A tiller sheave." This pulley wheel, apparently used to help turn the ship's rudder, becomes artifact number one for the 2002 expedition. He identifies the wood, only slightly grooved by shipworm, as *lignum vitae*, a very hard Central American wood used for such marine purposes.

"With oak it would last a year or two, but this is real tough stuff." He runs his hand lovingly around the bearings. "Boy, that's machine work. Pretty neat, huh?"

Broadwater is running what is undoubtedly one of the most important deepwater archaeological excavations in history and certainly the biggest project of his career, yet he takes time to lovingly examine every one of hundreds of artifacts that emerge from the ocean floor. Each small item, from buttons to lantern chimneys, tells a story, and even when big-picture events are looming, each deserves his undivided attention.

He also knows that each new artifact sets the turret recovery schedule back, and no one can afford to tarry. Each item has to be photographed where it lies, carefully removed, sent topside, tagged, and placed in water to keep it from disintegrating.

The diving part of the operation is already in high gear. Scholley is at the dive station checking the day's assignments, her wavy reddish-brown hair subdued in a ponytail. She seems all business at first, but her smile is quick and generous. She's already been down for an inspection tour of the wreck and feels good about how things are going. There are thirty-three divers from her command on the barge, only a fraction of those needed for round-the-clock operations, so divers from more than a dozen commands, including some from the United Kingdom, are rotating in. That many divers taking turns, getting their bottom time, eating, sleeping, and then doing it again, might create a logistical nightmare, but somehow it all seems to be running smoothly. "It's amazing how quickly the team gels," she says.

Her optimism is tempered by the realization that the target of this operation is one of the heaviest, yet most fragile, objects ever recovered from this deep in the ocean. Unlike the chunks of aircraft aluminum that these divers routinely wrest from the bottom of the sea, this is a national treasure. It would not do to mangle it or to have it fall to pieces.

Already the divers have begun preparations for removing parts of the hull and armor belt that are resting on top of the turret, but after thirty-six hours of storms, Scholley is nervous about the schedule. "We're all antsy because of the bad weather, and there's so much work to do." She shrugs. "We're never happy unless we're two weeks ahead of schedule."

That schedule could be stretched to the limit in the weeks ahead as Broadwater and Scholley lead their teams. As sailors and meteorologists have long known, the only predictable thing about conditions at Cape Hatteras is their unpredictability. The most favorable weather window has always been June through September, but that coincides with peak hurricane season. Experience with wind, high seas, and treacherous bottom currents has shown that it is possible to conduct diving operations only one day in three, so planning must include plenty of down time.

Then there is the turret itself, the iconic heart of a national historic landmark. Aside from the many dangers to the divers during much of the recovery, the most dangerous phase for the 120-ton turret is the lift itself. Unless it is done in optimal sea conditions, movement of the barge could cause the lifting gear to sway and turn the turret into a giant wrecking ball. In everyone's mind is a history of other recovery operations that successfully rigged large objects and raised them from the seabed only to have them dashed to pieces against the side of a barge or torn apart when they were lifted out of the water and the sudden lack of buoyancy concentrated all the weight on cables and lifting straps. For Broadwater and Scholley, the project will require persistence at times and the ability to compromise at others. It will rest heavily on both their shoulders. And in the end it might well call for something that neither could have planned for—incredible luck.

SEVEN

DARK MONSTER

SHORTLY AFTER noon on March 8, 1862, with a gentle northwest-erly rippling the water out on Hampton Roads, the quartermaster aboard the Union ship Congress turned to one of his officers: "I wish you would take a glass and look over there, sir. I believe that thing is a-comin' down at last." That "thing" was indeed the CSS *Virginia*, whose hour at last had come to wreak havoc on the ships of the Union blockade. One observer said the rebel ironclad looked like the roof of a barn with a chimney belching black smoke; another compared it to a "half-submerged crocodile." Gleaming with pig fat that had been slathered on its sloping sides to help deflect enemy shots, it appeared to still another observer as simply a "dark monster."

The Confederates were about to make a desperate move to break the stranglehold that President Lincoln and his strategists had used to shut down southern ports. The "Anaconda Plan," so named because of its intention of squeezing the South economically, was never fully carried out; the blockade was to have been accompanied by an overland flanking movement from the west. But the naval part was in full gear, with an aging fleet of wooden ships guarding the entrances to harbors all along the Atlantic and Gulf coasts. One of the biggest Union presences was in Hampton Roads, gateway to the Chesapeake Bay, Norfolk, Washington, and Richmond, now capital of the Confederacy.

Shortly after taking office as the South's secretary of the navy, Stephen R. Mallory, a former Florida senator and a keen observer of

European advances in the field of "iron-armored" ships, as he called them, made it clear to the Confederate House Committee of Naval Affairs that the South must have one, and soon. Such a vessel, he wrote,

> could traverse the entire coast of the United States, prevent all blockades, and encounter, with a prospect of success, their entire Navy.
>
> If to cope with them upon the sea we follow their example and build wooden ships, we shall have to construct several at one time; for one or two ships would fall easy prey to her comparatively numerous steam frigates. But inequality of numbers may be compensated by invulnerability; and thus not only does economy but naval success dictate the wisdom and expediency of fighting with iron against wood, without regard to the first cost.

Mallory dispatched agents to Europe to see about purchasing some of the iron-cloaked frigates being built there and studied plans for constructing floating batteries from scratch. There was not a moment to lose, he concluded, and these two options were taking too long. But it just so happened that a third option was available.

The *Merrimack*—her correct name, though often spelled without the k—had been an impressive fighting machine, a 4,636-ton, forty-gun steam frigate with a screw propeller built at the Boston Navy Yard in 1855. The pride of the U.S. Navy, first in a line of Merrimack-class frigates, she sailed first to Europe, largely to impress Old World powers, then around Cape Horn to serve as flagship of the Pacific Squadron. But her troublesome engine was in need of repair, and in February 1860 she was sent to the Gosport Navy Yard, the forerunner to the present Norfolk Navy Yard.

The Gosport Navy Yard, the largest and best equipped in America at the time, became a tempting prize a year later when Virginia broke off from the Union. With rebels almost at the gate, the commanders of the yard failed to slip the *Merrimack* out of their reach and were forced to put her to the torch, burning the ship to the waterline and sinking her into the mud of the Elizabeth River. There she might have stayed, but the wreck needed to be moved, and the new commanders of the yard had the blackened hulk raised out of the muck and placed in dry storage. It did not take them long to realize that there might yet be life in this sad vessel.

Conversion of the *Merrimack* at Gosport Navy Yard. (Mariners' Museum)

Beginning in July 1861, workers at the yard cut the ship down to her berth deck, then erected a heavy oak and pine casemate on top, slanting upward and inward at a forty-five-degree angle like the roof of a house. The Tredegar Iron Works in Richmond rolled out four inches of iron armor to be layered over the casemate. The old engines, once condemned by the navy, were again pressed into service. There were numerous delays. The South didn't have the industrial capacity to meet its war needs, and the ironworks was pushed to the limit. So desperate for iron was the Confederacy that old railroad and trolley tracks were melted down for armor. But this was a high-priority project, and shipbuilders toiled night and day. It was no secret what they were up to. Northern newspapers covered the progress of the new naval menace like a daily soap opera, and the Union at last tuned in with a hurry-up program to put iron on the water.

Rechristened the CSS *Virginia*, the ship that emerged was an ugly but lethal 262 feet, with a draft of 23 feet and a top speed of five knots. She carried two pivot-mounted 7-inch Brooke rifles, two 6.4-inch Brooke rifles, six 9-inch Dahlgren smoothbore guns, and just as menacing, a 1,500-pound iron ram. Union sailors either didn't know about the name change or simply refused to accord their adversary the respect of her new name. To them she was always the *Merrimack.*

Mallory had become increasingly excited about what his iron warhorse could accomplish. He suggested she might make "a dashing cruise" up the Potomac to Washington, and he even hinted that she "could doubtless go to New York. . . . Once in the bay, she could shell and burn the city and the shipping. Such an event would eclipse all the glories of the combats of the sea . . . and strike a blow from which the enemy could never recover."

The *Virginia*'s officers were more realistic about her shortcomings, including her deep draft and defective engines.

Unlike the *Monitor,* which filled her crew list in one day, the *Virginia* had a problem: a shortage of trained sailors, especially gunnery crews. So the ship's commanders recruited members of army artillery crews and brought them on board. There was no time for testing the guns, no time even to inform the crew of its mission. Many on that March 8 morning assumed they were going on a shakedown cruise. But flag officer Franklin Buchanan, a fiery navy veteran who had taken command of the *Virginia,* had other ideas. He would exercise his crew with live targets.

The air was electric with anticipation as news of the ship's departure spread along the banks of the wide Elizabeth River. "In an instant the city was in an uproar, women, children, men on horseback and on foot running down toward the river from every conceivable direction, shouting, 'the *Merrimac* is going down,' " wrote a Georgia infantry private who watched from the shore. "I saw the huge monster swing loose from its moorings and make her way down the river . . . a good portion of her crew were on top and received the enthusiastic cheers from the excited populace without a single response. Everything betokened serious business."

Shortly after 11:00 A.M., the monster made its way toward the waiting fleet of wooden Union ships, steaming like some armored, ominous, faceless gladiator into a confluence of history and place: Hampton Roads. Because forts on the north side of the Roads remained in Union hands while those on the south side bristled with rebel guns, it was literally a theater of war. This wide waterway that joins the Chesapeake Bay and several rivers—the James, the Nansemond, and the Elizabeth—was a nexus between the Union and the Confederacy, with extensions of its waters touching both their capitals. Seventy miles up the James lay Richmond, and sixty miles up the bay and another ninety up the Potomac River lay Washington. The South's fearsome new weapon, now steaming down the Elizabeth River, appeared to threaten Washington itself.

Ironically, on March 7 Secretary Welles, in his anxiety over the Confederate battery, had fired off telegrams to fleet commanders ordering them to send several ships in Hampton Roads, including the two old-line warships *Cumberland* and *Congress*, out of harm's way. They were to be sent up the Chesapeake Bay to the Potomac River, under tow if necessary. "Let there be no delay," he said. But there was. The blockade commanders couldn't get the ships out of the Roads in time, and on March 8, a clearly rattled Welles reversed the order. By now it was too late. His worst nightmare was already unfolding.

As the hulking Virginia steamed from the Elizabeth River into Hampton Roads, the wooden federal fleet, stretching from Newport News Point to Fort Monroe, lay waiting like ducks in a shooting gallery. The most tempting targets were just beginning to weigh anchor off the point. The attacker swung slowly, almost languorously, to port and headed right for them, prompting union ships and shore batteries to erupt with what should have been a withering barrage.

The quarry lay off the western edge of Newport News Point under the protection of 8,000 federal troops and their heavy artillery. But it was no protection at all. To the dismay of the shore batteries and the horror of naval gunners, the shells and shot bounced off the predator like spit wads. And she kept on coming.

The *Virginia*'s first targets were the *Cumberland*, a 1,726-ton sloop of war, and the *Congress*, a 1,867-ton sailing frigate, both with long and distinguished careers at sea and both completely dependent on sail power. The *Cumberland*, commissioned in Boston 1843, had served in the Mediterranean. She too had been at the Gosport Navy Yard but, unlike the *Merrimack*, had been towed out of the yard before its surrender. The *Congress* had sailed out of the Portsmouth Navy Yard in

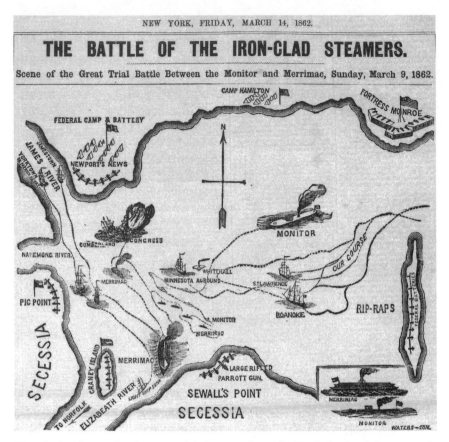

NEW YORK, FRIDAY, MARCH 14, 1862.

THE BATTLE OF THE IRON-CLAD STEAMERS.

Scene of the Great Trial Battle Between the Monitor and Merrimac, Sunday, March 9, 1862.

Map depicts (somewhat inaccurately) the area where the *Cumberland* and *Congress* sank, where the *Minnesota* lay aground, and where the *Monitor* and *Virginia* (*Merrimack*) met. (Mariners' Museum)

Kittery, Maine, in 1842, becoming flagship of the Pacific and Brazil Squadrons. She had joined the blockade in Hampton Roads in September 1861.

Heading straight for the *Cumberland*, the *Virginia* took advantage of a passing opportunity to maul the *Congress* with a broadside, leaving her grievously wounded. Now running at full speed, the *Virginia* rammed the *Cumberland*, burying her iron ram deep into the Union ship's starboard side below the waterline, at the same time reversing her engines. There was momentary panic aboard the *Virginia* when the ram stuck fast in the *Cumberland*'s side and both ships seemed about to go under. The engineers poured on the coals and the *Virginia* was able to back away, but the ram broke off in her victim like the stinger of a killer bee.

The *Cumberland*'s dauntless crew fired shot after shot at the assassin ship, with about as much effect as a popgun. So furious was the *Cumberland*'s response that the greased sides of the Confederate battery seemed to fry like bacon.

"Jack, don't this smell like hell?" one of the Confederate gun crew exclaimed.

"It certainly does, and I think we'll be there in a few minutes," came the reply.

The *Virginia*'s guns mauled the *Cumberland*, and rivers of blood and gore ran across the wooden ship's decks as she sank. Doggedly, the defenders kept firing even as the stricken vessel headed for the bottom, abandoning ship only when their guns went under.

It seemed to take forever for the *Virginia*, now lumbering up the James River, to turn—her helm hard astarboard, her keel slicing through the mud of the river—but at last it was the *Congress*'s turn to be mauled. In an attempt to avoid the *Cumberland*'s fate, the *Congress* was run into shallow water near Newport News—on the Union side of the James River—and grounded. Still, the ironclad was able to stand off about two miles and rake the wooden ship with broadsides. "The carnage, havoc and dismay caused by our fire compelled them to haul down their colors" and hoist white flags of surrender, reported flag officer Buchanan on board the *Virginia*.

Official telegrams between Union generals on shore offer an almost blow-by-blow account:

> The *Congress* has surrendered. . . . I expect to see her in flames soon. . . .
> We want blankets sent up to-night for the crews of the *Cumberland* and the *Congress*. The *Merrimack* has it all her own way this side of Signal Point and will probably burn the *Congress*, now aground, with white flag flying and our sailors swimming ashore.

As shallow-draft Confederate boats attempted to approach the beaten ship, Union army shore batteries at Newport News disregarded the surrender and opened up on them. Buchanan, furious over "this vile treachery," ordered the *Congress* riddled and burned with incendiary shells and white-hot cannonballs, heated on the ship's fire grates. "Plug hot shot into her and don't leave her until she's afire," he fumed. With that he leaped up on the deck of the *Virginia* and fired his rifle toward shore until a Union sharpshooter put a rifle ball in his thigh. He was helped below, still fuming.

At the end of the day, 121 men of the crew of 376 on the *Cumberland* had been killed, as had 240 of 434 on the *Congress*. Until Pearl Harbor, this would stand as the worst American naval bloodbath in history. And there might have been more carnage. Another Union prize, the USS *Minnesota*, had run aground, and the *Virginia* would have dealt with her next had the tide not been falling. It was time to retire for the night. As the *Virginia* headed for Sewell's Point on the Norfolk side of the Roads—where Confederate guns would protect her—she left one warship on the bottom, only its masts and yards standing above water, and another burning hopelessly. The slaughter would resume in the morning.

Just days before, a telegraph cable had been laid between Washington and Fort Monroe, the formidable Union stronghold overlooking the Roads that was never taken by the Confederates. Among the first dispatches to be sent was a telegraph from General John Wool relating the extent of the damage. A hurried meeting was assembled at the White House. According to a memoir by Navy Secretary Welles, Secretary of War Edwin Stanton was beside himself. What was to prevent the *Virginia* from ripping through the rest of the blockade and steaming into virtually any harbor in the North, laying waste to major cities like Boston, New York, or Washington? demanded the agitated Stanton, unknowingly echoing Mallory's most optimistic assessments.

With that, Stanton strode to the window, which had a commanding view of the Potomac River, and declared, "Not unlikely we shall have a shell or cannonball from one of her guns in the White House before we leave this room." Lincoln couldn't help a worried glance through the window. Even though Welles assured the gathering that the Confederate ironclad's draft was too great to negotiate the river's shoals, Stanton demanded to know what could possibly stop the "monster."

According to Welles, when he described the *Monitor* and her arma-
ments to the secretary of war, Stanton "turned away with a look of min-
gled amazement, contempt, and distress that was painfully ludicrous."
   And where was this *Monitor* anyway? No one seemed to know.

As THE little ship rounded the Virginia Capes on the afternoon of
March 8, the distant thunder heard by her crew was surely the anni-
hilation of the *Congress*. When a pilot who came on board confirmed
the devastation, the crew vowed revenge. The men were anything but
seasoned and were totally unacquainted with facing an enemy intent
on killing them. Now came the realization that the long-dreaded beast
was not merely girding for battle but was, then and there, on the loose.
How they summoned the courage after the near-disaster of their
maiden voyage is a wonder.
   "Oh, how we longed to be there," Keeler wrote his wife. "As we
neared the harbor," he added, "the firing slackened & only an occa-
sional gun lit up the darkness—vessels were leaving like a covey of
frightened quails & their lights danced on the water in all directions."
   They must have swallowed hard when they saw the devastation left
by their opponent. When they arrived off Hampton Roads around
9:00 P.M., the *Congress* was lighting up the night sky in her flaming
death throes.
   The scene would likely have been a prelude to further disaster if the
agitated Welles had had his way and the *Monitor* had abruptly departed
for Washington. Fortunately for the Union, when Worden pulled up
to the frigate *Roanoke* and reported to Captain John Marston, the senior officer in the squadron, the two men agreed that, in light of what
had just taken place, the *Monitor* had better stick around. This, after
all, was where the dreaded adversary stalked.
   Worden sent a message to Welles. "I have the honor to report," he
said simply, "that I have arrived at this anchorage at 9 o'clock this
evening, and am ordered to proceed immediately to the assistance of
the *Minnesota*."
   This seemed a preposterous assignment, a midget vessel going to
the aid of a giant warship. Indeed, when Worden shouted to the *Minnesota*'s skipper, Captain Henry Van Brunt, that he'd "stand by you to

the last if I can help you," the latter was heard to reply, "No Sir, you cannot help me."

Van Brunt was understandably unimpressed, although in his official report afterward he changed his tune. The *Monitor* came alongside, he wrote, "and all on board felt that we had a friend that would stand by us in our hour of need."

Shortly after midnight, just before the *Monitor* dropped anchor beside the *Minnesota*, the fires on the *Congress* reached her magazines, and the ship went up in a spectacular, though chilling, display of fireworks.

Keeler was on deck and witnessed "a scene of the most terrible magnificence" as a volcano of flame erupted. "Pieces of burning timbers, exploding shells, huge fragments of the wreck, grenades and rockets filled the air and fell sparkling and hissing in all directions," he related. "It did not flash up & vanish in an instant, but seemed to remain for a moment or two, an immense column of fire, one end on the earth the other in the heavens. It soon vanished & a dense thick cloud of smoke hid every thing from view. We were about two miles from the wreck & the dull heavy explosion seemed almost to lift us out of the water."

The *Monitor*'s exhausted sailors had arrived just in time to see what might lie in store for them in the morning. As Dana Greene, the ship's young executive officer, told his parents, "It went straight to the marrow of our bones."

H. Ashton Ramsay, chief engineer on the *Virginia*, had been standing on deck where the ship lay near Sewell's Point and observed "red-tongued flames running up shrouds, masts and stays, and extending out to the yard-arms." Occasionally flames would reach one of the loaded cannons, and a shell would hiss through the darkness. Then, at midnight, came the grand finale: "The magazines exploded, shooting up a huge column of firebrands hundreds of feet in the air, and then the burning hulk burst asunder and melted into the waters, while the calm night spread her sable mantle over Hampton Roads."

Before catching whatever sleep he could, Lieutenant Worden wrote a brief letter to his wife, saying the rebel ship "caused sad work amongst our vessels." But he added, with perhaps more bravado than the situation warranted, "She can't hurt us."

There was great excitement during the night, with frequent reports that the *Virginia* was coming. At 1:30 A.M. the crew was piped to quarters and told to weigh anchor. It was a false alarm, and half an hour later they dropped anchor again. The jumpy sailors remained watchful through the long night, hardly any of them laying down their heads.

On the *Virginia* it was quite another story. The men celebrated late into the night.

Lieutenant Catesby Jones had taken over for the wounded Buchanan. A Virginian, Jones was right at home on the ship now named for his state. He had served as ordnance officer on the *Merrimack* when the new steam frigate went into service six years before. When the war began, he became a Confederate navy lieutenant and was deeply involved in converting his old ship into the lethal battery she had now become.

The first day of the Battle of Hampton Roads—as it would later be known—was a bloody defeat for the Union and a heady victory for the suddenly potent Confederate navy. Stephen Mallory was later to crow to President Jefferson Davis about "this brilliant achievement, which will hold a conspicuous place among the heroic contests of naval history." He did not mention what happened the next day.

After making preparations for the morning, Lieutenant John Taylor Wood, an officer on the *Virginia*, would write, "We slept at our guns, dreaming of other victories in the morning."

While the rest of the crew dreamed, one of the *Virginia*'s pilots noticed an odd-shaped vessel gliding across the water, silhouetted by the blazing Union ship.

EIGHT

WHEN THINGS GO DOWN

O N THE dive platform at the verge of the Atlantic, three hardhat divers in black hot-water suits and red vests sit facing the water while teams of dive tenders get them ready. "On the side!" the master diver bellows, getting everyone's attention. "Moving divers to the stage!" The dive officers, tenders, console operator, communications operator, and stage handlers all echo the cry as two of the suited divers, looking like moon walkers, step onto the stage and stand back-to-back. One can watch this sequence dozens of times, but the precision and gusto with which Navy divers run it, the intricate ballet of people and machines, the mixture of caution and exuberance, is always riveting.

These aquanauts—sailor-athletes in superb condition, with muscles rippling from constant weight lifting and pushing objects around underwater—are about to be hurtled into inner space. They feel immense pride and passion for their work. You can see it in the iconic Mark V helmets that seemingly all have tattooed on calves or biceps or chests. You can hear it in their shouted commands and responses.

The Navy bought into this project not only to recover a treasured part of its history but to train divers in deep-ocean conditions. The lead group of the diving operation is Mobile Diving and Salvage Unit Two, from Little Creek Naval Amphibious Base in Norfolk, Virginia. MDSU TWO, like its counterpart MDSU ONE at Pearl Harbor in Hawaii, is an elite branch of the Navy. In peace and war, Navy divers take off at a moment's notice for all parts of the world to assist with the salvage and recovery of vessels and aircraft, battle damage assessment and repair, and harbor clearance.

The Norfolk command has five detachments, Alpha to Echo, each with sixteen divers, a dive officer, and a master diver. There are also unmanned underwater vehicle teams and side-scan sonar teams, as well as a shore detachment in Norfolk. Teams are equipped with fly-away diving systems. That means big stuff—recompression chambers and generators, portable offices, and hot-water heaters—all of which can be loaded onto C-130 transport planes and set up on ships, barges, piers, or beaches anywhere in the world. Occasionally that includes working in combat conditions. But unlike Navy SEALS, these divers are trained for defense, not for attack.

Both MDSU ONE and MDSU TWO were born in 1966 during the Vietnam War. Most of the work they do is unseen and unsung.

In recent years the divers of MDSU TWO have taken part in recovering victims of TWA flight 800 off Long Island, the terrorist bombing of the USS *Cole* in Yemen, the crash of John F. Kennedy Jr.'s plane off Martha's Vineyard, and many other disasters. They salvaged a spacecraft off Cape Canaveral and an SH-60 helicopter in 270 feet of water in the Red Sea. In July 2002, while much of the command's focus was on the *Monitor* expedition, MDSU TWO also sent several recompression chambers and master divers to help in the rescue of nine Pennsylvania coal miners who were trapped 240 feet underground—coincidentally, the same depth as the *Monitor* wreck. Because the miners were underground for three days, there was a chance they would suffer from the bends.

TWA flight 800 departed John F. Kennedy International Airport on July 17, 1996. Shortly after takeoff, the Boeing 747 exploded and plunged into the Atlantic Ocean off Long Island, killing all passengers and crew. Along with the Coast Guard, New York Police Department, and others, the Norfolk-based divers retrieved the bodies from depths of 115 to 130 feet in fifty-degree water that sometimes offered zero visibility. They spent ninety-eight days on site, working around the clock in twelve-hour shifts. "The aircraft was literally in millions of pieces, and we got every one of them; there were 216 victims, and we got every one of those," said Commander Bill Robertson, who was in charge of one of the recovery ships.

"I had little kids at the time and I'd go out on deck and they'd just recovered some little diapers or some Disney doll or something like that, and I thought, 'My God, there's a human side of this that will always affect me, I don't care what I do.' I think if you ask any diver and they say they weren't affected by it, they're lying to you. They're absolutely lying to you."

In 1999, MDSU TWO responded to another civilian tragedy when a private plane carrying John F. Kennedy Jr., his wife, and his sister-in-law had crashed off Martha's Vineyard. The divers conducted a meticulous search of the ocean floor in 114 feet of water and brought all three bodies to the surface.

Almost always, the divers' work entails recovering human remains, a job that most of them loathe but ultimately take pride in performing. The dead are comrades in arms or civilians whose families might at least take comfort from knowing they've been found. It's the right thing to do, they all know.

On board the barge, one of the T-shirts among the dive crew puts the job in perspective: WE'RE THE GUYS YOU WANT AROUND WHEN THINGS GO DOWN. Another implores, FLY NAVY—WE NEED THE WORK.

But not every salvage and recovery operation is cloaked in the overwhelming sadness of lives lost on the sea. Navy divers also have the opportunity to be part of historic and scientific operations. And one of the most prestigious in Navy history is taking place off Cape Hatteras.

A MASTER diver or chief petty officer usually runs the dive sequence, and there's no tolerance for error. As Jim Mariano, one of only about a hundred Navy master divers, puts it, "We accept nothing less than perfection and refuse to accept failure in any shape or form." That may be difficult for some to live up to, but when your life is on the line, divers say, it helps to know that the person calling the shots is uncompromising. Diving the *Monitor* is one of the most hazardous missions they'll ever encounter. The preparation goes by the book.

The three divers are quickly suited up. Two go down together, with the third standing by in case something goes wrong. They wear thin black dive skins underneath to keep from being scalded by the hot water pumped into their outer suits. These hot-water suits have special pouches for weights: thigh weights, calf weights, hip weights, vest weights—eighty pounds of lead. There's not much neutral buoyancy in salvage diving; these folks are going to the bottom, and only a winch and lift stage will bring them back.

Heavy yellow helmets are snapped in place and thick bundles of hoses and lines—"umbilicals"—attached. The blue line sends back depth information; the yellow carries a gas mixture to the divers; the small red one is for communications with the surface, but it also has a solid cable meant to be yanked and hauled on; the large red hose is for the hot water that will be pumped through their suits; the orange is for lights and camera.

The Navy does a lot of scuba diving, but for salvage jobs, which entail dangerous operations like cutting, welding, and hydroblasting, hard hat diving offers more protection. For one thing, the hard hats allow divers to talk with supervisors above and be guided while they work in heavy currents and seas. The hats also buffer the loud noises these activities, especially hydroblasting, produce. But ultimately the biggest reason for surface-supply diving is having an unending supply of breathing gas, compared with a pair of scuba bottles that would quickly be used up in deep water. Because the gas molecules are compressed, the deeper the dive the faster the gas is used. At 240 feet, scuba divers use seven times more than they would at 30 feet.

Dive tenders check everything: the helmet and the harness it fits into, the steady-flow valves and purge buttons, the connections to all the hoses, the dial-a-breath knob that regulates the amount of gas each diver receives, the "come-home bottle," an emergency gas supply that will give the divers a few minutes of air if the surface supply fails. They bathe the helmets with soapsuds to check for leaks. A console operator checks the gas pressure and the gas mix. The checks are not just performed by memory but follow a series of orders bellowed out by the master diver. And when everything is done, the master diver double-checks everything for both the "red," or lead diver, and "green," or secondary diver. OK, Red? OK, Green? OK!

The divers are led over to the stage, a sturdy two-person platform, and the tenders close the gate, making sure hands and feet are in the right place and umbilicals are positioned correctly. There are half a dozen further checks, including the manifold pressure on the gas supply and the winch connection, and finally, eyeball-to-eyeball contact with the divers.

"On the side, divers going up and over!" The winch begins to whine, the stage handlers throw their weight against the steel bars of the thousand-pound stage, thrusting it out over the water, and it plunges into the waves. Just underwater now, the divers do a final check of each others' connections, and the stage descends to twenty feet. After receiving OKs from both divers, the console operator switches from the normal topside gas mixture to the bottom mix, 15.5 percent oxygen and the rest helium. "Ventilate," the divers are told. They open the steady-flow valves to release the topside gas mixture. Two gushers of bubbles, blue green in the cobalt sea, pop to the surface. Then they're given the command "circulate," and they close the valves. Immediately the topside crew hears a slightly higher pitch in the sound the air bubbles make, the first sign of helium in the divers' helmets. "OK, Red Diver?" the master diver calls into his headset. "OK, Green Diver?"

As the divers answer, their vocal cords affected by helium, they sound comically like Donald Duck or one of the singing Chipmunks. But it is a welcome sound that means they both are now breathing the right gas for their new environment.

Helium, it has been found, is the best of the inert gases to use for deep diving. This avoids nitrogen narcosis, or what Jacques Cousteau called "rapture of the deep"—a three-martini drunken euphoria, usually beginning at one hundred feet, that can lure divers into reckless behavior. Like the reaction to nitrous oxide, or laughing gas, nitrogen narcosis is the toxic effect of nitrogen pressure on nerve conduction. It slows things down and makes serious situations seem trivial or even hilarious. In the worst cases, divers might remove their regulators or just forget all about decompressing on the way up. "I am personally quite receptive to nitrogen rapture," Cousteau wrote in *The Silent World.* "I like it and fear it like doom."

Decompression sickness, the "bends," on the other hand, is an explosion of nitrogen or helium molecules in the bloodstream. These gas bubbles can permanently damage muscles or organs if divers ascend too fast. An elaborate regimen of decompression stops must be observed on the way up, followed by time spent in a recompression chamber on deck. There also is the risk of a coronary or cerebral gas embolism, both of which can be fatal. This is serious business, with serious consequences.

When divers descend, they experience increasing atmospheric pressure. The rule of thumb is one additional atmosphere (the pressure of air at sea level) every thirty-three feet. Where the *Monitor* lies, more than two hundred feet below sea level, that's seven times the pressure bones and lungs and organs are normally subjected to. For divers, as for everyone else, the gasses they breathe pass through their lungs into the bloodstream and enter the organs and tissues. During a dive, the tissues absorb inert gases like nitrogen and helium in proportion to the surrounding pressure. The deeper the dive, the more gas molecules are absorbed. As long as divers remain under pressure there's little danger, nor is there much if they ascend gradually, pausing along the way to give the gas time to escape. But if they ascend too rapidly the gas forms expanding bubbles in tissues and bloodstream that can wreak havoc. Sometimes the damage is mild, a temporary tingling or numbness, joint pain, or dizziness, and this can be reversed by "pressing" the diver back down in a chamber and allowing the gas to escape gradually. At other times the damage is to the spinal cord or brain, causing numbness, paralysis, or brain damage. An arterial gas embolism, where bubbles interrupt circulation, can cause convulsions, unconsciousness, and death.

It is no surprise, then, that commercial and recreational diving organizations take the risks seriously. They require divers to be trained and certified. They develop bottom-time charts for various depths and decompression schedules for both time and depth. To reduce the danger, deep divers have developed mixed-gas formulas that include helium, which does not have the same narcotic properties as nitrogen.

For deep dives like those on the *Monitor*, the Navy uses a helium-oxygen mixture. This reduces the narcosis threat to zero, but helium, too, has a dark side.

Helium enters and leaves tissues much faster than nitrogen, and if dive tables are not closely followed it accelerates the speed of decompression sickness. Helium also tends to pull body heat away from divers faster than nitrogen does. The chance of getting "bent" goes up rapidly in cold temperatures. Divers don't like to be warm while they're working, but cooler temperatures are dangerous for divers on the stage during ascent.

Deep diving seems like an exact science, but it isn't. Divers all have unique physiological characteristics that affect whether they are likely to get bent. "It's different for everybody," says master diver Scott Heineman, a gentle giant of a man. "That's why diving medicine is just spinning a roulette wheel."

At twenty feet, the divers check each other's connections to make sure there are no leaks.

"Both divers leaving twenty feet," the master diver calls out, punching his stopwatch. This is when bottom time begins. Again, the call is echoed. "Give me depths every ten feet," he instructs the console operator. "Maintain minimal manifold pressure." The descent is slow at first, about thirty feet per minute. Tenders muscle the umbilical lines from their lockers, like firefighters uncoiling hoses, and walk each loop to water's edge, where other tenders shackle the lines to the stage cable.

As the divers descend, pressure immediately assaults their ear drums, and they must equalize the forces between middle and outer ear. Some are able to do it simply by swallowing, but the most common method is to press against a nose guard in the helmet and breathe out, forcing air through the Eustachian tube into the middle ear. Now the speed picks up, the console operator calls out each ten-foot interval, and the cartoon-voiced divers respond all the way down.

"Let me know when the bottom's in sight," the master diver tells the divers. When they do, the winch driver slows the stage. At 210 feet they stop. The divers give topside a quick impression of conditions—visibility, current, temperature—then leave the stage, descend to the bottom, and go to work. Usually they sprint to the wreck, trailing bubbles and umbilical connections. Divers know their time is limited, so they throw all the power their bodies can muster into the job, battling seven atmospheres of resistance.

On the TV monitor in the surface-supply shack, you can see the images the divers' helmet cameras send back, their gloves pawing through rubble around the turret, fish swimming through this video field of vision. The sound of their steady breathing, accelerated by the work they're doing, fills the shack: *ahh hahh, ahh hahh, ahh hahh.*

The young divers, when they land on the bottom, often take a second or two just to drink in the scene—and waste time doing it. "It's shell shock when they first get down there, you can tell," says Heineman.

> You can see what they're seeing through their camera. It's sensory overload. For some of these guys it's the first deep dive they've ever made, and here they are diving on one of the most storied warships in one of the most perfect diving scenarios: crystal clear water, seventy degrees, on a dive of a lifetime.
>
> You would notice if you talked to a guy who went down there and really did well, and you ask him, "What'd you see down there?" He'd say, "I didn't see a damned thing." They are so focused on the job. You got to go there, get off the stage, run over there, take this widget, do whatever, get your ass back, don't be a problem and don't get hurt and come back. In five years I went down there, made about forty dives, the only time I ever got a good look around was when the job was over and I'm on the stage and I'm just kind of looking as I'm coming up, a minute, minute and a half before it fades from sight.

Being distracted can be life threatening. One of the biggest problems young divers have is getting their umbilical hoses tangled or caught on something. The dives are primarily for training but also are designed for the maximum amount of work each time. The tendency is to stretch the limits.

One morning as a young diver is pushing a berm to clear space around the turret, a cloud of sand lifts off the seabed and visibility drops. At thirty-four minutes, Heineman tells him to head back to the stage, but soon notices the diver is having trouble. He tells him, "Hey, just grab hold of the umbilical and pull yourself back to the stage."

Another three minutes go by, and Heineman tells the other diver, "You need to help him get back." As visibility improves, Heineman sees that the diver's umbilical is in a big knot. "Man, come on, guys, let's go. We're going to be late. Let's go! Let's go! Come on!"

Heineman realizes the divers are in trouble. Forty minutes is bad, requiring extra time in the chamber, but he also knows that the real danger level, when the risk of decompression sickness goes up exponentially, is about fifty minutes. After that, they'd have to go into the diving bell used by saturation divers, come back to the surface, and spend almost three days getting all that gas out of their systems.

"All right, we're not going to make it," he tells them. "Throttle it down, take your time." They make it back to the surface and spend an extra hour in the chamber, much of it breathing pure oxygen. When the young diver emerges from the successful decompression, he's full of energy and ready to dive again.

It takes about four minutes to get to the bottom, and during that time some of the younger divers have a bit too much time to think—and worry. Some days, Chris Murray says, they get down there and can't even see the wreck. "You just go into a black hole. I'm sure there's a lot racing through their minds. You can get lost or disoriented. That's why we have umbilicals going through the stage. If nothing else, they follow it back and there it is." On a few occasions, Murray has had to lead young divers by the hand.

The overriding concern with the *Monitor* mission is not recovering artifacts but keeping the divers safe. "You never, never, never compromise diver safety for anything," Broadwater says. In talks with Murray he stresses, "If I ever ask you to do something that puts divers in harm's way, that's all you need to say. I'll never say another word." Murray knows that, and knows Broadwater is an experienced diver himself. Their relationship, stretching over several years, allows them to be completely honest with each other.

In an operation this big, with five hundred or more dives, there are bound to be a few injuries, a few slight cases of the bends. An hour after his dive, one of the divers complains that his arm is numb and cold. He assumes he's slept on it while in the chamber, but the condition persists. He is placed back in the chamber, pressed back down to sixty feet, and given oxygen to breathe. Over several twenty-minute, then thirty-minute, periods of inhaling pure oxygen, the inert gas escapes.

There are dozens of fouling incidents and a few "exceptional exposures" where divers have to be given extra decompression time. But nothing serious has yet marred the project.

Even veterans can get into trouble. Master diver Jim Mariano has been with the *Monitor* project all five years. Built like a fireplug and possessed of a can-do attitude, he's the quintessential Navy diver. And that can lead to too much confidence, especially when one of the other old pros like Heineman is supervising.

"We always have this thing about screaming to the bottom, as fast as the winch will go," Mariano says. "If I'm diving and he's supervising, he'll tell the winch driver to open it wide open. And we go screaming to the bottom. And this one dive I just happened to be a little clogged up." "Usually, if you squeeze," he says, referring to uncomfortable pressure on the eardrums, "it's within the first thirty feet. I squeezed at sixty-eight feet. I had to yell 'Stop!' " The winch driver had to raise the stage ten feet so he could clear the pressure, then the dive was resumed, but the slightest hitch is reason enough to get chalked up on the "Wall of Fame/Wall of Shame" board, a bitingly humorous account of daily performance kept at the dive station. "I was toast for a day or two," he confesses.

There is a dangerous alternative to stopping and raising the stage. In a dive I witness in early July—a dive of nearly forty minutes—one of the men has blood flowing from his right ear when his helmet is removed, and he looks woozy. He doesn't say anything, but the master diver stops him as he is being led to the chamber, then sends a medical corpsman in with him. The crew members crowd around the chamber window until they get an OK signal. It's painful, but he will heal. The diver failed to properly equalize on the way down and, rather than stop the descent, toughed it out. The result is a perforated eardrum. When the dive leaders asked him to stay a few minutes

extra to finish looping a cable around the armor belt, he didn't hesitate. The result could be permanent ear damage, possibly a lifetime of
hearing or balance problems, but he ignored the danger. "Typical
diver!" a teammate scoffs, but not without pride.

ON THE bottom, the divers have only twenty-two to twenty-five minutes to race to the work site and perform an agreed-upon task like removing debris or chunks of coal from the turret. Usually they're moving in current, so the sooner they get behind something, like the
turret or the hull, the better they can work. Sometimes the effort can
be dangerously close to exhausting, and breathing can become labored.

The pressure of seven atmospheres on the body isn't particularly
noticeable as long as the divers are breathing compressed gas—so
the pressure inside the lungs is the same as the pressure in the chest
cavity. But it can be fatiguing for even the strongest. In the long run
it takes a toll, and the hazards can be both serious and unpredictable.

Rick Cavey tells me the rule of thumb in deep water is that every
hour you work is like four hours on the surface. You're not only doing the job but fighting current, fighting the weight of umbilical hoses
and helmet, fighting to keep your balance, holding on, perhaps with
one leg, while calling on muscles that counterbalance that strategy.
You're also fighting to stay focused.

Lieutenant Commander Lori Yost, a physical education teacher
from Sewickley, Pennsylvania, and a Navy reservist, has just finished
her sixth dive on the *Monitor*. She's forty, and "as you get older this
stuff gets harder and harder," she tells me one day while she's acting as
tender, waiting for the divers to surface. She's tall, blond, and ath-
letic-looking, friendly and open, but also, it is clear, confident and focused.

On one of the dives she found herself in heavy current as she hit
the bottom and had to fight her way back to the stage. By the time
she got back she was exhausted and hyperventilating. She could barely
haul herself back up and collapse on the stage, seeing stars, fighting
panic. "Calm down, calm down, you're OK," she had to keep saying
until her breathing returned to normal.

She was caught in what divers know is a vicious cycle. Greater exertion produces a build-up of lactic acid in the blood stream, signaling the brain to breathe faster to restore the body's acid-base balance by lowering carbon dioxide. But breathing too fast can quickly drop CO_2 below normal, causing lightheadedness and panic—and even faster breathing. The only cure is to do the opposite, to slow everything down.

A high school and college athlete, Yost was superbly conditioned by the time she made it to dive school. Even so, she felt she had to prove she could do the job. If she could do that, she knew, the macho male divers would leave her alone. One of the ways the dive tenders pass the time while waiting for the divers to resurface is by playing Rock Paper Scissors, with the loser having to do a god-awful number of pushups. After she does those a couple of times, the men back off. Even so, every time she gets to the bottom she sprints to her assignment and makes sure the work gets done.

Being in the presence of the *Monitor* is a powerful experience, she says. "You can't dive on this and not be touched in some way, spiritually, emotionally, physically."

Divers all know what she means, even though they have little time to reflect while on the bottom. Down in the gloom, everything looks blue and black. Light filters down from above, but most of the color spectrum is gone. Brooding over everything is the iron ship with its upper hull, a wide belt of iron, resting on top of the upside-down turret. Soon the divers will knife through the armor and pry the belt off, and the turret will be exposed for the first time in fourteen decades.

The current claws at the divers as they move about the ancient wreck.

"Green Diver, make your way back to the stage," the master diver calls down on the two-way. The simplest way to do this is for divers to haul themselves back to the platform with the help of the umbilical lines. Now Red Diver—usually the more experienced of the two—follows. "Divers leaving the bottom!" the master diver wails. "Console, give me depths every five! Comms, every ten feet get an OK from the divers!"

Now, as the stage begins its ascent, the pace is far slower. They pause at 110 feet for seven minutes to begin decompression, the lower pressure allowing helium to begin leaving their tissues. At ninety feet they stop for five minutes, and the console operator switches them to decompression mix, 50 percent oxygen, 50 percent helium. They ventilate for twenty seconds to get the helium-rich bottom gas out of their umbilicals. Now their OKs sound slightly different. Even though they still have that Chipmunk voice, there's a change, a little more bass. It's subtle, but the master divers can hear it. They spend another three minutes decompressing, then travel again, oxygen now beginning to crowd out the helium. There are several seven-, nine- and thirteen-minute stops on the way up. By forty feet, their last stop, they have entered their surface decompression phase. From here, the entire team has five minutes to get them into the recompression chamber and drive the pressure back to fifty feet. If they're late getting to the surface or the tenders take too long, recompression time can go up an hour or more. Whenever the divers are subjected to exceptional exposure, official reports must be filled out, and much grief is given. It's worse than getting a bad report card. It means a diver's life has been endangered. While still underwater, the divers on the stage loosen the straps on their boots to help speed things up.

As they break the surface, the master diver screams, "On the winch, up four!" The stage flies up and over and slams onto the deck. The divers are led to the bench and the tenders, like race car pit crews, go into action. They remove the divers' helmets and peel off their boots and dive suits. As that's happening, the master diver checks their eyes and faces. Vision problems? Bloodshot eyes? Blood issuing from noses or ears? Facial features distorted? Now dive officers escort the divers to the chamber, and the master diver leans in to tell them to put on their "ears," the hearing protectors they must wear when high-pressure air screams into the chamber. The double hatches are snapped shut, and the console operator "drives" the chamber down to the fifty-foot pressure level.

Now the two divers begin the last decompression phase to get the rest of the helium out of their bodies. For the next two and a half hours they will don oxygen masks and breathe pure oxygen for fifteen-minute intervals as the pressure is reduced. All the while a chamber supervisor watches through a portal for signs of oxygen toxicity: blurred vision and dizziness, among other things.

All this for thirty to forty minutes of bottom time. One small job has been accomplished on the bottom, but hundreds more need to be done. Amazingly, the divers run these evolutions around the clock, with day and night shifts competing to pull off the most dives. This "sprint" diving, as Chris Murray terms it, is fine for most salvage efforts, and it worked well with the early dives on the *Monitor*, but for the sustained work required on the bigger jobs, where armor had to be cut away and lifting structures guided into place, something else was needed.

ON THE *Wotan*, right next to the surface-supply dive station but a world apart, is the saturation diving operation. The station is dominated by two cylindrical pressure chambers that look something like the containers on a tanker truck. In one, sat divers can decompress after several days at high pressure; in the other, divers can rest between work shifts while remaining at pressure. Up above is the "sat shack," a control headquarters that has room for four people but is often crammed with eight or ten.

This is the nerve center for divers who live and work under deep ocean pressure virtually around the clock. The heart of the operation is an onion-shaped bell that sends divers to the bottom for what must be considered one of the most unusual jobs in the world.

The bell is wrapped with emergency gas cylinders, but normally the divers receive all their life support, their gas, warm water, power and communications through tightly wrapped umbilical hoses and wires reaching to the pumps on the deck of the barge. When they exit the bell and drop down to the wreck, they trail a second life-sustaining umbilical, this one about 100 feet long, attached to the bell. As the shift changes, the first diver removes his helmet, but must now sit in the nine-foot-diameter globe fully suited up in case of trouble. With inside and outside pressure equal, the hatch stays open.

One day in July, as I watch the image from a video camera inside the bell, one of the divers is quietly reading. Soon, the head of the other diver emerges from below and his partner removes his helmet. And then plants a kiss on top of his balding head.

"Diver love," laughs one of the master divers.

The Global Industries system can house up to twelve people in the two pressure chambers, although the *Monitor* project uses only four divers at a time. Two divers per shift are lowered in the bell to 180 feet. One at a time, they drop down to the wreck, sharing a twelve-hour shift. That means four to six hours of unbroken, strenuous work for each of them before they ascend in the bell, clamber through an airlock into the pressure chamber, and rest for the next twelve hours while a second two-person team goes to work.

The transfer of the under-pressure, helium-saturated divers is accomplished with much less brio than with their sprint diver counterparts. At about noon and midnight every day their space capsule–like bell returns to the surface, where divers wrestle it into place over the pressurized living quarters. Still under pressure—and largely out of view of those on the outside—the teams trade places.

Because they work beneath the waves and weather, the saturation divers frequently work right through stormy conditions. The *Monitor* schedules call for about seven days of work—sometimes stretched to eleven—followed by sixty-six hours of decompression.

Although a few halting steps were taken earlier, the Navy did the pioneering work in saturation diving in a project known as Genesis, beginning in 1962. Navy divers were exposed to various levels of pressure for prolonged periods, breathing in an environment that was mostly helium. The most notable test came in 1964, when three divers spent twelve days at nearly two hundred feet, with no ill effects other than thermal discomfort. Almost simultaneously, Cousteau and his associates began their *Conshelf* experiments in the French Riviera and the Red Sea. Cousteau's team lived in large cylindrical habitats that included living quarters and dive stations. During their stay, they made several deep excursions, returning to their habitat to sleep and cook their meals. The experiment, which Cousteau turned into an Academy Award-winning documentary, *World Without Sun*, in 1964—and then a book of the same name—helped popularize the undersea world.

The next phase of the Navy's involvement with saturation diving was born in heartbreak. In April 1963, the nuclear-powered submarine *Thresher* sank while conducting deep diving exercises off Cape Cod, with the loss of all 129 crew members. It came to rest at 8,400 feet, far too deep for divers or submersible craft to investigate, but public outcry over the loss was a catalyst for deep ocean research.

The following year brought the first of the Navy's *SEALAB* projects and its first aquanauts. During *SEALAB II* in 1965, three teams of divers spent ten to sixteen days each 205 feet down in the La Jolla Canyon off the California coast. They succeeded in speaking with an astronaut circling Earth in a Gemini space capsule and with Cousteau at the bottom of Monaco harbor. Former astronaut Scott Carpenter was one of the team members. For the Navy it was a heady time, a golden age of deep sea exploration. And then, just as quickly, it ended. Barry Cannon, one of the *SEALAB III* aquanauts, died in an accident involving a rebreathing apparatus, and the public outcry this time shut the program down.

But it didn't shut saturation diving down completely. The Navy developed sat systems for use in deep diving missions, and it maintained the Naval Experimental Dive Unit—which provided the saturation divers for the *Monitor* project—in Panama City, Florida. But because most Navy dive operations take place in relatively shallow water, the bulk of the work was carried out by surface-supply, or "sprint," divers. In the early 1990s the Navy decommissioned the last of its sat diving platforms.

Another sub disaster reawakened the Navy's interest. It was August 2000 when the Soviet submarine *Kursk* sank in the Barents Sea. The world watched helplessly as 118 men died at a depth of 330 feet.

The Russians, fearing disclosure of military secrets, declined American help, but this might not have made any difference. The depth was then just below Navy fleet diving capability, although saturation divers often operate at one thousand feet, and even deeper on rare occasions. It was clear that the Navy, lacking its own saturation system, should take a look at using one of many now being widely used in private industry. The *Monitor* project offered the perfect opportunity for testing.

With the go-ahead from top Navy brass, master diver Chuck Young did the research and recommended the use of a civilian system for the 2001 engine recovery. A team of top Navy dive officers looked at what various companies had to offer, making sure that diver safety wouldn't be compromised, and chose the Global 1504 Sat System. There was no question about its usefulness. With often-brutal sea conditions between June 17 and July 25, 2001, saturation divers spent all but forty-eight hours working on the bottom, accounting for 70 percent of the total workload. "This is incredible when one thinks of the unpredictable sea conditions frequently encountered off Cape Hatteras," said Chris Murray. The same system was chosen for the turret recovery expedition in 2002.

Experienced though most of the sat divers are, their work is flat-out dangerous. Young, a twenty-year veteran who convinced Captain Murray he should use saturation diving in the first place, is evidence enough. In 2001, while divers were preparing to bring the *Monitor*'s engine up, he was cleaning up the area around the reversing wheel in the engine room with a hydroblaster when several deck plates, each weighing two hundred pounds or so, crashed down on him. He was trapped in a sitting position, his helmet wedged between the plates, his "come-home bottle" hissing as the gas escaped. In total darkness, cold and alone, he realized he was still able to breathe. "Whew!" he said to himself, "my umbilical hasn't been pinched."

"Bryon," he called to master diver Bryon Van Horn, who was running the dive, "Don't panic, but I've got a little bit of a problem here."

His dive partner Keith Nelson, who was then in the bell, dropped down to the wreck. Typical for him, he talked a mile a minute while surveying the problem; then, using a six-foot pinch bar, he lifted the plates. It was enough to free Young's helmet and come-home bottle and allow him to crawl out of the rubble. "Thank God Nelly was able to figure out how to get me out of there," Young said.

Because the work is exhausting, much of the time sat divers spend in decompression is given to sleeping. They don't have much appetite, at least not then, but meals are passed to them through airlock windows. The food, compressed by the weight of several atmospheres, is inevitably chewier. No popcorn or marshmallows, thank you. Certainly no lemon meringue pie. They seem to spend many of their off hours reading Clive Cussler novels, and others of that genre. *Blackhawk Down* is another favorite this summer. And this year, for the first time, the chamber comes equipped with a video player. It isn't such a bad deal, some of them say; they eat and sleep, people bring them food, they read, they watch movies.

But diving can be a miserable experience. On some days the diving bell bounces up and down as much as ten feet in the water column, causing divers' ears to pop constantly. They have to wear heavy equipment, breathe through a mask, be constantly cold or constantly hot, work in cramped conditions, get hurt, suffer from exhaustion, and then spend days trapped in decompression. "I wouldn't mind working four hours, but I wouldn't want to be locked up for ten days, no way," a surface-supply diver tells me.

One of the sat divers got sick while on the bottom and had to be brought back to the chamber and carefully watched by doctors. In that high-pressure, oxygen-rich, moist environment, germs are hard to kill and infections almost impossible to cure. Sat divers say their knees pop and crack when they bend until more fluids can be introduced.

There could be long-term consequences to sat diving, including bone loss from constant pressure. That's why divers are encouraged to drink plenty of milk and keep exercising. Unlike some commercial sat divers, who may take two weeks off after a dive and then go down again, Navy divers usually don't do more than two or three dives every year.

And yet, for many who make their careers in this extraordinary field, there is nothing on earth like their experiences at the bottom of the sea. Especially at night, some report, there is a kind of total focus and serenity down there. Because the plankton can be thick as a snowstorm and reflect light from divers' helmet lamps, many prefer switching off their lamps and working entirely by feel and instinct.

"It's a whole different world down there at night, a lot closer in to you," says Rick Cavey.

> Survival and every breath you're taking is something that's on your mind. Every time you reach out and touch something, you have to think about it. That takes away the problems of the world or anything else that

happens to be on your mind and gives you that focus. It's hard to get in that state in the real world, but when you're in the water and your very survival depends on that focus, it's a kind of euphoric feeling. The bubbles all around you give you the feeling you're doing everything right. You don't have gravity working against your body. You're totally concentrated on where you're going to put your foot, like rock climbing. Your world becomes an envelope around you that you can see and touch and taste and feel.

The skills of a diver are as perishable as those of a professional athlete, like shooting a basketball or swinging at a baseball. Working underwater, turning a wrench or screwdriver or swinging a hammer, is a delicate art. Divers have to know how to position and brace themselves, especially with current running. They have to take account of the refracting property of water and realize that things are not where they seem to be.

When they get out of saturation after nearly two weeks, the divers feel a rush. The first breath of fresh air, the first sunlight, makes them almost keel over from dizziness. For a couple of days they just want to sleep, eat, and sleep again to get ready for the next time.

What both saturation and surface-supply divers like about it is doing a job few others are able to do. Like Carl Brashear, the famous Navy amputee who made master diver, they feel that they, like those in the movie about him, are men and women of honor. When they reenlist or gain promotions, most have their ceremonies performed underwater. Several reenlistments are planned in the shadow of the *Monitor*.

IN THIS early phase of the project, the divers' first major job is to remove a thirty-ton section of the ship's hull and armor belt that landed on top of the turret when the *Monitor* flipped over. Because the turret broke free, part of it was already accessible, but about nine-tenths is still covered. The heavy belt made of oak and pine plated with iron, which protected the ship from heavy cannon fire, is proving as tough as it was 140 years before. A wire sling is rigged up, with two small cranes dragging it back and forth like a band saw, but that doesn't work. Then hour after hour, day after day, the saturation divers use three different tools to rake at the armor belt. First, there's the hydroblaster, a 20,000-pound-per-square-inch water jet that cuts through metal—and could take off a foot if a diver isn't careful. Second, is a hydraulic chisel. Third, is an exothermic torch that burns oxygen and magnesium.

"Hot! Hot! Hot!" one of the dive officers calls out from the control shack as 440 volts of electricity surge through the torch, igniting the elements. "Everything your momma told you about electricity and water, it's all true," says Chris Murray. "You can feel it in your teeth." But they do it anyway. On the TV monitor in the shack, an arc of fire and smoke can be seen as the torch blasts away. "Cold! Cold! Cold!" the officer announces as the session ends. And still the belt stubbornly hangs on.

In a kind of tag team match, the divers attack the belt and the remaining hull section 'round the clock. With the cutting torches they burn the heads off spikes that hold the armor in place. They use pry bars to remove sections of iron, peeling the plates off like layers of an onion. When at last they reach the soft pine and oak backing, they figure it will be easy now. But the wood resists almost as steadfastly as when it stood against a fusillade of heavy shot from a determined enemy.

NINE

SLUGFEST

FOG LAY heavy over Hampton Roads on the early morning of March 9, 1862, but it soon burned off as a red, angry sun rose. Already, soldiers and spectators had begun to line both shores, just a few miles apart, Northerners stretching along Union-held positions from Camp Butler to Fort Monroe, Southerners craning to see from vantage points at Craney Island and Sewell's Point. Small boats ventured out to get ringside views. French and British warships, whose commanders were more than a little interested in the outcome, waited and watched.

The *Virginia* crew was still celebrating. "We began the day," said seaman William Kline, "with two jiggers of whiskey and a hearty breakfast."

It was an ideal Sunday for church, observed Richard Curtis, another member of the crew. But alas, the morning's calm "was soon to be broken by the roar of cannon and angry men seeking each other's lives."

Although exhausted and sleep deprived, the *Monitor*'s crew was hellbent on revenge. John Driscoll, the twenty-six-year-old fireman from County Cork, Ireland, recounted that Captain Worden came down from the turret as they were wolfing a breakfast of canned beef, hardtack, and coffee. Worden reminded them that they had all volunteered and that now was the time, seeing what the *Virginia* had done to those warships, to change their minds about being on board. They could be taken off to a nearby ship. They must have swallowed hard, but the sailors were not about to desert their captain. "He was answered by every man jumping to his feet and giving three cheers," said Driscoll.

It had still been dark when Driscoll and two others were sent on deck to screw iron plates over the port lights, remove deck stanchions, and take down blower pipes and smokestacks in preparation for battle.

The scene that greeted the *Monitor* crew as the sun rose might well have given them pause. All that was left of the *Congress* was blasted and charred debris floating on the water. And not far from where they lay at anchor, the *Cumberland*'s three masts stuck out of the water at an angle, with a tattered pennant dangling from one of them. It must have been chilling to realize that many of those who had died were wounded sailors who could not get off their ship as it went down. But this morning there was scarcely time for reflection. The *Monitor*'s officers sighted three steamers lying under Sewell's Point, one of them the *Virginia.*

The rebel ironclad wasted no time in getting underway, steaming across Hampton Roads toward Fort Monroe, then describing a wide, slow arc as she entered the north channel and moved west. There was no doubt what the attacker was up to as she headed toward Middle Ground, where the *Minnesota* still lay aground—and, unbeknownst to the *Virginia*'s crew—where their enemy lay in wait.

As the *Virginia* approached, William Keeler recalled, "we slowly steamed out of the shadow of our towering friend."

Even though the strange silhouette may have been spotted during the night, no one on board the *Virginia* seems to have made the connection to the Union's long-awaited ironclad. Rebels standing watch assumed it was some sort of water tank coming to the *Minnesota*'s aid. Others thought it was a raft helping to lighten the ship. An oarsman on a small boat bearing spectators described it as "a tin can on a shingle."

Lieutenant James Rochelle on board the CSS *Patrick Henry* was amazed at what he saw. "Such a craft as the eyes of a seaman never looked upon before—an immense shingle floating in the water, with a giant cheesebox rising from its center: no sails, no wheels, no smokestack, no guns. What could it be?" The cheesebox-on-a-shingle description would become an enduring nickname.

Lieutenant John Taylor Wood would later claim he knew at once that it was Ericsson's *Monitor.* If so, it was more than a little upsetting. "She could not possibly have made her appearance at a more inopportune time for us," he would write, "changing our plans, which were to destroy the *Minnesota,* and then the remainder of the fleet below Fortress Monroe." But as she stalked across Hampton Roads and made directly for the *Minnesota,* the *Virginia* paid no attention to the little ironclad.

Within a mile of the grounded ship, completely ignoring whatever nuisance was now lying in its path, the *Virginia* opened fire. "A puff of smoke arose from her side," said Keeler, who was on the *Monitor'*s deck with the ship's surgeon, Daniel Logue, "and a shell howled over our heads and crashed into the side of the *Minnesota.*" "Gentlemen," Captain Worden barked at the men, "that is the *Merrimack,* you had better go below." They needed no further encouragement.

Down below, where the only light was what seeped from the turret and flickered from lanterns, the sensation of not being able to see where they were or where the enemy lay was suddenly brought home. "I experienced a peculiar sensation," Keeler confessed. "I do not think it was fear, but it was different from anything I ever knew before. We were enclosed in what we supposed to be impenetrable armour—we knew that a powerful foe was about to meet us—ours was an untried experiment and our enemy's first fire might make it a coffin for us all."

One of the *Virginia* crew made a similar observation. "Our vessel never having been tested before, and her model being new and unheard of, many of those who watched us predicted failure," said Dinwiddie B. Phillips, the Confederate ship's surgeon, "and others suggested that the *Virginia* was an enormous metallic burial case, and that we were conducting our own funeral."

The combatants were about to make history by shooting at each other from behind heavy armor. There were other ironclads in the world, most notably in the English and French navies, but none had been tested in combat. Hence the presence in Hampton Roads of a kind of foreign spectator fleet, ready to report back to its commanders.

Inside the Yankee iron challenger, the suspense was dreadful. Except for the captain and helmsman peering through slits in the pilot-house walls, and gunners looking over the barrels of their weapons, no one, especially not the engineers and coal heavers in the engine room, could see anything. "We were all in absolute blackness," said fireman Driscoll, "excepting the dim rays . . . we got from the oil lamps."

"My only view of the world outside of the tower was over the muz-zle of the guns, which cleared the ports by a few inches only," said Dana Greene.

The first confirmation most of the *Monitor*'s crew had that a battle had been joined was the howl of gunfire as the *Minnesota* unleashed a broadside at her attacker. Because the speaking tube between the *Monitor*'s pilothouse and turret did not work as planned, Keeler was pressed into service as messenger, running from one to the other.

"Paymaster, ask the captain if I shall fire," demanded Greene, who was directing the *Monitor*'s guns. "Not yet," Keeler called out after hus-tling to the pilothouse and back. "Be cool and deliberate. Don't waste a shot."

Worden maneuvered the *Monitor* alongside the *Virginia* as the turret slowly revolved, locking in on the enemy. Then he gave the order to commence firing.

"I triced up the port, run the gun out and fired," Greene related. There was an earsplitting roar in the turret as the immense cannon hurled 168 pounds of solid iron at the other ship. It was 8:20 A.M. The battle had begun.

As though not believing what had just happened, the *Virginia*'s gun-ners again blasted away at the *Minnesota*, and the Union ship returned fire. Then Greene pulled the lockstring on the second gun, and there was no longer any doubt. "You can see surprise on a ship just the same as you can see it in a human being," Peter Truscott, a twenty-three-year-old seaman on the *Monitor*, would write. "And there was surprise all over the *Merrimac*."

"Our second shot struck her and made the iron scales rattle on her side," reported Keeler in a letter that was smudged with dirt and pow-der. "She seemed for the first time to be aware of our presence and replied to our solid shot with grape and canister which rattled on our iron decks like hail and stones."

"Well, the damned fools are firing canister at us," scoffed one of the *Monitor*'s crew. Officers on the rebel ironclad may have known right away, as Wood claimed, that it was the Yankee ironclad. Catesby Jones, commanding the *Virginia*, also claimed that he immediately recognized the "Ericsson floating battery." But it seems they had no inkling before this moment that their adversary was there and ready for battle. The *Virginia*'s magazines were loaded not with heavy shot to take on another ironclad but with explosive shells, hot shot, and canister to rip apart and incinerate wooden adversaries.

The once-disparaging Captain Henry Van Brunt of the *Minnesota* likely stood with his mouth open. The improbable ship, "much to my astonishment, laid herself right alongside of the *Merrimack*, and the contrast was that of a pigmy to a giant. Gun after gun was fired by the *Monitor*, which was returned by whole broadsides from the rebels with no more effect, apparently, than so many pebble stones thrown by a child."

The two ironclads now gave each other their undivided attention. The *Monitor*, taking advantage of her agility and revolving turret, did not have to square off with the Virginia before letting loose with her guns. Both sides scored direct hits without doing much damage, except perhaps to the eardrums of the gun crews. Like heavyweight boxers, they stood toe-to-toe, occasionally touching each other as they exchanged blows. So intense was their firing, the ironclads were enveloped in a heavy cloud of black smoke. At times, witnesses on shore couldn't see either of the combatants.

The *Virginia* altered course, swinging away from the *Minnesota* and into a giant S turn. The *Monitor*, much more agile than her opponent, set the pace of the battle, passing port-to-port, then ducking around behind and pursuing as a bird might chase an offending cat. They ranged across almost the breadth of Hampton Roads, looping, dodging, feinting, shadowing, and all the while erupting with whatever guns either could bring to bear on the other. Inside the *Monitor*'s cramped turret, some twenty men operated the giant eleven-inch guns. Rather than drop the heavy port stoppers (the shields that protected the crews) after every recoil, then raise them again—a tremendous effort—the gunners found it simpler to turn the turret away from the enemy after each shot, reload, swing back around, and fire again as the target came into view—"On the fly," as Greene put it. He was acutely aware that if an enemy gunner succeeded in firing an exploding shell into the turret, the mayhem would have been devastating.

This was the *Monitor*'s baptism by fire, the first time the crew had ever tested her turret or fired her guns in action. In the turret, brawny gunners were stripped to the waist, their bodies black with powder and smoke, dripping perspiration. When the turret first received a direct hit, there was a sudden intake of breath that was not released until the crew realized the shot had only dented the iron plates.

The turret was only twenty feet in diameter, with two thirteen-foot cannons and crews of eight to ten for each. The explosion of each shot must have been deafening, the air filled with gas and smoke and shouting. It was a dangerous place to be, not so much because of enemy fire but because the 17,000-pound guns recoiled with a velocity that could kill or maim. The moving guns rode on gun carriages, with arresting gear that had to be adjusted as the tracks warmed. It must have been fresh in the gunners' minds how, in their first and only trial, the massive guns had become airborne when the cranks were turned the wrong way.

George Geer had changed from fireman to shot handler during the battle and must have grunted from the effort needed to pick up the heavy cannonballs—a two-man job—and hand them to the gunners. All that time he worried about what would happen to his "Matty" and their two young children if he were to die. "I often thought of you and the little darlings when the fight was going on and what should become of you should I be killed," he would write, "but I should have no more such fears as our ship resisted everything they could fire at her as though they were spit balls."

Conditions were much the same on the *Virginia*'s gun deck. In at least one instance when the *Monitor* fired at close range, opposing gunners near the impact were stunned nearly senseless, eardrums bleeding from the blow. Adding to the hellish conditions, engines just below them poured out heat and smoke as the ships jockeyed for position. And the *Monitor*'s guns were accurate; they fired every seven or eight minutes, in Wood's estimation, "and nearly every shot struck."

The *Virginia*'s smokestack was shot away, reducing the draft of her engines and therefore her already limited horsepower and mobility.

Inside the engine room, conditions were hellish. "The noise of the crackling roaring fires, escaping steam, and the loud and labored pulsations of the engines together with the roar of the battle above and the thud and vibrations of the huge masses of iron being hurled against us, altogether produced a scene and sound to be compared with the poet's picture of the lower regions," according to H. Ashton Ramsay, the *Virginia*'s chief engineer.

The *Monitor* received at least nine direct hits to her turret. Even though the turret included a shield to protect against flying bolts, some of the men inside thought they were being bombarded by bolt heads that went flying when the turret was struck. One man was struck in the head by a flying object and had to be taken below to recover. Others were no doubt left with nasty bruises.

All of the hits from heavy shot were the result of friendly fire—shots fired at the *Virginia* by the *Minnesota*. With the *Monitor* often lying between the larger combatants and the Union gunners firing low so that the shot skipped across the water, some errant hits were inevitable. One shot struck about a foot from the starboard gun port, apparently while the turret was turned away from the enemy. It must have been a shock to the *Monitor*'s gun crew.

Truscott was in the turret when a ball struck a few inches from his head. "The shock was so fearful that I dropped over like a dead man," he recalled. The next thing he knew he was below, with surgeon Logue bathing his head. The injury, Logue reported, "did not result in total insensibility, but the circulation remained depressed for some time." He administered stimulants and brought the man back. Acting master Louis Stodder had been bracing his knee against the turret wall when the shot struck. "I was flung by the concussion clean over both guns to the floor of the turret," he remembered.

The ironclads fought through the morning, actually touching each other five times, according to one account. At about 11:00 A.M., almost three hours into the slugfest, the *Virginia*, with twice the draft of the *Monitor*, ran aground and was pummeled with shot after shot, causing some of its iron plates to crack. A few more minutes of this might

Battle of the ironclads, March 9, 1862. (Oil painting by Thomas Skinner, Mariners' Museum)

have meant the end. Frantically the engineers poured on the coals, and a cheer went up as the ship groaned and escaped the shoals.

Catesby Jones, in his account of the battle, complained that his gunners hardly ever got good shots at their opponent, while those on the *Monitor* were able to pick their spots, rarely missing. All the while, the *Monitor* worked its way around the *Virginia*, seeming to probe for weak points. At one point, the frustrated *Virginia* gunners stopped firing. What was the point, one of them complained, if their best shots simply ricocheted off the upstart's impenetrable hide? Never mind, said, Jones, he had an idea. With that, he sent the lumbering giant directly at the *Monitor*. The *Monitor*'s quartermaster, Peter Williams, reacted to the lumbering charge by throwing the helm hard to starboard. The glancing blow knocked the chimneys off several lanterns below but did little damage. "She gave us a tremendous thump, but she did not injure us in the least," said engineer Alban Stimers, adding that the sharp-edged deck of the *Monitor* sliced through part of the rebel ship's bow, tearing into the oak beneath the iron skin. Greene took the opportunity to give the *Virginia* both guns at close quarters. "Both shots struck about half-way up the shield abreast of the after pivot," Lieutenant Wood related, and the impact seriously dented the shield. "Another shot in the same place would have penetrated."

The gunners could not keep many of the 168-pound cannonballs in the turret. They were so heavy that if they rolled around the floor they could easily shatter ankles. With the supply running low and no way to hand up more ammunition while the turret was in motion—the shot lockers and the turret deck openings had to be lined up—Worden ordered the ship to disengage.

While they were at it, he instructed Keeler to dole out shots of whiskey to all hands. Keeler, a teetotaler, wouldn't touch the stuff even then.

The relentless *Virginia*, meanwhile, used the lull to take a couple of deadly shots at the *Minnesota*. "I opened upon her with all my broadside guns and ten-inch pivot—a broadside which would have blown out of the water any timber-built ship in the world," the *Minnesota*'s Van Brunt related. "She returned my fire with her rifled bow-gun with a shell which passed through the chief engineer's state-room, through the engineer's mess-room amidships, and burst in the boatswain's room, tearing all four rooms into one, in its passage exploding two charges of powder, which set the ship on fire, but it was promptly extinguished."

Wood hoped the *Monitor* was out of action, but more heavy blows from the little ship's guns "soon undeceived us." The two went at it again. It was after 11:00 A.M. now, three hours into the slugfest, and neither opponent showed signs of quitting.

It was Worden's turn now to try ramming the *Virginia*, hoping to strike her stern and disable her rudder and propeller. It might have been all over for the enemy ironclad, since she would have been instantly transformed from fearsome warship to battered sitting duck. But the *Monitor*'s steering mechanism malfunctioned, and she narrowly missed the *Virginia*.

The attempt backfired. As the *Monitor* glided past its stern, one of the *Virginia*'s gunners took aim at the pilothouse and fired just as Worden was looking out through the viewing slit. Keeler, who was standing nearby waiting for an order, wrote that a "flash of light and a cloud of smoke filled the house. I noticed the Capt. stagger and put his hands to his eyes—I ran up to him and asked if he was hurt. 'My eyes,' says he, 'I am blind.' "

With the assistance of the surgeon, Keeler related, "I got him down and called Lieut. Greene from the turret. A number of us collected around him, the blood was running from his face, which was blackened with the powder smoke." "He was a ghastly sight," according to Greene, "with his eyes closed and the blood apparently rushing from every pore in the upper part of his face."

Worden told Greene to take command. The young officer immediately gave orders to withdraw from the fight and helped lead Worden to a sofa in his cabin. Worden's only plea was that the *Monitor* stick to its mission of saving the *Minnesota*. But members of the crew urged Greene to do more, to get back into the fight and, if possible, sink their adversary.

When he took over in the damaged but still usable pilothouse, Greene realized the moment had passed. The *Virginia* was steaming away. The *Virginia* took some parting shots at the *Minnesota*, but by now the tide was going out, and pilots on board warned that the heavy, deep-draft warrior could be stuck out in the Roads until the next high tide. Jones couldn't understand why the *Monitor*, which appeared undamaged, had retreated to shallow water, but he could wait no longer. Judging that the *Monitor* was not coming back out, the decision was made. Shortly past noon, the *Virginia* headed toward the Elizabeth River. Even though the *Monitor* attempted to get back in the action, each side believed the other had retreated, and both hurrahed what they thought were victories.

Just under four hours after the first shots were fired, one of the most important battles in American naval history was over. Neither ironclad had won. Not a sailor on either side was killed. But both had made huge statements. The *Virginia* had shown that wooden ships were a thing of the past. The *Monitor* had stopped the naval equivalent of a speeding train in its tracks.

Assistant Secretary of the Navy Fox, who had journeyed from Washington to witness the battle, gushed in a telegraph to Ericsson, "Your

noble boat has performed with perfect success." What he did not mention was that, for better or worse, the nature of naval warfare had
changed forever. Within days of reading the dispatches from Hampton Roads, the Royal Navy, the preeminent naval force in the world, is-
sued orders to build no more wooden ships.

An editorial in the *Times of London* put it this way: "Whereas we had
available for immediate purposes one hundred and forty-nine first-
class war-ships, we have now two, those two being the *Warrior* and her
sister *Ironside* [both ironclads]. There is not now a ship in the English
navy apart from these two that it would not be madness to trust to an
engagement with that little *Monitor*."

There was a sense, as Nathaniel Hawthorne wrote shortly after the
battle, "that the age of the majestic, wooden man-of-war had passed
in one afternoon and that the era of the mechanized iron and steam
warship had arrived the following day."

TEN

IT'S A MAN'S JOB, MA'AM

THE NAVY diving community is a testosterone-fueled world peopled largely by males rippling with muscles, painted with tattoos, and bristling with pride. Speed and power are their gods, loyalty their bond. On board the *Wotan*, one T-shirt asserts that there are only two kinds of women: those who have Navy divers and those who want Navy divers. But this particular community at this particular time is under the command of a woman—a smart, capable woman who can hold her own with the best of these hard-body males.

Commander Bobbie Scholley, head of MDSU TWO and tactical head of dive operations on the barge, decides to go for a plunge one morning in early July. Looking relaxed and well rested, she emerges from the women's quarters wearing black dive skins, her red hair held back in a band, carrying a mug of coffee. She walks to the lead dive chair and sits down beside master diver Brick Bradford. They grin at each other like old friends, but when their helmets are snapped on they are all-business—like astronauts about to go into space.

Although Scholley's name is Barbara, she has seldom been called anything but Bobbie, a nickname she got from her dad, Bobbie Lee Aten. Her tomboy ways did nothing to change her moniker. When she was in grade school, her family went camping and boating almost every weekend. She loved the water that arced behind her father's powerboat as they flew up and down the Illinois River. On water skis she dared to jump the wakes of lumbering barges. Though the river wasn't the ocean, it was water, and she qualified as a water rat.

Scholley grew up in Normal, Illinois, 800 feet above sea level. She went to Normal Community High School, where she was president of her senior class, and then to Illinois State University, right there in town. It was no wonder, then, that after graduating with a degree in biology she left Normal to join the Navy and see the world. She'd enroll in officer candidate school, she thought, sign on for four years, and then decide about the rest of her life.

She received her commission in 1981, a time when the Navy was beginning to bring women onto ships, and Scholley saw the makings of not just a four-year hitch but a career. In her first job on a submarine tender, watching Navy divers at work, she was so intrigued by what they did that she had to see if she could do it. Even though she had never even snorkled, in 1983 Scholley convinced her commanding officer to support her application for Navy dive school.

Once there, she was pushed to what she was sure was her limit—physically, emotionally, and academically—and then beyond it. There were times at the bottom of a pool when she couldn't breathe because those darned helmets, designed for men, didn't fit properly. She should have been frightened, but there in the water she was calmly stubborn. There was no way she was going to give up.

When she graduated from dive school, the certificate meant more to her than her college degree or her Navy commission. Diving for the Navy would be her career. Scholley returned to the sub tender as diving and repair services officer. She had various assignments, including in 1992 the command of the USS *Bolster*, a 213-foot rescue and salvage ship. This made her just the fourth woman in history to take command of a U.S. Navy–commissioned ship.

During the salvage and recovery of TWA flight 800 Scholley coordinated all fleet operational units, including two salvage ships and two amphibious support ship, and supervised two hundred Navy divers.

She joined MDSU TWO in 1995 and began scheduling dive shifts for the *Monitor* project in 1988. On October 12, 2000, just after Scholley took command of the unit, terrorists detonated explosives beside the guided-missile destroyer USS *Cole* as it was refueling at a port in Yemen. The explosion ripped a 1,600-square-foot hole in the hull, killing seventeen sailors and wounding thirty-nine. A detachment of divers flew out of Siganella Naval Air Station in Italy and was on scene within forty-eight hours. Scholley, along with dive officers and FBI agents, flew out of Norfolk on a Navy plane. A day later, she joined the divers. Their task was to locate the missing sailors, help stabilize the ship, recover evidence, and perform structural inspections.

The blast was devastating. According to a report by Captain Murray and Michel Leese, a diving project engineer, port and forward bulkheads were blown inward, all nonwatertight doors had broken from their hinges, filing cabinets lay scattered across the deck, and visibility was less than three inches. Because of scorching air temperatures, the divers worked in water that was about ninety degrees—a dangerously dehydrating environment. Frank Perna, chief warrant officer in charge of the detachment, said Scholley not only dived with the team but dealt with Navy top brass, the *Cole*'s commanding officer, and the FBI, allowing his divers to concentrate on the job.

It fell to Scholley and the team to retrieve the remains of sailors trapped belowdecks. "It's part of our job, and you do it and you don't think about it at the time," she said. "But you think about it afterward. That's the tough part." In fact, recovering the dead left nightmarish memories. The bodies had been in the water for a few days and, "as you can imagine, that was just horrible, absolutely horrible."

It took three weeks, but they were able to recover the bodies of all of the sailors, who received full military honors as they were escorted off the ship. The team then began inspection dives to assist naval engineers in determining how much of the *Cole*'s structural strength had been lost. Finally, they helped maneuver the damaged destroyer into position as a heavy-lift transport ship took it on board for the trip back home.

Scholley says she felt the most fear not while diving in the bombed-out hull but while leading the divers through the streets of the city of Aden. "We had to transit back and forth through the city, and we didn't know who were bad guys and who were good guys, and we were obviously a group of unarmed Navy divers."

Yemeni security guards were not used to dealing with women in positions of authority. "As the only female with the detachment, I'm sure she felt a little uneasy," said Perna. The divers had to pass through three checkpoints, and at each one she received more attention than necessary. She was relieved to find that they were leaving on a Navy ship rather than a military aircraft and wouldn't have to go through any more checkpoints.

It would be difficult to take anything positive away from such an experience, but Scholley at least had this: the close rapport she developed with the divers. They were the ones who formed the core dive team for the 2001 expedition to recover the *Monitor*'s engine.

For dangerous diving, the *Monitor* mission has no equal because of the depths, the weights the divers have to deal with, the currents, and the complexity of the mission, especially the number of divers from many different commands. With 160 divers, Scholley feels the weight of responsibility for each one. No commanding officer ever wants to lose a sailor, whether in combat or in an operation like this. Since this is not combat, any loss of life or injury is completely unacceptable.

Says master diver Scott Heineman, "Anybody gets hurt, you can have all the 'atta boys' you want but if you have one 'ah, shit,' it's all done. Everything you've done to that point is absolutely erased. The government does not look well on injury. Equipment is bad, but personal injury—you're gonna get hammered."

Scholley became Murray's replacement as head of MDSU TWO in 2000 as he moved up from commander to captain and to a desk job in Washington, where he became head of Navy divers for Naval Sea Systems Command. They had a long, solid relationship built on professionalism and trust, but it was hard to escape the fact that she was taking over a project he had started and nurtured for years.

She delights in the memory of her first dive on the *Monitor* with Murray. Conditions couldn't have been better, with visibility that exceeded a hundred feet; amberjacks and monitor fish swam placidly nearby, and soft corals swayed in the current. She walked over to the fantail and then into the engineering space. The reversing wheel for the main engine looks just like a ship's wheel, so she couldn't help but stand there and put her hands on it as though she were driving a ship. As she stood there in full dive gear, she could imagine those sailors from 140 years before, turning the wheel to reverse the steam engine. It was one of those defining moments that connected her to the *Monitor*.

Jim Mariano, the project master diver, with his stocky, muscular build and gung-ho personality, looks and acts the part of a Navy diver as much as anyone on the project. He frequently kidded Scholley, "You've got to do a man's job down there, ma'am." He probably got a punch in the arm, or at least the verbal equivalent. But his assessment was loaded with respect. "The first time I ever dove with her was on Flight 800. I asked the master diver, 'Why do I have to work with her? I want to go down and get something done.' He told me to shut up and get in the water. She got in the water, and I turned around and she was gone. She was already working. After that, she stood up with the best of them."

Scholley is very much aware of the culture of what she calls "hairy-chested, knuckle-dragging deep-sea divers with tattoos all over," and underwater she works hard to match them stroke for stroke. It was the first time she had met Mariano, so she had to show what she could do. "There was no way I was going to let these guys know that I couldn't do just as well as they could, considering corresponding sizes and all that stuff."

She may be no match for most of the men in physical strength, but she has no equal in the tenacity department. It isn't so much a stubborn streak that pits her against the challenges of her job as it is the thrill of being there and doing it well.

This is Scholley's second summer out on the barge, and she seems to know every inch of it, trodding upon its steel decks and stairways dressed in khaki shorts, sleeveless shirt, and black combat boots. She has a wholesome, girl-next-door appearance, with frizzy auburn hair, hazel green eyes, and a dazzling smile. She exudes confidence. After twenty-one years in the Navy, she's used to dealing with men, often bulked-up men, and she can dish it out with the best.

"It's a man's world," she acknowledges, "and it's a very physical world and a very dangerous world, but the beauty of it is if you're capable and you're professional and you do what you're supposed to be doing, then you earn their respect. Oh, my gosh, this group of elite people, Navy divers, it's a family, and once you're a member, people will do absolutely anything for you. I just can't believe that I'm fortunate enough to be part of this family."

Still, it irritates the old guard if she happens to make a slight fashion statement, such as trying to get the women divers to wear the same color shorts.

"This isn't a damn press opportunity, ma'am, with all due respect," Mariano tells her one day.

Rick Cavey jumps all over him. "You've got to lighten up, master diver," Cavey warns.

There's a small problem brewing between Scholley and the old-boy network—divers going directly to Captain Murray with their problems. Going around her, in other words. It isn't surprising, since Murray has been out here so long and is so much one of the guys, so much the godfather of this operation. But Scholley isn't having it. As she writes in her journal on July 3: "Frustrated with flow of communications going directly from CWO to Capt Murray."

Chief Warrant Officer Cavey, who has planned and carried out the whole operation, knows there are tensions. How could there not be with two high-ranking, highly experienced divers more or less bumping into each other on the barge? Even though they had the same roles during the engine lift last year, she as overall commander, he as head of Navy divers, it still isn't easy for Murray to take a backseat, especially now, at the grand finale. It isn't so much that Cavey goes around Scholley to Murray, it's more that when Murray likes an idea he runs with it. A thousand-pound gorilla if ever there was one.

That same day, she makes Heineman, a powerful diver and hugely respected leader, her command master chief—a shrewd move. Although Cavey is, in effect, executive officer on board, Heineman, one of the senior enlisted men there—and a long and close friend—becomes her special advisor and advocate. There's a later entry: "Had good talk with CWO about communications flow."

What that "good talk" was like is not hard to guess. Scholley is a good listener, but she has no trouble speaking her mind. She knows that getting the turret off the bottom while protecting the lives of everyone on the barge is her responsibility, and hers alone. If she's in charge, she's going to be in charge.

Heineman calls Scholley a "fabulous communicator. Maybe it's a woman's touch and maybe it isn't, but she can walk into a room and get people to think in a common way for a common goal. And do it in such a way, even if it's an extremely unpopular thing to do, she's going to get you to not feel bad about it."

This is not to say she isn't racked by doubts, especially given the footsteps she walks in. Sometimes, she realizes, she's second-guessing herself. "Am I really the right person here?" she wonders. "If I fail, are people going to second-guess me because I'm a woman? Am I getting enough information from the right people? Am I listening to my people enough? Am I supporting John Broadwater enough? Are the master divers going to Captain Murray because they don't have trust in me?" On the other hand, she knows her strengths, especially in choosing the right people and relying on them, letting them do their jobs and not tying their hands.

Self doubts aside, she has no problem speaking her mind with the male divers. Still, it's good sometimes to take refuge from them. Her three-bunk stateroom near the dive station is the only place where Navy regulations allow women to be berthed. Including rotation changes, four women play a role: Scholley, Commander Gina Harden, Commander Karen Shake, and Lieutenant Commander Lori Yost. They usually have different shifts, so they are rarely in the stateroom together, but the night before Harden is to leave, Scholley asks Cavey to schedule the women for "training" in her quarters. They spend the evening telling jokes and sea stories and almost certainly ragging on the men.

Out on the barge, Scholley considers herself on duty round the clock and manages to spend time with both day and night shifts. The operation, after all, runs twenty-four-seven, and she knows those extra hours at night demonstrate that she doesn't have favorites. "That means," she says late one evening on the barge, "I can take a nap anytime I want."

Like the other divers, Scholley spends time pumping weights in the exercise gym on the barge, but she has a more serious addiction, a voracious appetite for science fiction novels. She devours about one book a week, usually in the David Weber genre of space battles and futuristic naval warfare. And Clive Cussler, the prolific writer-diver-adventurer, ranks way up on her list, with his Dirk Pitt, specialist in nearly impossible underwater rescues, an almost-real hero. In the run-up to the turret lift, Cussler comes out with *Valhalla Rising*, a page-turner in which Pitt puts the kibosh on a blackguard adversary who tries to blow up futuristic yachts with hundreds of passengers. Our hero suffers not a scratch or even a frown. Scholley barely has time to think on the barge, but every so often she'll sneak up to the helicopter deck—it's on top of the berthing quarters and serenely quiet—with her escape novel and CD player and tune out the madness below. It's often only a few minutes until someone finds her, but the time is blissful.

The role Scholley is playing is anything but fiction, and she has an awareness of the moment she's in, like the strong connection she feels to the men who lost their lives on the *Monitor.* "It happens every time you go down; you feel that camaraderie with those sailors of 140 years ago. You kind of get goose bumps because you think back to what those men were doing—it's really hallowed ground. We've come so far because of what these men did and sacrificed."

SCHOLLEY SITS on the dive bench exchanging greetings with some of the divers. There's no more than a few seconds' delay, but Chief Steve Janek, running the dive, rolls his eyes. This is no time for chitchat. "All right, guys, let's put a fire under this," he barks. "Get her dressed up."

Several tenders help her into the dive suit. As she tugs at blue diving gloves, one of them slides over the wedding band on her left hand. She's married to former Navy SEAL Frank Scholley. She and Frank—an engineer now pursuing a second career—joke that they've spent so much time apart chasing their careers that when they do get to see each other it's like a honeymoon all over again. When they travel they try to meet at a spot convenient for both, but that's a bit more difficult when she's sixteen miles out at sea. Scholley is 43—old enough to be the mother of half of the divers out here. She and Frank have been too busy with careers for children of their own, but that might soon change. They've begun to explore the idea of going to China and adopting a child, perhaps twin girls. And also, nudging from the back to the front of her mind, is the idea of retiring. She could stay in the Navy, but there is no chance of becoming a diver-admiral. Besides, admirals don't have as much fun as divers, and she's had all the fun she ever wanted. Being a mom at last is beginning to crowd out other goals. After, of course, getting this turret on deck.

Her boots are shoved on, and the big yellow helmet is lowered over her head, fitted into its collar, and snapped snugly in place. All elements of the umbilical are attached: water, depth, communications, camera, gas. And just like that, she and Bradford are over the side and down with an explosion of green bubbles and Chipmunk voices.

"Officers rarely dive," says Cavey, "but Bobbie makes a point of getting in the water. She's probably in the top ten of all the people out here in the amount of dives on the *Monitor*. Even guys who might have an old-fashioned view of men and women respect someone who does the job as well as or even better than they can. Bobbie's carved a huge slot in the diving Navy for women."

As Scholley and Bradford descend through the water column, bubbles rise around them. At 100 feet, a barracuda lurks nearby. At 210 feet the platform stops, and both divers step off and drop to the wreck.

Scholley feels the same old thrill. "It's kind of like you're walking on clouds down there," she tells me later, "although you have this incredible drag on you from the current and the umbilical, your very heavy helmet and suit become neutrally buoyant. I feel very comfortable and very serene."

This morning's job is to remove debris near the turret, but there's always a secondary agenda. "Keep an eye out for artifacts, Red Diver," urges John Broadwater. Through her helmet camera, the monitor in the communications shack shows gloved hands pawing through rubble. An eel scoots out of the way. A coral branch waves in the current. She tosses a piece of debris into the recovery basket. Jeff Johnston, watching the image from Scholley's camera, shows sudden interest, but it isn't much. "Historic junk," he pronounces.

"Looks like a rim from a '67 Chevy," says Cavey.

She claws her way next toward a cavity left last year when the engine was removed, looking for a place to run a cable to help saw away the armor belt, an ingenious cutting technique. The cable will be pulled back and forth by two winches, acting like a bandsaw. She doesn't find one and makes a mental note that a hole will have to be punched through. She'll discuss that later, after she gets out of decompression.

Thirty minutes on the bottom is quickly over, and the divers return to the stage.

"Everything OK?" Janek asks.

"OK," she says.

"Hoo-yah!" he announces.

"Hoo-yah!" she agrees.

It's the language of divers, and she knows it well.

ELEVEN

EVERLASTING IRON

LATE IN the afternoon of March 9, Union Secretary of the Navy Welles received the telegram from Fort Monroe he so desperately wanted. It was excellent news, even if slightly inaccurate. The *Monitor*, it said, "had encountered and driven off the *Merrimac*." On Monday, March 10, the *New York Herald* reported that the dispatch "has created the wildest excitement in the city." No less fevered was the elation on the Union side of Hampton Roads. As fireman George Geer wrote to Martha one day after the battle, "Our ship is crowded with Generals and Officers of all grades both army and Navy. They are wild with joy and say if any of us come to the Fort we can have all we want free, as we have saved 100s of lives and millions of property to the Government."

It's a wonder they were able to celebrate after days without sleep. "My men and myself were perfectly black with smoke and powder," Dana Greene, executive officer on the *Monitor*, wrote to his mother and father. "All my underclothes were perfectly black, and my person was in the same condition. . . . I had been up so long, and under such a state of excitement, that my nervous system was completely run down. . . . My nerves and muscles twitched as though electric shocks were continually passing through them. . . . I layed down and tried to sleep—I might as well have tried to fly."

The next morning the now-heroic ironclad did a turn through the battered but saved fleet. "Cheer after cheer went up from the Frigates and small craft for the glorious *Monitor*, and happy indeed did we all feel," Greene related. A few days later, the *Monitor* sailed close to Newport News, and it seemed the whole Union army turned out to cheer. As paymaster Keeler observed, "Thousands & thousands lined the shore, covered the vessels at the docks, & filled the rigging. Their cheers resembled one continuous roar." Bands played "See, the Conquering Hero Comes" and "The Star-Spangled Banner." "Iron sides and iron hearts" was one of many slogans he heard.

Above the Potomac, where good news had been scarce, the reaction verged on the ecstatic. The *Monitor,* so recently sneered at, was now a national treasure, and her crew, rank recruits who had learned to live and fight on an untested vessel in the heat of combat, were instant heroes. If you could not see the valiant little ship in person, you could soon buy *Monitor* playing cards, cigars, hats, and flour. There was even sheet music. One catchy tune of the day was "Monitor Grand March."

The little upstart of a warship, as well as its ponderous but deadly opponent, changed the nature of naval warfare. After the engagement, there was hardly another order for a traditional wooden warship anywhere in the world. Ericsson and his partners received orders for as many new *Monitor*-class ships as they could produce. In all, sixty-six of the half-submerged vessels were built, and many would remain in service well into the next century.

But it was hardly the way sailors wanted to go to war. "How can an admiral condescend to go to sea in an iron pot?" Nathaniel Hawthorne sniffed facetiously. As part of a rambling tour of Civil War Virginia for the *Atlantic Monthly,* the famous novelist joined the throng of observers who came to see the curious warship. "What space and elbow-room can be found for quarterdeck dignity in the cramped lookout of the *Monitor,* or even the twenty-feet diameter of her cheese-box?" he asked in his essay attributed to "a Peaceable Man."

> All the pomp and splendor of naval warfare are gone by. Henceforth there must come up a race of enginemen and smoke-blackened cannoneers, who will hammer away at their enemies under the direction of a single pair of eyes; and even heroism—so deadly a grip is Science laying on our noble possibilities—will become a quality of very minor importance, when its possessor cannot break through the iron crust of its own armament and give the world a glimpse of it.

The *Monitor* was not a vessel at all but a machine that

> looked like a gigantic rat-trap. It was ugly, questionable, suspicious, evidently mischievous,—nay, I will allow myself to call it devilish; for this was the new war-fiend, destined, along with others of the same breed, to annihilate whole navies and batter down old supremacies. The wooden walls of Old England cease to exist, and a whole history of naval renown reaches its period, now that the *Monitor* comes smoking into view; while the billows dash over what seems her deck, and storms bury even her turret in green water, as she burrows and snorts along, oftener under the surface than above.

Hawthorne, however, couldn't help being impressed at the accommodations below decks. "It was like finding a palace, with all its conveniences, under the sea," he went on.

> The inaccessibility, the apparent impregnability, of this submerged iron fortress are most satisfactory; the officers and crew get down through a little hole in the deck, hermetically seal themselves, and go below; and until they see fit to reappear, there would seem to be no power given to man whereby they could be brought to light. A storm of cannonshot damages them no more than a handful of dried peas.

Hawthorne's "Peaceable Man" essay inspired his friend Herman Melville to take a crack at the notion of ironclad warriors in a series of Civil War poems. "In the Turret" finds the *Monitor*'s captain "sealed as in a diving bell" and facing the possibility that it could be his iron coffin, a remarkable echo of paymaster Keeler's dread: "Stand up, thy heart; be strong; what matter/If here thou seest thy welded tomb?" And in "A Utilitarian View of the *Monitor*'s Fight," Melville sees a small silver lining in the demise of heroic encounters. "War shall yet be, but warriors/Are now but operatives; War's made/Less grand than Peace."

It is clear that Jules Verne was also inspired by the *Monitor*. In his *20,000 Leagues under the Sea*, published in 1870, the professor who is trying to solve the mystery of an underwater phenomenon considers several hypotheses, including a narwhal-type beast and a kind of "submarine Monitor." As it turns out, the *Nautilus*, Captain Nemo's electric-powered, water-ballasted, deep-diving undersea voyager, is indeed an iron submersible with all the comforts of Ericsson's vessel and numerous futuristic inventions, including a chamber that allows deep-sea explorers to exit and walk on the bottom.

The *Nautilus* may have been a cross between the *Monitor* and the *Alligator*—the navy's first submarine. The *Alligator* was designed by French inventor Brutus de Villeroi, who was once Verne's math teacher. The cigar-shaped sub, with openings for oars and an airlock that allowed divers carrying explosives to swim to targets, paid a brief visit to Hampton Roads early in 1862, its mission to clear obstructions in the James River. The river proved too shallow for the sub to operate safely, and it was sent back to Washington for modifications, including a hand-cranked propeller. The following year, under tow and heading for Charleston, the *Alligator* began taking on water off Cape Hatteras. Because it threatened to sink the tow ship, it was abandoned and probably drifted hundreds of miles before finding the bottom.

The *Monitor* may have become world famous, but she was surely nowhere better appreciated than in official Washington. After his injury, with one eye blinded and his face permanently blackened, Lieutenant John Worden returned to his K Street home in Washington to recuperate. It was there that a deeply appreciative Lincoln paid him a visit: "You do me great honor, Mr. President," said Worden, lying abed with his head swathed in bandages, "and I am only sorry that I can't see you." "You have done me more honor, sir, than I can ever do to you," the president replied.

What the *Monitor* had done was immediately restore the strategic balance to Hampton Roads, which the *Virginia* had abruptly upset. The rebel ship would not only have done in the rest of the wooden fleet there but denied General George McClellan the ability to land troops at Fort Monroe for his much-anticipated march on Richmond. Now, as long as the *Monitor* held the *Virginia* at bay, the March 17 Peninsula Campaign could begin. This naval stalemate was fine with Lincoln, and he specifically ordered that the *Monitor* not take any unnecessary risks. "It is directed by the President," Gideon Welles said in a telegram, "that the *Monitor* be not too much exposed; that under no event shall any attempt be made to proceed with her unattended to Norfolk."

Orders were orders, but they were humiliating to the *Monitor*'s sailors, who were itching for a rematch as much as were the *Virginia*'s. The Confederate ship had a surprise waiting, a newly installed twelve-foot ram capable of reaching beneath the *Monitor*'s armor belt to its thin underbelly.

There were other ideas. "A few days later we went down again to within gun-shot of the Rip Raps [a manmade island], and exchanged a few rounds with the fort, hoping that the *Monitor* would come out from her lair into open water," Lieutenant John Taylor Wood was to write. Had she done so, the rebels planned to attack using gunboats, with boarding parties assigned to place wedges under the turret to keep it from turning, cover the pilot house with tarpaulins, climb to the top of the turret and smokestack, and drop hand grenades inside.

That's exactly what the Union commanders feared. Time after time the *Virginia* came out to the Roads, spoiling for a fight, and time after time the *Monitor* declined to take the bait. In a ponderous dance, the two steamed back and forth under the guns of Fort Monroe and Sewell's Point, neither foolish enough to come within range of the other's shore batteries.

The day after the battle, Greene was replaced by the first of a series of more experienced officers. Lieutenant Thomas Selfridge, a Naval Academy graduate who had recently served on the *Cumberland*, came on board briefly, then Lieutenant William M. Jeffers, another Annapolis product, took over and incurred the instant dislike of the crew. "Our new Capt. is a rigid disciplinarian, of quick imperious temper & domineering disposition," Keeler wrote. One of his first actions was to put the enlisted men on half pay, holding the rest for a time of his choosing to discourage desertions. Fireman George Geer, who was scrimping to send money home, was beside himself. He couldn't even get his grog allowance, he wrote, because it was money "the Captain wants for his own gutts. He is a damd old Gluttonous Hogg, and I hope the curse of Hell will rest upon him." Everyone else felt the same, he said.

Some of the *Monitor*'s crew never got over the fact that, even though Worden was injured, they failed to chase the *Virginia* and sink her.

Furthermore, it was galling that their hands were now tied. Greene's actions gnawed at him for the rest of his life. He served in several other commands and at the Naval Academy, but it seemed he was dogged by the missed opportunity. In 1884, twenty-two years after the battle, he wrote a lengthy article for *Century* magazine on the challenges and difficulties he faced. It was similar to the long letter he had sent to his parents after the battle, and again it painstakingly recounted his actions.

"We of the *Monitor* thought, and still think, that we had gained a great victory. This the Confederates have denied. But it has never been denied that the object of the *Merrimac* on the 9th of March was to complete the destruction of the Union fleet in Hampton Roads, and that in this she was completely foiled and driven off by the *Monitor*, nor has it been denied that at the close of the engagement the *Merrimac* retreated to Norfolk, leaving the *Monitor* in possession of the field."

In December 1884, shortly after sending the article to the magazine from his post at Portsmouth Navy Yard in New Hampshire, Greene ended his life and his misery with a pistol shot.

BY MID-SPRING 1862, the "Monitor Boys," as they liked to call themselves, had grown bored by the lack of real action. The weather was unusually warm, almost balmy. "We are having very easy and very lazy times laying here waiting for the *Merrimack*," George Geer wrote to Martha. "I have been in the Navy one month to day and I have worked so hard time has sliped by very quick, but know [*sic*] we are doing nothing and it commences to drag very slow." "I done the Cook a favor," Geer added, "and on Sunday morning he gave me half of a Mackrel and two bisquit. I thought when I was eating them that perhaps you was eating the same but then I had no Willey to give some to, no Wife to pour out a good cup of coffee, no Sunday paper to read, no little Gilley to talk to. Oh when I get home again I will know how to apreciate a loving Wife's society, although I cannot love you any bettor than I always have."

Quarters on the *Monitor* were cramped and afforded little privacy. With only partitions separating the officers' staterooms, nearly all conversations were shared. And then there was the vessel's tomblike construction. "I am tired of everlasting iron," complained Keeler. "The clank, clank, clank, while I am writing this, of the officer on the deck as he paces back and forth on the iron plates over my head."

Keeler was on deck the morning of April 11 when the *Virginia* made an appearance, gliding over the smooth waters of the Roads with other steamers and gunboats. "As she slowly approached in advance of her attendants she seemed like some huge gladiator just entering the vast watery arena of the amphitheater, while on the opposite shore the *Monitor* steamed forth her defiance with the attendant fleet as spectators in her rear—then they stood on the edge of the arena, each hesitating to advance. . . . The same comedy I suppose will be enacted day after day for I don't know how long, though how soon it may be turned to tragedy none of us can tell."

He compared his ship to a fragile piece of china that an owner might display but never use for fear of breaking it. The crew, in Keeler's words, was "ready, willing & anxious for another interview," so it was galling, especially the day the *Virginia* delivered the insult of a single shot as she turned and steamed away. Local newspapers didn't make it any better by constantly ridiculing the opponents as cowards. But the simple fact was that stalemate equaled checkmate for the South, victory for the North.

Life aboard may have lacked the drama of battle, but it wasn't all that disagreeable, at least for the officers. On May 6 Keeler went ashore at the Rip Raps, where a fort helped guard the entrance to Hampton Roads, and strolled "among bright yellow daisies." General John Wool (for whom the fort would later be named) picked him a bunch of sweet-smelling mignonette, which the paymaster dutifully sent home to Anna.

The next day the *Monitor* and her crew had the ultimate in high-power guests. President Lincoln, accompanied by Secretary of the Treasury Salmon Chase, Secretary of War Edwin Stanton, General Wool, and others, came on board. Lincoln had a "sad, care-worn and anxious look," Keeler observed. "When he turned to us I could see his lip quiver and his frame tremble with strong emotion and I imagined that the terrible drama in these waters . . . was passing in review before him," Keeler related to his wife. Lincoln declined a drink of whiskey and opted for water instead. "As the president and his party left us," Keeler wrote, "we gave them three hearty cheers."

Shortly afterward, the *Monitor*'s crew could hear the rumble of heavy artillery and wagons rolling by, as well as the tramp of horses and the shouted orders of officers. This was the much-delayed Peninsula Campaign. It was now underway but would soon fizzle when McClellan's forces ran into determined Confederate opposition. The campaign had been designed to make a quick end of the war, but the end was nowhere in sight.

It looked as though the *Monitor* was stuck playing cat and mouse with the *Virginia*. George Geer wished "she was at the bottom for then we could have a hand in the attack on Yorktown but now we must lay here and watch for that devilish mashine while the rest of the gunboats can have the fun."

Geer had no idea how soon he'd get his wish. On May 10, as Confederate troops moved to defend Richmond, Norfolk and its navy yard fell to Union forces, leaving the rebel ironclad without a home port. It was doubtful that she could get past the guns at Fort Monroe and flee to the open sea, so the Confederate commanders decided to send her to help with the Richmond defenses. There was one problem: with a draft of 23 feet, they'd never get the *Virginia* over the eighteen-foot shallows at the entrance to the James River unless they could lighten the load. As tons of material were thrown overboard, the balky old ship rose in the water, but not enough. Persistent wind out of the west had further dropped the river's depth, and it would be impossible, pilots said, to pass the shoals into the main river. At midnight, flag officer Josiah Tattnall gave the order to destroy the *Virginia* by running her aground at Craney Island and putting her to the torch.

From where they lay at anchor, the *Monitor*'s sailors could see a bright light over Sewell's Point. It grew in intensity until about 4:00 A.M., when there was a sudden flash and a dull, heavy report. Their old nemesis had come to this. The fire had reached the eighteen tons of powder in her magazine, and the resulting explosion was thunderous. Though they cheered, there was a note of sadness that the once-dreaded ironclad had died by her own hand rather than in a fair fight.

Later that morning, orders came to move to Norfolk, and the *Mon-*

itor crew witnessed the now-silent guns at Sewell's Point. A squad of sailors went ashore, Keeler recounted, marched over the earthworks, and hoisted the Stars and Stripes over the rebel fort. Another Union flag now flew from Craney Island, where, as Keeler recounted, "a blackened sunken wreck was pointed out as all that remained of our old foe."

Things were moving fast now. The next morning before sunrise the *Monitor* was steaming toward Richmond in company with the *Galena*, one of the two other, more conventional, ironclads that had been built in the race to compete with the *Virginia*. They were to open up the James River to federal traffic, but the attempt was a bloody fiasco. Hemmed in by rebel forces—some of whom had been sailors from the *Virginia*—at a bend in the river known as Drewry's Bluff, the *Galena* was nearly ripped to pieces. While the *Monitor* sat helpless, unable to elevate its guns sufficiently to fire at the enemy, the rebels fired shot after exploding shot, piercing the *Galena*'s armor. Thirteen Union sailors were killed and eleven were seriously wounded.

"I went on board the *Galena* at the termination of her action," Keeler told Anna, "and . . . she looked like a slaughter house . . . of human beings." The mission was a total failure. George Geer, in his letter home, said the *Galena* "proved no better than a wooden vessel." He went on deck, he said, "and counted 17 holes in her side."

The *Monitor* was struck three times, once squarely in the turret with an eight-inch shot, twice in the side armor near the bow. Beyond a few bent iron plates, there was no real damage except perhaps to the sailors' pride.

William Jeffers, the *Monitor*'s unpopular new commander, fired off a blistering report to Commodore Louis Goldsborough, head of the North Atlantic Blockading Squadron. The guns couldn't elevate, he complained. Ventilation was "intolerable," with temperatures reaching 140 degrees during the engagement. The vessel made only six knots. He was disgusted with the ship's performance and took the position that "for general purposes, wooden ships, shell guns, and forts, whether for offense or defense, have not been superseded." The *Monitor*'s flaws, however, remained a closely guarded secret. The Union was about to invest millions in a new class of ironclad warships.

The night after the Drewry's Bluff disaster, the *Monitor* anchored off City Point on the James River. Keeler was ready to turn in when the cry went up, "Boat Ahoy," followed by a musket shot that rang through the muggy night air and a stampede of steps up to the turret. The officers were concerned about being boarded and gave instructions to shoot anyone approaching who did not answer immediately.

Keeler rushed to the turret and saw a trembling black man in a boat on the water below, with sailors training guns on him. He was Siah Carter, almost certainly an escaped slave from nearby Shirley plantation. He implored them not to shoot and said over and over that he was a black man.

His owner, he said, was a colonel in the Confederate army, and he'd been taken with other slaves to work on the defenses at Yorktown, then to build a road from Yorktown to Williamsburg. His owner had gone off with the army to Richmond but had warned the slaves that if they fell in with the Yankees they'd be thrown in the river with weights tied to their necks. The talk hadn't frightened Carter, however. He had escaped and now had come down to the ship to see what he could do to help the Union. He was hired as first assistant to the cook.

Historic records indicate that "Sigh" Carter was born on the Carter plantation in October 1839, which would have made him twenty-two at the time of his escape, and he had become one of five hundred slaves owned by Hill Carter. Siah Carter—apparently the same—signed up for a three-year term as first-class boy.

The Carter plantation dated to 1611, just four years after the first English settlement at Jamestown. Ann Hill Carter, wife of Light Horse Harry Lee and mother of Robert E. Lee, had once lived there. Siah Carter's real name was Siah Hulett, but all the slaves on Hill Carter's plantation took the owner's last name. Carter, almost certainly the black man posing in the foreground of the most famous picture of the *Monitor*'s crew, served on other Civil War vessels until 1865. He then married Eliza Tarrow, also born a slave on the plantation, and the freed couple helped populate their part of Virginia with thirteen children.

Three other onetime slaves—Robert Howard, Daniel Moore, and Robert Cook—would join the *Monitor* later, when the ironclad went

Monitor crew. The man kneeling forward right is believed to be Siah Carter, an escaped slave who came aboard in May 1862 as first-class boy. (Photo by James F. Gibson, Mariners' Museum)

to Washington for repairs. Former "contrabands," as they were called, were not to be hired at a level above landsman, the lowest crew designation, but they could then advance to seaman, fireman, and coal heaver, Secretary Welles declared.

From May until late August, the little ship and her crew lay baking on the James. They were supposed to support the Peninsula Campaign, but it wasn't going anywhere. For some, the only diversion was the daily grog ration, though not everyone participated. Those who declined got five cents a day extra. Fireman George Geer, ever eager to save a few pennies, wrote to his wife, "I believe I have not told you before how much my Grog is. By not drinking it I get $1.25 per month, which will most cloath me."

In July, the navy disallowed the ration and banned alcohol completely on warships, but there seems to have been no rush to remove

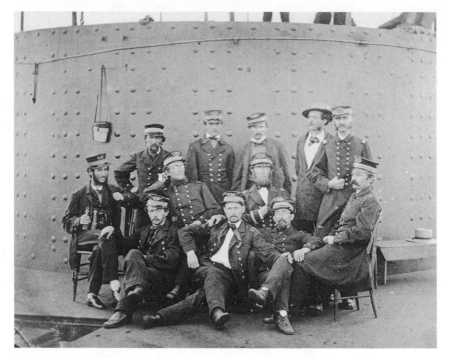

Monitor officers pose in front of the turret, July 1862 (not all have been identified). Back row: George Frederickson (left), Dana Greene (third from left), Isaac Newton (right); middle row: Louis Stodder (left), William Keeler (second from left); front row: Robinson Hands (left). (Photo by James F. Gibson, Mariners' Museum)

the stores of spirits already aboard. The tedium that settled upon the crew may have led some to seek oblivion in the hidden casks of stored rum.

A log entry for September 2: "At 6:30 the wardroom steward (Lawrence Murray), being drunk and disorderly, was placed forward of the pilothouse and placed in double irons. On leaving him, he immediately threw himself over the side and never afterward appeared at the surface. Search was made but in vain."

Shortly after the grog ration was disallowed, a new item began appearing on board the *Monitor*: bottles of Gray's Hair Restorative. History does not record a sudden inclination among sailors to pay attention to their hairlines.

There were rumors that a "new *Merrimack*," the CSS *Richmond*, would soon attack, and the *Monitor*'s mission was to lie in wait. The sailors were largely kept below because of the dangers of rebel sharpshooters, so it was hot and confining. On August 19, newly arrived engineer George White wrote to his mother: "There are more mosquitoes than I ever saw up the Mississippi. They are a great source of trouble to us." The men's clothes were soaked by perspiration, and the only escape from the heat was to sleep out on deck, where they were drenched by the dew. They were, Keeler complained, "prisoners in the bowels of our iron monster."

TWELVE

LUCY'S THE TURRET

IN A pep talk one July morning in 2002, Chief Petty Officer Steve Janek praises his divers for their work the day before. "We are now deemed the wrecking crew!" he proclaims. But then he adds (perhaps because someone might be listening), "An archaeologically correct wrecking crew!"

Janek well knows the value of the ship they are diving on. "This is our history," he says. "This is where it all started." But he also knows you don't whip up enthusiasm among young divers by telling them to be careful about nicking an artifact or bumping the turret. There's a delicate mix. "It's a little old lady trapped under a building, and we gotta get her out safely."

The old lady, of course, is the *Monitor*'s turret. Millions are being spent to raise it from the bottom of the ocean—all 120 tons of it plus the guns and gun carriages it holds—and to restore them. A new wing of the Mariners' Museum is to be virtually built around the turret. It will not do to have this piece of history, once invulnerable but now in danger of collapse, come up in pieces.

The Navy diving community knows its importance, but hauling tonnage off the ocean floor as fast as is safely possible is their specialty. The day and night shifts compete fiercely to log the most dives—five dives to a shift if possible—and they heap scorn on anyone who slows things down. Furthermore, planning, while nice, is time consuming. The divers pride themselves on improvising on the spot, and they are very, very good at it. The archaeological community lives by caution and planning, with backups and fallbacks. Yet each group knows that if things were left entirely to the other, the turret could either be wrecked or not come up at all. This tension dogs the recovery mission day in and day out—and makes things interesting. Miraculously, it seems to work.

Divers are careful not to bruise the turret. They've worked in and around it, night and day, for months, and there have to be times when they smack into it with tools, shackles, or lifting gear. So as not to alarm John Broadwater or Jeff Johnston, those ever-present archaeological nags, they begin using a code name for it—"Lucy." As in "I just crashed into Lucy."

Broadwater, manager of the *Monitor* Marine Sanctuary and now head of the *Monitor* recovery effort, is always popping in and out of the saturation shack. "He has a tendency to get excited quickly," says master diver Chuck Young. This goes on for weeks until finally Broadwater confronts one of the master divers: "Lucy's the turret, right?"

"No, of course not," the diver replies, failing to stifle a huge grin.

Many of Broadwater's archaeologist colleagues warned him that he couldn't trust a bunch of Navy salvage divers with something as significant as the *Monitor*; they were bound to harm it. "What's the alternative?" he'd ask. "Do we let nature rip it apart?"

Broadwater wants the turret recovered as much as anyone, maybe more, but he's haunted by the thought of it falling apart on the way up. "The last thing we want," he tells a group of divers one night, "is to bring up a turret kit."

"John is our good angel," says Rick Cavey. "He's the one who stands over our shoulder and says, 'Hey, don't do that; instead of using a jackhammer, let's use a chipping hammer.'" The suggestions always mean more time, but the divers understand.

Because Broadwater and Johnston are not salvage experts, they feel obliged to be devil's advocates, always asking whether certain approaches will really work. They know this can seem annoying, but being wrong is unthinkable. There is sure to be a classic standoff between wanting to bring the turret to the surface and making sure it is intact, yet they know that the Navy also has a huge stake in doing it right and that trusting this better angel is the best course.

The responsibility is split, but if it ever comes down to jeopardizing any of the historic parts of the ship, the final decision is Broadwater's alone. Still, he's got to rely on the divers' judgment about what is possible.

This burden of responsibility inspires caution at a time when the divers are most eager to get the turret on deck. Chris Murray begins to worry that Broadwater and Johnston's concerns are tying the divers in knots. Being smothered by busywork makes his blood boil. Murray, more than anyone, knows that time is precious. There are times, he feels, when you just have to say this is as good as it's going to get and move. Forty-five days is not a lot of time for a project of this magnitude, and delays, most of them inevitable, have already gnawed away most of their cushion. Further setbacks could push them right to the edge.

To Broadwater, bringing the huge artifact up safely is both a burden and an opportunity. As he told me one day before the mission began, "To see that turret come up, all intact and set down on the barge—I think a lot of us are going to consider that a major day in our lives."

It is an archaeologist's dream come true. Since the *Monitor* sank more than a century ago, very few people have seen it. Even after it was found, it was much too deep for most divers to get to. So it is virtually intact, still containing everything that was in it the day it sank. "Knowing you've got a deepwater wreck that's virtually pristine, and then the whole separate dimension of knowing it's the *Monitor*, the Navy's first ironclad ship and the first modern warship, and knowing all the history that's behind it and all the stories about it and the epic battle of Hampton Roads—it's just about an icon of American naval history; put all that together and it's pretty awe-inspiring," Broadwater says. "The icing on the cake is we're saving parts of the *Monitor* so that millions of people, instead of a handful of divers, will get to see these things."

If Broadwater sometimes takes the role of good cop in the NOAA operation, his loyal sidekick Jeff Johnston doesn't mind being the not-so-good cop. He probably knows more about the *Monitor* than anyone in the country, including Broadwater. Even though largely self-taught, he is the consummate historian, with more passion than most. When Johnston first went to work for the chief archaeologist, Broadwater told him to read everything he could get his hands on, especially the correspondence and drawings of John Ericsson and the accounts of the men who served on the *Monitor*. He should become, Broadwater told him, the expert on how the ship was built. Johnston went for it, soaking up everything he could, imagining what it must have been like on board. Now he spends days and nights staring at video monitors, running on coffee, cigarettes, and adrenaline. He seems one with the wreck.

Johnston grew up in Portsmouth, Virginia, across the Elizabeth River from Norfolk and next door to the shipyard where the *Merrimack* became the *Virginia*. As much as anyone can be, he was steeped in local history, with a touch of the *Monitor* story flowing in his veins. His great-granduncle, William Johnston, served as gunner's mate on the *Virginia* and may have helped put some of the dents in the Union ship's turret. If the turret ever comes up, he vows, he'll "put a touch" in every one of the dents.

With this heritage going for him, it isn't unusual to see Johnston wearing a CSS *Virginia* cap, with long hair flowing from the back like one of Moseby's raiders, but with the possible exception of Broadwater, he is the closest thing to the complete *Monitor* junkie.

In 2001, the year the engine was retrieved, Broadwater and Johnston began dividing the twenty-four-hour clock into day and night shifts, with night-owl Johnston taking the night trick. He likes it, especially being able to watch the images pouring back from divers' helmet cameras, their lights sometimes reflecting off shiny objects like lantern chimneys or medicine bottles that might not be seen in gloomy daylight.

"The artificial light also brought out the incredible colors that are not seen in the ambient light during the day," Johnston writes in an NOAA log entry. "At night, corals, anemones, and sea fans glow with a vibrant brilliance. The varieties of marine life on the wreck also change at night as the nocturnal creatures emerge to feed and the smaller reef fish hide so as not to be fed upon. Even though we at the *Monitor* sanctuary primarily view the wreck as a cultural resource, seeing the colorful life on the wreck—especially at night—reminds us that we also have a beautiful artificial reef here."

Ericsson's correspondence tells Johnston that the top of the turret was not very strong. The top, which is now on the bottom because the turret is upside down, was supported by inverted railroad rails mounted on a perimeter roof rail, with a layer of perforated iron plates on top. "He designed it to be able to swap the guns out," Johnston says. "That told us it was only lightly bolted in place. It was a compression fit, all these pieces laminated on top of each other and rested on that roof ring. It was never designed to support all that weight."

In other words, with two 17,000-pound guns and several tons of concreted mud and silt still in the turret, it would be foolish to lift it without first reinforcing the roof. Losing the contents of the turret would be a disaster. The Navy knows that and NOAA knows that, yet the pressure is mounting to get the turret on the barge.

They lose everything if the roof falls off, Johnston knows. So what if they have to leave the turret on the bottom? Yes, he'll feel bad about not recovering it, but how bad would he feel about being pressured into lifting the turret too soon and dumping the contents onto the bottom of the ocean?

Johnston is the most aggressive of the artifact protectors. This raises the hackles of some of the divers, but they respect him. "You need people like Jeff," says master diver Chuck Young. "You hate him, but you know the guy really is right." Johnston has done his homework and seems to have a sixth sense when something's about to go wrong. He can be enjoyable to be around, wry and funny, Young says, "but when he puts his *Monitor* hat on, he's strictly business."

Scholley has another take. If they follow Johnston, the turret may never get off the bottom. But she knows, too, that if the Navy has things its way, the turret might come up in pieces.

JOHN BROADWATER would just as soon be down there with the divers. He has scuba dived on the wreck several times, an impressive accomplishment. Recreational divers seldom go below one hundred feet because of the danger of nitrogen narcosis. Deeper, "technical" diving requires advanced training and the use of sophisticated mixed gases. He and several NOAA divers have often done cleanup work and assessment after Navy dives and brought up some of the smaller artifacts. But in 1998, while the *Monitor*'s propeller was being freed and raised, he suffered the bends, sustaining damage to his inner ear. It appeared to heal with no noticeable symptoms, but NOAA doctors have ordered him to stay out of the water.

"It looks like my diving days are over," he laments. "It's killing me. My favorite is the hands-on part, and staying out of the water has been a real struggle." At least he knows what it's like down there on the ocean bottom, breathing mixed gases, fighting the currents, drinking in the aura of that hallowed sanctuary.

It does not make things easier that the project has ingredients similar to some well-known maritime and space disasters. Back in his office in Newport News, Broadwater has on his desk a copy of *Hardluck Ironclad*, a book by Edwin C. Bearss, on the near disastrous recovery of the USS *Cairo*. This Civil War ironclad was sunk by a Confederate mine on the Yazoo River near Vicksburg, Mississippi, on December 12, 1862. Pressed for time and running short of money, salvors in 1965 pushed ahead with a recovery attempt and just about ripped it apart— something Broadwater vowed never to repeat. Also on his mind was the terrible tragedy of the space shuttle *Challenger*. Again, delay followed delay and, under pressure, NASA made the decision to proceed with the flight. And here they are, with time and money beginning to run short. Was this to be his *Cairo*? His *Challenger*?

An inner voice constantly whispers: Let's stop and re-evaluate; maybe it's better that you leave the *Monitor* alone, that nature go ahead and destroy it rather than have you guys destroy it.

"It's good to have that little voice," he says, "but sometimes you wish you could shut it off."

Sleep is not easy. Unlike Johnston, who seems to thrive without it, Broadwater needs at least five or six hours a night to keep sharp. He worries about being in a situation where his brain isn't working. Worrying about sleep does not promote more of it.

If only everything would work out perfectly; if all their concerns could be addressed; if the weather would cooperate; if the funds would hold out—there is no end of things to worry about, and Broadwater's face shows it. He looks haggard half the time and is constantly besieged by people wanting a moment, half a moment, ten seconds of his time. "I'm going to start wearing a disguise," he says ruefully.

Broadwater wears the conservationist hat constantly but never seems self-important about it. He has a puckish sense of humor. As saturation divers are entering their compression chamber one sultry summer day, he pokes his head into the portal just before it's shut. "Have a good one," he tells them, "but just remember: Jeff and I will be watching you every moment."

It's true. The two of them are constantly watching the dive monitors. But it isn't just to make sure no one goofs. Sometimes, it seems, Broadwater is having the time of his life, as if he were down there with the divers and can't wait for the next discovery. In the communications shack next to the dive station, listening to the voices of the divers, to their breathing, glued to the video monitors and wearing a headset, he doesn't try to hide his enthusiasm. "If you can get in closer and get a little more detail, it would be helpful," he tells one of the divers as he watches the image coming back from the diver's camera. "Wow!" he exclaims as the camera pans over some detail of John Ericsson's invention. "Oh, yeah, Green," he says to the diver in the secondary, or green, position. "That's a good shot. Neat!"

His excitement over each little step reflects a growing respect that has developed between the NOAA and Navy teams. After five years of working together, learning from mistakes and improving the art of deepwater recovery, their comfort level has risen. Besides, the Operations Manual states how the command structure works. Broadwater has the final say. "It's sort of like a prenuptial agreement," he says. "You love and you trust your partner, but it doesn't hurt to kind of have things spelled out."

On the barge late one night in July, Broadwater stands near the railing that overlooks the place where the *Monitor* went down. An orange two-thirds moon hangs over the gently rolling sea. A large dolphin fish, looking blue-green, splashes in the lights off the barge. In the distance, off to the northwest, the Cape Hatteras Lighthouse—a different structure but not unlike the one the *Monitor* sailors saw 140 years ago—flashes every seven and a half seconds. A kind of closure is near.

"I can hardly wait," he says.

THIRTEEN

ORDERS AT LAST

T HE PRISON term that paymaster Keeler lamented was finally coming to end. On September 30, 1862, the *Monitor* received orders to proceed to the Washington Navy Yard for repairs. Her engine was in need of attention, and after seven months in salt water, her bottom was so fouled she needed a tug for the long trip up the Chesapeake Bay and the Potomac River. Smooth as the ride was, water broke across the deck, forcing the crew to stay below, close the deck lights, and endure the stifling air.

The arrival in Washington provoked a kind of frenzy. Thousands of visitors and gawkers, including whole regiments of soldiers, descended on the yard; carriages lined the docks, and crowds of visitors streamed onboard.

"Our decks were covered & our ward room filled with ladies," Keeler complained. And on retreating to his stateroom, he found several women "making their toilet before my glass, using my combs and brushes. We couldn't go to any part of the vessel without coming in contact with petticoats." Near dinnertime the crowd was so large that marines had to be posted to keep people away or they probably would have eaten all the food. As it was, they helped themselves to doorknobs and just about everything else that wasn't locked away.

At last the crew left for much-deserved furloughs while their iron home underwent several changes. Davits were added for new lifeboats; new, telescoping smokestacks and higher fresh-air intakes replaced the old ones; iron patches covered the shot marks made by both the

Virginia and the *Minnesota,* stamped appropriately to indicate where the shots came from. The ship had become an instant icon. Her eleven-inch guns were engraved, as though autographed, with the words MONITOR & MERRIMAC/WORDON and MONITOR & MERRIMAC/ERICSSON.

Also added was an inch-thick rifle screen, including stanchions and awning, to protect those on the turret from musket fire. The berth deck was raised, lowering the ceiling considerably but making it wider. Black walnut steps now led down from the berth deck to the wardroom. The ship was given a fresh coat of white paint inside, and new oilcloth was laid on the floors. "With our bright lights burning at night our Ward room looks as bright & cheerful as could be desired," Keeler would write to Anna.

The men had families to visit and lives to resume, if only briefly. Twenty-three-year-old James Fenwick went home to Boston. Born in Scotland, he had signed on as seaman, and by November 7 he had been promoted to quarter gunner. The short, scrappy, blue-eyed sailor, who proudly wore the tattoo "J. F. R. Dundee" on his right shoulder, was at least once clapped in irons for brawling, but on this occasion he was presumably on his best behavior—and in a hurry. During his ten-day leave he married his sweetheart, Mary Ann Duffy, and before returning to the ship he left her in a family way. He rushed back to the ship only to find that others had just gone on furlough. In his only letter home, he regretted he had not stayed longer.

If there were delays in getting underway again, it wasn't because there was a shortage of big ideas about the *Monitor* and what she might next accomplish. "It would be a grand stroke to take a couple of steamers, tow these vessels down in good weather, and clean out Wilmington and its railroad connection," Assistant Secretary of the Navy Gustavus Fox wrote to Acting Rear Admiral Samuel P. Lee on November 7. That, then, was to be the *Monitor*'s new mission—to serve, along with the other ironclads that were by this time coming out of northern shipyards, as an offensive strike force.

Among the other changes was the appointment of a new captain, the ship's fourth and last. Commander John Bankhead, forty-one, was a native of Charleston whose family had strong ties to both Virginia and South Carolina. It is certain that he had felt enormous pressure, like many other sons of the South, to resign his commission and join the Southern cause. One of his brothers, a Memphis lawyer, became a colonel in the Confederate army, and one of his cousins became a general. But Bankhead, as well as another brother, who was in the army, remained loyal to the Union flag.

He had been in the navy for twenty-four years and clearly liked the life. A bachelor who was fond of good wine and cigars, he was considered witty, gallant, and courtly, and he apparently liked that image. One photograph captured him in full uniform, with long flowing hair and ferocious side-whiskers, standing with one hand on the hilt of a magnificent sword. During his previous command on a gunboat, he affixed a pair of silver coffin handles—given to him in jest by a Charleston socialite—to the paneling over his stateroom door.

He was ambitious, too, and not shy about using his shipmate ties with Gustavus Fox, now assistant secretary of the navy, to promote his cause. Like other junior officers before the war, he had been stuck in the unexciting Coast Survey, charting the waters of the Carolina inlets and sounds. Should the need arise for a lieutenant commanding a naval ship in those waters, he wrote to his friend, "I hope you will bear me in mind." Apparently Fox did just that, because he was quickly given a series of commands on gunboats that were sent to attack coastal fortifications. He acquitted himself well, although he had a reputation, as one of his commanders put it, as a "daredevil."

While serving on a blockade vessel near Charleston, Bankhead must have voiced his ambitions to flag officer Samuel DuPont. When DuPont wrote to Fox that Bankhead "wants an iron vessel," the suggestion was quickly acted upon. On September 10 Bankhead arrived in Hampton Roads to take command of the *Monitor*.

Based on his experience with the Coast Survey in and around Wilmington, Bankhead informed Acting Rear Admiral Lee that the *Monitor*, with its eleven-foot draft, could not make it up the Cape Fear River in winter but if there were no obstructions in Old Inlet, the alternative route on the other side of Fort Fisher, he could slip behind it and strike.

By November 12 the *Monitor* was back in Hampton Roads, and rumors were circulating that the ship would be heading out soon, probably to Charleston. Several new members of the crew came on board, including a new surgeon, Grenville Weeks, "quite a young man & I think withal a little self conceited," in Keeler's estimation.

On December 6, Keeler wrote of having spent the previous day holed up in his stateroom while a cold northerly brought constant wind and rain and waves washed over the ship's decks. In the wardroom, the officers sat around the table, reading, writing, and talking. "The dash of the waves as they roll over our heads is the only audible sound that reaches us from the outer world. One would hardly suppose from the quiet stillness that pervades our submarine abode that a gale was raging around us."

Keeler did not mention any excursions the ship might have made, but at one point the *Monitor* may have gone out and run hard aground on an oyster reef, damaging its propeller. Over a century later, when the ship was found, three out of four of its cast iron blades showed evidence of striking something hard and unyielding while running fullspeed ahead. If so, the incident was kept quiet. Who wanted to inform Washington that the ship, just back from extensive repairs, would have to be taken off line again?

HOPES THAT the *Monitor* and other ironclads could be used to bombard Fort Fisher had faded after reports reached Washington that, though the Old Inlet channel was just barely navigable, obstructions would be difficult to clear because the channel ran under the heavy guns of another Wilmington bastion, Fort Caswell. The alternative was to head for Charleston, where the ships could attack Fort Sumter, but that was left up in the air.

On Christmas Eve, the *Monitor* at long last received her orders. In a confidential message, Lee ordered Bankhead to "proceed in tow of the Rhode Island, with the *Monitor* under your command, to Beaufort, N.C., and wait further orders." The *Monitor* would be accompanied by the new ironclad *Passaic*.

The *Monitor*'s legacy included the construction of more ironclads, all of them based on the same design. The Passaic-class vessels, however, were bigger and perhaps better, with thicker hulls, larger guns, better steering, and a pilothouse that sat on top of the turret, revolving with it, instead of forward where it got in the way of the guns. They were 200 feet long and 45 feet in beam, compared with 173 and 41.5 for the original.

Admiral Lee advised the *Monitor*'s commander, "Avail yourself of the first favorable weather for making the passage." It would be several days before that occurred.

On Christmas Day, warships in the Roads—American, French, and English—set up a din of gunfire as much to celebrate as to practice, and shore batteries at Fort Monroe answered exuberantly, filling the still air with smoke and bravado.

In late afternoon the officers sat down to a gluttonous feast that included turkey and enough meat to supply a chophouse. There were oranges, pineapples, apples, figs, raisins, and five kinds of nuts; peaches, strawberries, and quince; mince and apple pies and cakes; and cider as well as blackberry and currant wine.

If George Geer was any judge, the enlisted men did not dine so well. The crew might have thought the food the cook served was "splendid," he told Martha, but that was only because the "poor devils" had no experience with her kind of cooking. She was lonesome, he knew, and he assured her that he had no time to enjoy himself, that he stayed busy most of the day. "I hope next year we may spend our Christmass and New Years both together," he wrote, "and every one hear after."

On one of their last days before departing, some of the sailors went ashore and caroused with counterparts from English warships that were anchored nearby, engaging in minor fisticuffs.

On December 28, both Keeler and Geer sent letters home that reflected the excitement of their preparations. The weather was foul, but not enough to prevent Keeler from going on deck that morning to listen to a brass band on the English ship *Ariadne* strike up "God Save the Queen" and "The Star-Spangled Banner." In his writing to Anna, he professed his wish to "whisper in your ear our destination & plans. . . . You will have to nurse your curiosity and patience for a little while, when we hope again to make 'the little *Monitor*' a household word."

Geer, who may not have gotten the message about keeping their orders secret, told Martha that he expected they would bombard the fort at Wilmington and then move farther south to Charleston. The new ironclad *Passaic* was now lying nearby, and another, the *Montauk*, skippered by their now-recovered, former commander John Worden, was due to arrive; two others were expected to join them.

This was going to be a far larger expedition than he had expected, Geer told his wife: They would likely pound and capture just about every fort still in rebel hands, including Fort Sumter. It would not last long, he boasted, "when us three Iron Clads get up close to it, especially when these two new ones with their 15 in. guns get to hammering away at it."

Geer's guess was on the money, even though navy brass still had not figured it all out. In a confidential memo to Welles on that same date, December 28, Admiral Lee wrote, "I shall not dispatch the ironclads from Beaufort until I receive a satisfactory report as to whether or not the obstructions at Fort Caswell are removable while under the hostile guns of the fort." In other words, sending them to Wilmington was almost certainly off the table. It would be Charleston.

There was one problem that neither Keeler nor Geer nor Lee mentioned. To get there, the ironclads would have to go by way of the Graveyard of the Atlantic, an area of vast shoals and conflicting currents off Cape Hatteras. Keeler described it as "the Cape Horn of our Atlantic coast."

Cape Hatteras is close to where the warm Gulf Stream and the southern extension of the cold, south-flowing Labrador Current brush against each other. Not infrequently, the exchange of energy produces quick and violent storms. Add to this the fact that Cape Hatteras sits thirty miles offshore at the edge of Diamond Shoals, an eight-mile plateau of shallow, shifting underwater sandbars, and you have the makings for deadly conditions. Furthermore, when things turn rough, this zone is far enough out to sea to make running for shelter a doubtful option. More than six hundred known shipwrecks attest to its treachery.

Just before they left, Jacob Nicklis, a twenty-one-year-old seaman who had just joined the crew, wrote to his father, a custom tailor in Buffalo, New York. "Do not answer this letter until you hear from me again, which I hope will be shortly," Nicklis said. "They say we will have a pretty rough time going around Hatteras, but I hope it will not be the case."

FOURTEEN

SELF-EXILE AT FORTY FATHOMS

L ATE IN June 2002, as Broadwater and Johnston are changing shifts at midnight, the two lean on the barge railing. A waxing orange moon illuminates a gently rolling sea. Chris Murray comes down from the sat shack. "All in all, it's been a good day, I'd say," Murray offers. "We're making a lot of progress." "Yes, indeed we are," Broadwater says. "I think this will look even more exciting in the morning."

But morning comes and goes, hours stretch into days, and still the tenacious armor belt hangs on. Maybe, Broadwater speculates, the pine and oak boards, backed by iron armor, have become petrified until they're almost like rocks. The belt resists even the efforts of the cable bandsaw. The crew is beginning to fret over the timetable and the worsening conditions. The seas are giving them trouble too, coming at the barge from the side and causing a roll that makes the stage and diving bell plunge up and down. They decide to reposition the barge to bring it head-on into the seas, adjusting the cables that moor it to the eight sunburst-pattern anchors.

Up in the tower control room, television monitors watch each of the barge's corners. A screen, informed by a Global Positioning System, shows the barge's position relative to the wreck. Deck foreman Greg "Big G" Clavelle, gloves stuffed in his boots, is throwing levers. He's six-three, 270 pounds, the smallest of the boys in his family. A brother played football for the Green Bay Packers, a sister played basketball for Louisiana State University.

"Snug up on number 6, slacken number 8," chief warrant officer Rick Cavey tells him. "All right, I'm moving west a little now." When the levers are thrown there's a *pwish!* as air brakes grab and hold. On screen 2, a giant barracuda hangs like an evil blimp.

Outside, the cables scream as the *Wotan* does its ponderous dance. Now, all night long, the divers saw away at the armor belt with their improvised cable saw, and saturation divers rake it with hydroblasters.

The next morning, Sunday, small gray-and-white birds zip across the water, skimming the surface like touch-and-go planes. At a private gathering on the fantail of the barge, a couple of cooks read aloud from the Bible.

Below, the divers continue to blast and saw at the armor belt until it seems to be hanging by a thread. They pry at it with the help of a seventy-five-ton lift, and finally, on July 5, it gives way with a violent jerk that sends it crashing into the turret. There are gasps in the control shacks, but cameras show no noticeable damage. What was holding everything up, they realize, was one of several steel spikes that John Ericsson used whenever he had wood butted together. The turret, thank goodness, is not as fragile as they feared and might survive other insults.

The belt of iron, oak, and pine, which was supposed to take twenty-four hours to remove, has taken five days. But at least now the target of this massive enterprise is completely exposed. After the sediment settles, the barge crew flies the remotely operated vehicle (ROV) over the site and gets back clear images of what needs to be done. The top of the turret is obscured by iron deck plates, hull framing, and debris. As these are removed, the full extent of the next phase becomes clear.

The *Monitor* carried about eighty tons of anthracite coal in its bunkers, and it's apparent that, either when the vessel's port quarter crashed onto the turret or soon after, when part of the deck gave way, tons of coal were dumped into the turret. The divers also encounter iron concretions, a thick layer of compacted silt, and a species of dead coral with branches that stick together like Legos—and grab diver suits like Velcro. Tons of this material will have to be removed by hand, each handful hoisted to the surface and examined.

By noon on July 9, about half of the coral layer has been removed, but the weather is beginning to worsen, with wind and seas from the southwest growing and building through the night. The next morning brings winds of over thirty knots and swells of five to seven feet, with periodic squalls and thunderstorms. Strong currents force surface-supply diving to be suspended, but saturation diving continues. Now in the turret, these divers are surrounded by a cloud of silty debris that rises around them as they blast through coral and coal with pressure hoses. Through topside video monitors the divers appear to be standing in a tub of dry ice. Lights from their helmets look like car headlights in fog. Next they encounter a layer of soft gray clay, and the work accelerates. They use a powerful hose that sucks the clay out through wire baskets, filtering out anything that might prove valuable.

The archaeologists are getting excited because they know what's coming. First the divers uncover a series of metal plates they know were part of the recoil mechanism for the gun carriages, then the carriages themselves, and finally the muzzle of one of the huge eleven-inch guns. This ends any speculation that the cannons tumbled free when the turret flipped over. Later the second cannon, along with the port stoppers—the four-ton iron pendulums that covered the gun ports—emerges from the sediment, coal, and debris.

At the same time, two-person teams of sprint divers, working around the clock, clear a six-foot-wide swath around the turret so that the Spider—the twenty-five-ton lifting device—can be lowered and secured around it. Around 3:00 A.M., Commander Karen Shake, one of the divers on the night shift, is working to clear a large fragment of deck plate near the turret when she notices shards of glass.

Johnston gets on the headset and watches the images from Shake's helmet camera as she paws through the sediment and uncovers two glass lantern chimneys in remarkably good condition. Into the basket they go, and up to the surface. The site proves to be a treasure trove of artifacts as the next divers find numerous fragments of lantern chimneys and glass bottles. There is more: several broken parts from hydrometers—the instruments that measured salinity—and an intact thermometer.

Johnston's mind is racing. On the television monitor he spots segments of wood that certainly are not deck fragments. It appears they have dug into the remnants of a storage cabinet that was once located at the extreme end of the lower hull aft of the Monitor's engine.

As morning dawns, saturation divers are sent to investigate further, and the artifact beat goes on, yielding several large brass bearings for the main engine, numerous firebricks, more hydrometers, and porcelain cabinet knobs. Cabinet knobs! A void in the coal and debris suggests that the space was once occupied by a storage cabinet that held spare engine room instruments, chimneys for lanterns, and bottles. Amazingly, many of the hydrometer tubes contain paper scales that have weathered the sea for 140 years.

When the *Monitor* went down, Johnston theorizes, "whatever was not secured in the aft area of the ship tumbled into the aftmost sections of the hull. Unfortunately, the falling bearings, firebricks, and chain destroyed this cabinet."

History may seem to have vanished with many lost Civil War wrecks, but not with the *Monitor*. Because the ship went down intact, she took many of her secrets with her, locked in an iron time capsule that would slowly be opened as parts of the ship are brought to the surface. One can tell, for instance, how dark it must have been below—especially in places like the engine room—by the number of lanterns that are being found.

There are dozens, maybe hundreds, of other secrets buried with the ship, and those secrets will be kept a while longer. Future expeditions will concentrate on the living quarters, the mother lode of artifacts. On one of his earlier submersible dives, Johnston noticed an iron box that seemed to have tumbled out of the captain's quarters. Its contents could be highly interesting. The engines and gear that made the turret revolve are also high on the archaeologists' lists. Then there was the galley stove. What stories could be imagined if that were found! And, last but not least, the safe in paymaster Keeler's stateroom. What if fragments of his wife's letters have survived? The turret is undeniably a big deal, but the personal items, some no more than fragments, might have even more stories to tell.

The *Monitor* has much to teach everyone who investigates her, and one of the main lessons seems to be patience.

Engineers who studied the turret came up with the solution for raising it—an eight-legged steel Spider that would clutch the turret like an octopus, each leg locking in place under the cylinder. The device would be lowered from the deck with its legs splayed out. When it reached the turret, divers would activate hydraulic valves to close the legs in a clawlike embrace. The problem is that the excavation around the turret isn't quite ready. The divers were supposed to dig down to the bottom of the turret before the operation started. But the weather has not cooperated, and lift team leaders begin to worry about the schedule. They'll just have to hope for a window of calm conditions and go for it—get that lifting frame down and locked in place. Everyone hopes that the heavy Spider legs will sink into the sand and eliminate the need for more digging.

The Spider was designed by Phoenix International of Landover, Maryland, a company that does a lot of heavy-duty underwater engineering for the Navy. Representatives from the company would see the process through from design to lift. Phoenix orchestrated most of the project, from hiring Manson Gulf and arranging for the barge, the saturation system, and an ROV to handling all the logistics, including food, transportation, and accommodations.

Phoenix received the go-ahead for the project in early February 2002. At the time there was no working concept, yet the barge was set to leave Houma, Louisiana, on May 28. There were still substantial unresolved issues. For starters, how could they safely lift nearly three hundred tons of turret? The crane was rated at five hundred tons, but when it leaned out over the water, that rating dropped to three hundred tons. This meant that, to lighten the load, divers would have to excavate while the turret was still on the bottom. Second, the engineers had to come up with a lifting structure that would safely deposit the turret on deck without losing a single piece of it. There were a few competing designs, but the clawlike Spider, both powerful and simple, won the day.

Everything went well through all the meetings held with NOAA, the Navy, and the Mariners' Museum. Computer trials again and again showed the Spider closing down on the turret, ensnaring it, and lifting it. But the clear need was to support the contents of the turret, a need that hadn't yet been met to everyone's satisfaction.

Broadwater and Johnston had insisted on inserting a steel lifting platform under the roof of the turret. But of course the turret would have to be raised, if only a few feet, before it could be set down on the platform. What if the turret contents at that moment simply explode onto the ocean floor? This is the archaeologists' worst nightmare.

At a "stakeholders" meeting at the Mariners' Museum on March 20, 2002, there was unanimous agreement that they would move the turret over to a lifting platform before the lift. What they didn't agree on at that point was how to connect the turret and the platform. There were other issues, like designing a sprinkler system for keeping the turret and its contents wet on the long ride back to Hampton Roads, but that had been done the year before with the engine, and it shouldn't be a problem. Coupling the Spider with the lifting platform and supporting the roof would be.

When a final meeting was held in May at the Little Creek Naval Amphibious Base in Norfolk, it was clear that there were still problems, and there were only twenty days to go before the barge was to leave for Hatteras.

Jim Kelly, Phoenix's chief engineer for the project, had called for the turret to be quickly set down on the lifting platform and locked in place with "stabbing guides," steel spikes on opposite sides of the platform that would marry with bell-like receptors attached to the Spider's legs. But there was a rift in the company. Senior engineers felt it would be dangerous to set the turret on the platform, especially if it was moving in the water column. Instead, they suggested that while the turret and Spider were suspended over the platform, the platform would be raised from the bottom by hydraulic cylinders. This would be the only safe way to wed turret and platform, they argued.

The problem, Kelly felt, was that the hydraulic system left a four- or five-foot gap between turret and platform that could allow the contents to escape if the roof collapsed. He stubbornly fought for the guides, much to the company's displeasure.

Eric Lindberg, the company's engineering manager, said the idea of stabbing guides was "predicated on an optimum sea state," which was hard to predict and impossible to count on. If it got down to a time crunch at the end, he felt, "you were pretty much in the hands of fate."

At the meeting, which was attended by several divers, including Commander Scholley, all in camouflage fatigues, Kelly demonstrated the lift with a computer graphic presentation, showing not the system he preferred but the one the company had insisted on: hydraulic lifters. He was uncomfortable with the design, but rather than saying so, he passed a note to Johnston: "Ask me how far below the roof the platform is." When Johnston obliged and Kelly answered, Johnston and Broadwater looked at each other in disbelief.

Johnston then said, "When did we get to a point where we decided not to support the roof?" Broadwater said it wouldn't take much of a surge for the contents, including possible human remains, to spill out if the roof collapsed. "The potential for irreplaceable damage is great," he said.

The meeting broke up, but was followed by a hurried "engineering sidebar." When it ended, NOAA and the Navy had sided with Kelly. Phoenix senior engineers continued to think it would be risky, that rough seas could be dangerous not only for the turret but for the divers. The burden would be on Kelly to see that it worked.

It was clear to him at this time, however, that his days with Phoenix were numbered.

AFTER WEEKS of hard work underwater, go-ahead is given to put the Spider down. The order is a huge morale booster. On July 17, shortly after dawn, the big crane swings into action, picking the device up off the deck and lowering it just below the surface. Divers follow to open the Spider's legs to fifteen-degree angles. Surface conditions are rough, with strong currents and wave surges, so as they work they wrap their legs around the Spider's crossbeams to keep from being sucked away.

Later, as the Spider descends, Broadwater watches anxiously. What if its legs sink straight into the seabed and the whole lifting structure crashes down on top of the turret? Instead, something quite unforeseen happens. Some of the legs land where the armor belt now rests, jamming into deck plates. These legs stop, while opposing legs keep going into the sand. The leggy structure slumps over and some of the legs slam into the turret.

Scholley is horrified and feels a knot in her stomach. Oh, my gosh, I just broke the turret, she thinks. But when the ROV goes in for a closer look with its video eye, it appears there's no major damage. A couple of small concretions—merged iron and shell formations that will eventually be removed anyway—were knocked off. But still, it's heart-stopping. "John," she tells Broadwater, who was watching from the saturation van, "I'm so sorry!"

"It's OK, Bobbie, it's OK," he says. "We didn't break anything."

But the hasty mistake costs the mission several days as divers have to go back and redig the footings. Combined with other delays, the Spider glitch helps build the kind of tension that the mission cannot afford to shoulder. It suggests that the mission could fail. The only way to regain the momentum is to do the redigging with surface-supply divers while positioning a saturation diver in the turret to continue excavating. It will have to be a full-court press. Several divers, including Scholley, take turns digging and trying to muscle the legs into place. It's slow going. Way, way too slow.

TOWARD THE end of July, the divers realize that because of all the extra work they are running out of bottom-mix breathing gas, the precise blend of helium and oxygen needed for work in the deep ocean. They'd planned for forty days, and within thirty the mix is nearly used up. The gas expert, Jim Mariano, has had plenty of experience mixing gases, but rarely at sea. Now is the time for him to concoct what he likes to call his "witch's brew."

Mariano knows all the formulas and equations for gas mixes and decides he can make a rack of bottom-mix gas from what is already on board, by delicately mixing straight helium and fifty-fifty helium and oxygen. He has to "sniff" the cylinders with an oxygen analyzer. A mixture that is too "sweet," with too much oxygen, is dangerous for divers. Oxygen toxicity can cause symptoms from mild to severe: a roaring in the ears, blurred vision, vertigo, twitching facial muscles, dizziness, and worst of all, full-blown convulsions.

The first batch is a little sour, too much helium, so he dumps straight oxygen into the mix. Just right.

WHILE TIME and gas and money are beginning to wear thin, another drama is unfolding behind the scenes.

Chris Murray, who was once in command of the *Monitor* expeditions, was promoted to captain in October 2000 and now runs all Navy dive operations from behind a desk at Naval Sea Systems Command in Washington. But he can't stay away from this final chapter. He is on board to make sure things run smoothly, to keep the money pipeline from Washington flowing, and to work with the saturation divers. But he's no longer in charge of day-to-day operations. The problem is that his former subordinates keep going to him for advice and, in effect, going around their new commander, Bobbie Scholley.

Murray met Scholley right after dive school in Newport, Rhode Island. One day they dived together for lobsters, and when they rose to the surface it was evening; fall had arrived, and suddenly there was a three- or four-foot chop. Getting back in was going to be tough, but Scholley was there all the way, "so she had gained my level of confidence as far as a diver goes the first time I met her," Murray tells me.

This is a sticky situation. Scholley is newer at this; Murray outranks her, even though she is due for promotion to captain. She is in tactical command of the barge, responsible for the safety of the crew, responsible for the success of the mission. But he is in charge of Navy divers, every one of them; he has the longest history with the project; this is one of the highlights of his career; people are looking to him for leadership. And he wants badly to be here at the grand finale.

Murray thinks it over. He and Scholley have a long history of command together, and they look up to and respect each other. Even if there is a delicate dance as they try to avoid stepping on each other's toes, each finds it reassuring to have the other to rely on.

A man of few words, Murray doesn't waste any. He'll take himself out of the equation. He decides to go where he can be most useful and where no one can reach him. He'll go into saturation.

Scholley needs to be able to walk through this alone, Murray decides. Rather than standing in the shadows, he wants it known that she's in charge. He has full confidence in her and knows this will show everyone that he does. And she deserves to have her due.

"Hey, I'm going down," he tells Scholley. "You've got it up here. I can probably do better down there."

It's simple, but maybe too simple. Murray is about to experience days of galling frustration as delays continue to push the recovery back. He's sentenced himself to working long shifts on the bottom, unable to participate in critical decisions that will need to be made.

But for all of that, there are moments of serenity. On one of several dives that begin at midnight and last until the sun comes up, Murray is so totally focused on the work that he doesn't notice the hours fleeting by. The soft glow from the windows of the diving bell, suspended just above him, is a comforting presence. And then there's the sunrise. One morning, with visibility at least a hundred feet, little fish begin coming out of the wreck, swirling around him, and the sun streams down through the water column. Above, a crisis may be building, but for the moment at least, down at the bottom of the ocean, he feels invigorated and flooded with peace.

FIFTEEN

COLD GREY MANTLE

Finally, on December 29, 1862, the weather cleared. A light breeze over Hampton Roads barely rippled the water. It was time to go. Commander Bankhead ordered the crew to prepare the *Monitor* for sea. According to standard navy practice, that meant sealing everything, including the turret. The weight of the 120-ton turret, riding on top of a brass deck ring, was supposed to provide all the seal the ship needed, but the *Monitor*'s commanders, not trusting the turret to seal itself, decided to raise it and stuff the opening with oakum, just as they had done before shipping out of New York. But this time, as fireman George Geer later told his brother, they didn't bother treating the oakum with tar. Perhaps no one remembered that terrifying night in March when the *Monitor* almost didn't make it to Hampton Roads; when the waves battered the turret, opened gaping holes in this very same packing material, and allowed water to enter in torrents that, together with other leaks, reached the fires in the boilers and created deadly fumes, just about doing in the engine room crew.

The other sealing they did that December day was vital. The iron port stoppers meant to close the gun ports were dogged down with wooden bucklers bolted to the outside and caulked tight. The two big guns were slid back on their carriages amidships and secured. A temporary helm was installed on top of the turret so the ship could be steered from there rather than from the more vulnerable pilothouse. Geer related that he "secured the hatches with red lead putty and for the port holes I made rubber gaskets, one inch thick and in fact, had everything about the ship in the way of an opening water tight."

There were sixty-three men on board, eleven of them officers.

At 10:00 A.M. the *Montauk* arrived, in company with the tow ship USS *Connecticut* as well as the ironclad *Passaic*. But the *Montauk*, with John Worden now in command, experienced engineering problems and had to put in for repairs. She would not be able to make the trip.

As final preparations were being made, the *Rhode Island*, a powerful side-wheel steamer that had once been a merchant ship, held gun exercises out on the Roads and then pulled alongside the *Monitor*. After two stout hawsers were secured to the ironclad's forward bollard, a sailor sewed sailcloth chafing gear around them at the point where they passed through the forward chocks. Even though the *Monitor* had been provided with new davits, it was decided that her lifeboats might not survive on the deck in rough seas. They were placed aboard the *Rhode Island.*

At 2:30 P.M., the *Rhode Island*'s paddle wheels began to roil the placid waters of Hampton Roads. The towlines pulled taut, and the *Monitor* was finally underway, riding comfortably on the smooth wake of the side-wheeler. Though under tow, the ironclad also ran under its own power to help with stability, air circulation, and the operation of its pumps. As the pair passed Willoughby Bay opposite Fort Monroe, they were joined by the ironclad *Passaic* and her tow ship, the *State of Georgia.* The procession moved slowly out through the lower Chesapeake Bay, toward the venerable Cape Henry Light and the waiting waters of the Atlantic.

At 5:40 P.M., Ensign Albert Taylor, standing watch on the *Rhode Island*, noted that Cape Henry "bore west distance 4 miles." Now only a brief ocean passage stood between the crew and their next adventure.

Commander Bankhead reported that the weather was "clear and pleasant, and every prospect of its continuation." As they crossed from bay to sea at about 6:00 P.M., the watch on the *Rhode Island* logged the winds at one to three knots out of the southwest, with barely a ripple on the water. It was warm for December, a balmy fifty-eight degrees. Several sailors ventured out on deck to breathe the fresh air, a rare event aboard a ship so low in the water that the only safe place to ride above deck was the top of the turret.

"General joy was expressed at this relief from long inaction," remembered Grenville Weeks, the young surgeon. "The sick came upon deck, and in the clear sky, fresh air, and sense of motion, seemed to gain a new life."

The engine ran with a reassuring thump, slow as a resting athlete's heart. The barometer held steady.

"At sundown," the log on the *Passaic* noted, "U.S. Steamer *Rhode Island*, with Iron Clad Steamer *Monitor* in tow, in sight four miles astern." On the *Monitor*, Weeks took note of "glorious clouds of purple and crimson" as the sun dipped below the horizon. It was "a suitable farewell to the Virginia Capes."

It is not clear whether Commander Bankhead was relying on anything except the ship's barometer and the appearance of the westerly sky when he declared that there was "every prospect" that fair weather would continue. Other than the barometer, the wind, and a few weather proverbs, there were almost no tools then for forecasting weather. Captains kept a keen eye on the horizon for signs of change; they knew that any sudden drop in barometric readings meant trouble and that abrupt wind shifts could signal approaching weather, and they certainly knew what storm clouds looked like. And whenever they met another ship, especially one coming from the direction they were heading, they would "speak" the ship—pull within shouting distance and exchange information about conditions they might have experienced.

But Bankhead and his officers did not seem to have the slightest notion of what was coming their way. Nor did Keeler. "Everything passed quietly and pleasantly that afternoon and evening; a smooth sea and clear skies seemed to promise a successful termination of our trip and an opportunity of once more trying our metal [*sic*] against rebel works. . . . " Who could blame a ship's crew, lionized after their first outing and then cooped up below decks for the better part of nine months, for itching to get back into action?

The little squadron found plenty of company off the Virginia and Carolina coast. A matter-of-fact entry in the *Rhode Island*'s log read: "At

9:30 sighted 2 sail, one standing to the Northward and Eastward, the other standing to the Westward. At 10 sounded in 12 fathoms water . . . sighted sail standing to the Northward and Eastward. At 12 sounded in 13 fathoms water."

They had chosen a route that would save time by skirting the North Carolina coastline and, once they reached Cape Hatteras, take them inside the Gulf Stream. This powerful "river in the ocean," as it had recently been called, moves north at two to four nautical miles an hour. The stream is part of a huge wheel of current that picks up the sun-warmed waters of the western Caribbean, flows north through the Gulf of Mexico, bends around Florida, and then bowls northward until it encounters the abruptly shallow shelf at Cape Hatteras known as Diamond Shoals and veers off into the North Atlantic, ultimately warming the European subcontinent. Off the North Carolina coast, especially in winter, it creates a steam bath of warm, moist air.

Sailing south against the Gulf Stream can be risky, especially in winter, since the prevailing northerly winds meet the stream head-on, turning it into a nasty washing machine. In southerly winds the stream is less boisterous, but it is still a powerful force, making passages south slow and uncomfortable. Dodging the stream—running close to the shoreline and, ultimately, close to the shoals—can also be risky.

There were no lighthouses between Cape Henry and Cape Hatteras, so a night passage along the coast meant holding a relentlessly steady course. Stephen D. Trenchard, captain of the *Rhode Island*, instructed the officer of the deck to keep "a very bright lookout" and take frequent soundings to check for depth. This meant dropping overboard a weighted line marked in increments of six feet, or fathoms. The sounding shortly after midnight of the first night off Currituck Beach, North Carolina, was thirteen and one-half fathoms: eighty-one feet. That would have put them about ten miles offshore. From later soundings, it seems they were able to hold a remarkably steady course, running due south or south-by-east through the night.

During that long first night the weather held, the little ship towing easily at five to six knots. The only problem was air. With more than sixty people sleeping below, by dawn the quarters on the berth deck were more than a little close. Several of the sailors ventured on deck the next morning, filling their lungs with fresh air and lingering even as ocean spray dashed over them.

Already, though, there was a force at work that only the most seasoned salts among them might have recognized.

At 5:00 A.M., two hours before sunrise, Bankhead reported, "we began to experience a swell from the southward with a slight increase of the wind from the S.W., the sea breaking over the pilot house and striking the base of the tower, but not with sufficient force to break over it." The sister ship *Passaic* also observed a "light swell from the Southward." Bankhead didn't seem to notice, but Keeler saw something else.

"Tuesday morning," he wrote, "cloud banks were seen rising in the South & West & they gradually increased till the sun was obscured by their cold grey mantle."

Keeler was occasionally guilty of flowery prose, but this in fact was a very specific observation. What he saw was a reaction between cold, dry air that was being pulled from over land around the bottom of a low-pressure system and warm, moist air hovering over the Gulf Stream. When a cold front plows into this giant hothouse, it produces squalls and strong winds that kick up the water and eventually, as the low sweeps by, clock around to the northwest. The low-pressure systems that move up from the south are often called Cape Hatteras lows, a name strikingly appropriate in this context. It appears that just such a low, caused by warm air rising, probably as far south as the Gulf of Mexico, was marching up the Atlantic seaboard. Imagine a spinning air mass, hundreds of miles across, turning counterclockwise as it moves north. On a ship off North Carolina you would begin to experience winds out of the south as they wheel around the bottom of the circle. As the counterclockwise vortex spins around the center of low pressure, it drags dry, cold air down from the west and north, likely the Great Lakes region. This chilly, dense air, whipsawing around the low, ducks under the warm, moist air over the Gulf Stream like a wedge and generates a bank of clouds and a band of rain. All along the interface between cold and warm air, this "cold grey mantle," which could be several thousand feet high, presides.

The approaching weather might not have been a major problem

for most ships at sea, but for a small ironclad that surely had one of the lowest profiles of any ship in the world, it was going to make things more than a little interesting.

At 6:40 A.M. the convoy paused. The watch on the *Monitor* had discovered that the constant working of the towlines in the chocks was wearing through the chafing gear and threatening to sever the lines. With the procession stopped, some of the men went forward with great caution, watching out for the seas that occasionally washed over the deck, and added more protection to the stout lines.

By 8:00 A.M. there were broken clouds ahead, but nothing to suggest that a storm was approaching. The weather was still balmy for winter on the Atlantic: sixty-four degrees by 9:00 A.M., according to the log on the *Rhode Island,* and getting even warmer as the day wore on. The low had not yet arrived. In fact, they were still basking in a high-pressure zone of warm air, a Bermuda high, but the early morning swells, driven by the southerly winds, were enough to cause seas to break over the pilothouse and strike the base of the turret. Bankhead observed that the oakum under the turret was already beginning to loosen as the tower "worked" from the slight pitching and rolling the *Monitor* experienced. But the engineer reported that the bilge pumps kept things nice and dry. There was nothing to worry about, they all thought. "Felt no apprehension at the time," Bankhead reported.

By mid-afternoon the wind was blowing Force 2, a mere four to six knots. Even though seas occasionally rolled over the *Monitor*'s deck, conditions were still calm enough for a little sightseeing.

"We amused ourselves for an hour or more," Keeler related, "by watching two or three large sharks who glided quietly along by our sides observing us apparently with a curious eye as if in anticipation of a feast." If they had been on the deck, with sharks rising on passing waves, the men and sharks might have seen eye to eye. Keeler added this observation: "We made no water of consequence; a little trickled down about the pilot house and some began to find its way under the turret."

But the log on the *Rhode Island* shows a subtle change. The barometer was starting, ever so slightly, to drop as the low approached. It was certainly not a "bomb," as seafarers call sudden plunges in pressure, but a change it was.

AT 1:00 P.M. on December 30, the quartermaster on board the *Passaic* noted in the ship's log: "Saw U.S. Steamer *Rhode Island* with Ironclad Gunboat *Monitor* in tow, bearing 4 miles W.S.W., steering S.W. by W."

The *Passaic,* herself under tow by the *State of Georgia,* was the first of a ten-ship class of 1,335-ton ironclad "Monitors," the much-heralded new breed of warships inspired by their celebrated 987-ton namesake. In all, thirty-five of these formidable new vessels would be built during the Civil War.

"She [the *Passaic*] is truly a fine vessel, a great improvement on the *Monitor,*" wrote Isaac Newton, the former engineer for the *Monitor* who became superintendent of ironclad construction. But this "great improvement" was itself already in trouble. The *Passaic*'s log entry, in a firm, practiced hand, finds the "latter part of the ship making a quantity of water. One watch constantly bailing water from under turret."

At the time the convoy was making only three knots, apparently because the *Passaic* and her consort were now in the north-rolling Gulf Stream, bucking winds of up to sixteen knots and slamming into water that measured seventy degrees. Unlike the *Monitor* and *Rhode Island,* the *Passaic* and the *State of Georgia* had accepted the discomfort of the Gulf Stream for the relative safety of deeper water. The *State of Georgia*'s log also mentions sighting the other ships and then records, matter-of-factly, that all hands were assembled on deck to commit to the sea the body of landsman William H. Kearney of New York, who had died that morning of acute laryngitis. The burial took place in rough seas under cloudy skies.

The *Rhode Island*'s log entry for 4:00 P.M., December 30, reads: "Wind, S. W. by W. Force 2. Weather, b.c. [broken clouds]. Air temperature, 68, water 69. Barometer, 30.12." By 8:00 P.M. the water temperature would rise to seventy degrees and the air to seventy-four.

From these increases, it is clear that the *Monitor* and *Rhode Island* had entered the warm waters associated with the Gulf Stream—perhaps not the fast-flowing stream itself, but close enough to feel its effects. For a brief period, conditions seemed to hold. But then the wind began to build, until by late afternoon it was blowing from the southwest at about sixteen knots. According to Keeler, the sea was "rolling with violence across our deck, rendering it impossible to remain on it without danger of being swept off."

Surgeon Weeks had another observation. "As the afternoon advanced, the freshening wind, the thickening clouds, and the increasing roll of the sea gave those accustomed to ordinary ship-life some new experiences. The little vessel plunged through the rising waves instead of riding on them as they increased in violence . . . so that, even when we considered ourselves safe, the appearance was of a vessel sinking."

Life below was again becoming uncomfortable. Off-duty sailors, unable to sleep and feeling the effects of the rolling seas, clustered on the turret and watched waves dash over the pilothouse. "I'd rather go to sea in a diving bell!" one of them declared.

"Give me an oyster scow!" another lamented, "—anything!—only let it be wood, and something that will float over, instead of under the water."

Some of the junior officers, who as yet had little respect for what the sea could do, hurrahed when the big waves reared up and engulfed the little vessel, but it is not hard to imagine what it was like for the majority of the sailors who were confined below decks as the ship pitched and rolled. Water finding its way under the turret made things "wet and cheerless below," Keeler reported. Seasickness and that old *Monitor* scourge, poor ventilation, must have begun to take their toll in misery. Some of the sailors may have fortified themselves with a little something extra. The navy had banned drinking on board, but had never ensured that existing stores were removed. Keeler, a teetotaler and a stickler for details, noticed something odd about the door to his storeroom off the berth deck, where two barrels of whiskey were kept. But this wasn't the time to investigate, not with sixteen knots of wind pushing seas over the deck.

The average mature wave height for sixteen knots of wind is about six feet. That's fine for most boats, but not for one whose deck was not much more than a foot above the water.

Sixteen knots is considered a moderate breeze on a scale that was developed by a onetime commander of a forty-four-gun British man-of-war. Sir Francis Beaufort, born in Ireland in 1774, had an illustrious career with the Royal Navy and, after years of observation, hit upon the idea that levels of wind behavior could be identified on a scale that warship captains would recognize. His scale ranged from virtually no wind at all, Force 0, to a hurricane, Force 12. The Beaufort scale became mandatory for log entries on all Royal Navy ships in 1838 and carried over to American sailing vessels. Although Beaufort did not then assign specific wind speeds to each force, other than "light," "gentle," "moderate," "fresh," and so forth, the designations had clear implications for the amount of canvas that could be flown. A Force 7 moderate gale, for instance, meant double-reefed topsails. A Force 12 hurricane was one "which no canvas could withstand."

Forces 0 through Force 4 were described in part by the speed at which a "well-conditioned man-of-war" might travel, according to Beaufort's scheme. Forces 5 through 9 were related to the missions that could be carried out, such as being "in chase, full and by," as well as sail-carrying ability. In Forces 10 and higher, however, missions were to be abandoned and efforts turned instead to surviving to fight another day.

Later mariners, eager for wind speed numbers, filled them in. Thus Force 4, a "moderate breeze," was said to range from of eleven to sixteen knots, while a "fresh breeze" was considered to be seventeen to twenty-one knots. When sailors spoke of the wind "freshening," that carried a specific meaning.

THE *MONITOR* and *Rhode Island* were now in sight of Cape Hatteras Light, sixteen miles off their starboard quarter. The lighthouse had been built in 1802. In 1852 it was raised to a height of 150 feet and fitted with a "first-order," or largest, Fresnel lens, which could be seen twenty miles out to sea. These lenses, invented in 1822 by French physicist Augustin Fresnel, have intricate honeycombs of glass prisms that bend light and concentrate it into a powerful beam. At the onset of the war, the light was disabled by Confederate troops, but by June 1862 Union forces had put it back in service. The rebels had made off with the first-order lens, but the slightly smaller second-order lens that replaced it produced a light that could easily be seen.

Just before dark—sunset that day was at 4:58 P.M.—Bankhead had the *Monitor* pull alongside the *Rhode Island*. Because the *Monitor* had no mast from which to suspend signal lanterns, the only way to communicate was by scribbling messages on a chalkboard and holding it up for the other ship's crew to read. The commander was not overly concerned, but to be on the safe side he advised Captain Trenchard that if they got in trouble during the night, they'd display a red lantern from the turret.

When the officers sat down for dinner at 5:00 P.M. they were "cheerful and happy," Keeler noted, even though the sea was rolling and foaming over their heads. The sun had just set and darkness was coming on fast. Nevertheless, all were laughing and "rejoicing that at last our monotonous, inactive life had ended." But after dinner, while the stewards were clearing the table, some of the officers ascended to the top of the turret, and what they saw might have made them wish for monotony. "The wind was blowing violently; the heavy seas rolled over our bows dashing against the pilot house & surging aft would strike the solid turret with a force to make it tremble, sending off on either side a boiling, foaming torrent of water."

They could still see their ironclad companion. Shortly after 6:00 P.M., the watch on the *Rhode Island* reported sighting the *State of Georgia* with the ironclad *Passaic* in tow.

And then apparently a squall arrived. From 6:00 to 8:00 P.M., the *Passaic* began laboring in a head sea. "Leaking badly forward in anchor well," the log reported. "Hands bailing water from under berth deck and passing it into fire room, and from there pumped out." The big steam pumps on board the *Passaic* weren't working, so the crew had to resort to a small hand pump and buckets. It was a slow, tedious, backbreaking job.

The freshening breeze blew as strong as twenty-seven knots, according to *Passaic* logs, building powerful waves, ten feet high or more. Captain Percival Drayton, in his report to Rear Admiral Samuel P. Lee, said he began to notice that the ironclad's "forward iron projection thumping into the sea was gradually making a large opening there, through which the water poured in a large stream, and I am seriously of the opinion that a few hours of a very heavy sea, end on, would go far to rip the whole thing entirely off of the main body." Had the top and bottom halves of the ship separated, she would have sunk immediately.

On the *Monitor* at about 7:00 P.M., there was a moment's hesitation. The ships were now south of Cape Hatteras, and the plan was, if the weather turned foul, to duck into the safe haven of Hatteras Inlet, just south of the cape. A report in the *New York Herald*, based on later interviews, indicates that Bankhead considered heading for safety but believed that the weather was clearing—the moon at that moment shone bright in a cloudless sky—and elected to plunge ahead.

No sooner had he made that decision than the wind picked up and the waves began to break. That ended any chance of running for cover, because southerly winds would have kicked up breaking seas in the south-facing inlet, making it impassable.

Then one of the towlines connecting the two vessels parted, worn through by prolonged chafing, and the *Monitor* began to yaw and roll severely. Even larger gaps between the turret and deck appeared, and the water level in the bilge began to rise.

By 7:30 P.M., about fifteen miles south of Cape Hatteras shoals, Bankhead noticed that the wind had hauled more to the south, building in strength and causing the seas to rise. The *Monitor* yawed even more, swinging back and forth across its course.

Surgeon Weeks, who was standing on the turret, noted: "At this time the gale increased; black heavy clouds covered the sky, through which the moon glimmered fitfully, allowing us to see in the distance a long line of white, plunging foam, rushing toward us. . . . A gloom hung over everything: the banks of cloud seemed to settle around us; the moan of the ocean grew louder and more fearful."

SIXTEEN

MICHELANGELOS OF THE DEEP

O N JULY 26, 2002, at about 9:00 A.M., a morning when light seems to pour down from the surface, senior chief Wade Bingham is excavating in the turret near one of the guns when he discovers something that looks and feels like a collarbone. He gives it a slight tug and finds that it won't budge. It must be attached to something. With an edge in his normally matter-of-fact voice, he tells topside that he is touching something that appears to be a bone.

Bingham is at the end of an extraordinary fifteen-day shift in saturation. Another diver fell sick, and he is glad to be able to extend his shift five days. To some that might seem a punishing ordeal, but not to Bingham. "There's nothing better than walking on the bottom of the ocean," he says, "and the advantage of being a sat diver is that we can do it all day long if we want to." Even so, this could be numbingly boring work, identifying each handful of coal or silt before introducing it to the nozzle of the suction hose. Each piece will end up in a basket, to be lifted to the barge and pawed through again, so it's tempting to cut a corner or two at this stage to speed things up a little. But Bingham, forty-two years old, is a methodical worker who is going by the book.

His announcement of finding a possible bone sets off archaeological alarm bells throughout the barge. Night owl Jeff Johnston had just been watching the divers from the sat shack, kidding with the master divers about what they'd do if they found a "dead Yankee." "Nothing," he'd joked in his best Tidewater accent.

He's gone down one set of stairs from the shack and up another to the galley for coffee. Now he hears his name called over the intercom and rushes back. "We've found a dead Yankee," they tell him.

Eric Emery, a forensic archaeologist from the Army's Central Identification Laboratory in Hawaii (CILHI), is on board for just this possibility. The laboratory, now called Joint POW/MIA Accounting Command—representing all branches of the military—has the responsibility of bringing home and identifying the remains of lost service members. Emery designed the protocol to be followed if remains were found and has closely watched the excavation of the turret, but the divers were getting down toward the roof and nothing had been found. His schedule calls for him to head back to Honolulu the next day, leaving careful instructions about what to do in the unlikely event that human remains are discovered. Emery has just come off the night shift but rushes to the sat shack. "You better look at this," Johnston tells him.

The picture is murky at first, a lot of silt from the excavation obscuring the view. Emery asks Bingham to dig around the bone so they can see it better on the topside monitors. Rick Cavey happens to be down on a surface-supply dive—part of his job that morning is to conduct a re-enlistment ceremony for one of the other divers on the bottom, a common event in this community—and the dive officer asks him to climb into the turret and train his camera where Bingham is pointing. As the sediment cloud settles again, the divers below and archaeologists above realize that these are indeed human bones.

Last year a false alert was sounded when a bone found in the vicinity of the engine turned out to be from an animal, most likely from the cook's dinner preparations. But this is quite another matter.

Finding human remains is what the archaeologists and divers have hoped for and dreaded. It might add a personal dimension to the expedition, but at the same time it could seriously delay the lift. On his way back to the surface, Cavey realizes that the schedule for raising the turret is now in jeopardy, and his original hunch that this was a two-year project is being borne out. "If we've found bodies, there's just no way we're going to be able to move fast enough, honorably and fast enough, to get the job done," Cavey concludes.

Emery puts on a headset and talks Bingham—and the divers who follow—through a series of procedures, much as a crime scene investigator would do. They bring the ROV into the turret so the video images will be sharp. They take measurements to pinpoint the location and to photograph and videotape the bones. The location will be part of an assessment of what happened when the sailor drowned. All heavy excavation work stops, and the job turns to a gentle process of exposing the bones by painstakingly clearing away the hard, coal-infused sludge around them.

On missions, Emery characteristically wears a tiny silver and gold crucifix on a chain around his neck. He has never been a strongly religious person, but it helps him to remember why he got into a profession that involves finding and identifying human remains, often in dangerous conditions where it seems only a miracle keeps him safe.

In May of 1999, while he was a graduate student in Texas A&M University's underwater archaeology program, Emery was at Lake Allyon, high in the Andes Mountains of Ecuador. He and the other students dived in the ice-encrusted lake in search of evidence of a pre-Inca civilization that flourished throughout the Andes. Unfortunately, local miners were led to believe that the archaeologists were diving not for artifacts but for veins of precious metal in the lake. The miners, the researchers believed, were bent on doing them harm. There were six members of the team, and a helicopter was sent to evacuate them, three at a time. It was the first time Emery had ever ridden in a chopper.

Shortly after takeoff, as they were gaining altitude, there was a metallic sound, and the helicopter began to spin out of control. Somehow the tail rotor had become separated or disabled. They were going down. In the midst of their wild, spiraling plunge, the pilot had the presence of mind to crash into a mountaintop lake rather than the side of one of the ragged mountains or a precipice dropping off into an intermountain chasm.

Some of his memories are clouded because of long periods of unconsciousness, but Emery remembers coming to amid a snarl of twisted metal and wires, with freezing water gushing into the cabin. The water was cold enough to take his breath away and to remind him he wasn't dead yet. He couldn't talk or yell because the cold water seemed to squeeze the breath out of his chest. The helicopter had begun to turn over as the cabin filled with water, and Jon Faucher, Emery's tent mate and a fellow Texas A&M student, was already underwater. Faucher was able to surface and wriggle out through an opening in the cabin, but when Emery tried to follow he couldn't move. His seatbelt was jammed from the impact, and he was trapped.

Things were happening fast. Emery yelled to his friend that his belt was jammed. Then the top-heavy helicopter flipped upside down. Frantically, Emery fought to keep his mouth above the surface. He slammed his fists, feet, and even his head against anything that seemed to show light, but the belt held him in his seat. Water flooded the cabin and soon his lungs, and he blacked out.

Somehow Faucher, who had broken his back in the fall, was able to get hold of a small knife and, in blinding pain, dive down to the wreckage. He cut through Emery's seat belt, but the shoulder belt still held. He had to return to the surface for air, then dive again to sever the other belt and pull his friend to the surface. Emery had been submerged for at least five minutes and possibly as long as twenty, long enough in either case to have died, but Faucher got him to shore and immediately began to resuscitate him. Emery was brought back from the dead. Perhaps it was the water temperature that saved him, but it was also the courage and determination of his friend. And the villagers, the very ones they had suspected of wanting to harm them, wrapped the men—Emery, Faucher, the pilot, and a third passenger—in plastic tarps and fed and tended them until another helicopter could break through a thick cloud cover and lift them out.

Emery's second helicopter ride went better.

Weeks later, after being released from a hospital in Quito, Emery was recuperating at a small hotel in the city when a woman at the front desk who had prayed for his recovery gave him the crucifix.

Soon after, Emery went looking for what he calls "archaeology with a purpose" and landed a job with CILHI. "I wanted to be able to apply my skills to something that would make a contribution to other people's lives," Emery says later in an e-mail from Iraq, where he was serving the needs of soldiers there during the war. "I can never repay Jon Faucher for what he did that day, but I can devote my skills to something I now believe in dearly . . . that you should never leave anyone behind."

EMERY DOES not care to reflect on how his experience helped him understand what the *Monitor* sailors went through in their last moments, but it certainly helped ignite a passion for doing his job, and doing it right. "It is vitally important," he says, "that you capture how the remains appear, how they are positioned, where they are located, because that is what essentially allows you to reconstruct and develop hypotheses about what happened, how they came to rest there, what was going on inside the turret—all that rests on the ability to document properly before anything is moved." Down on the bottom off Cape Hatteras, each new bone is photographed and mapped in place with the help of a grid of PVC pipe and nylon string. Like a clock face, the turret is divided into twelve segments, each one a bone zone.

The long-lost sailor appears to be lying with one arm and his head over the hatch that once opened to the top of the turret, almost as if he had been trying to climb out when the ship flipped over and went down. His skull and part of his neck bones are white, while the rest of the skeleton, in contact with iron, is stained burgundy. Part of his body is wedged under the breech of one of the cannons. The gun does not appear to have struck him, they later realize, because there is no evidence of blunt trauma.

Field notes made by Wayne Lusardi, archaeological conservator for the Mariners' Museum, show the position of the skeleton "on the starboard side of the turret between gun and turret wall. The skeleton lies parallel to the gun, head toward the muzzle, face down."

The bones had been entombed in cold, silty clay and sealed off from the corrosive sea by layers of coal and coral—apparently effective preservatives, because the condition of the skeleton is remarkable. Emery, a diver who specializes in underwater recoveries, believes the victim must have been covered with coal and silt soon after the ship sank because of the "articulation" of the bones. They are connected just as they would be if covered with soft tissue. Normally the action of current and scavenging by sea creatures would have destroyed or scattered many of them.

Emery is amazed at the condition of the bones. "If they weren't pinned in the event itself, they would have had to come to rest in a suspended state and somehow biodegraded without a single bone being moved out of the way by waves or current or just the suspension of the water."

There are more than two hundred bones in the human body, and every one of them seems to be there. After measurements are taken, they will be brought up on deck and transported to Hawaii. In due course, using all the forensic tools available, the victim might be identified.

The discovery changes everything, Jeff Johnston feels, because now it is doubly clear that the contents of the turret are as important as the turret itself. The *Monitor* is no longer just a historic wreck but the resting place—now no longer final—of a person who had lost humankind's age-old battle with the sea. Everyone on the project can relate to that. After Johnston posts a list of the sailors who died, the salvage team begins calling the remains "Bob," for Robert Williams, a Welshman who went down with the ship. The skeleton is large, they realize, and a photograph of the crew taken in the summer of 1862 shows him towering over most of the others. But there were others of his stature, so this is no more than a hunch.

From the outset, NOAA and the Navy agreed that they would follow the full military protocol for human remains, treating the bones with dignity and honor. They would be transported under lock and key to CILHI where forensic scientists might eventually identify them. And someday, if relatives could be located, the lost sailors would be returned to their hometowns or buried at a national cemetery—and not as unknowns. "They're still due the honor and respect of a full military burial," Emery says.

The divers, who well know what it is like to recover human remains from the ocean, agree. "I'm a sailor, and that's the Navy down there," says Bobbie Scholley. "Even if it does hold us up," Jim Mariano adds, "that sailor needs to come home. World War II, that's something special. But the Civil War? Off the *Monitor*? Somewhere in the United States, somebody will get a really cool letter."

Over several days, through work that is as intricate as surgery, as

Monitor crew, July 9, 1862. At right, standing with arms crossed is fireman Robert Williams from Wales. (Photo by James F. Gibson, Mariners' Museum)

painstaking as sculpture, the divers reveal almost the entire skeleton. Emery can't get over how well it's working. Parts of the skeleton are encased in a solid concrete of silt and coal, so the excavation has to be done with a hammer and fine chisel, with Emery asking the divers to train their cameras on a portion of the skeleton, a little to the left, a little to the right, gently tapping around the bones. The divers have not had previous experience or training at this delicate art, and to be able to do what they're doing by following his suggestions over the comms is remarkable. They are Michelangelos, Emery concludes, down there with a chisel, revealing the figure within the stone.

Chris Murray spends a memorable night with Bob. It is one of his loneliest dives. The victim is still concreted to the top of the turret, and Murray has to tunnel under him. Then Murray finds himself face to face with the skeleton, or face to rib cage. He can't help being a little unsettled, what with topside getting on his nerves, making jokes and eerie sounds, trying to spook him.

One by one Murray frees the bones, places them in plastic bags and then Tupperware-type containers, and locks them in a small cage to make sure they are going to the surface. "When you're down there working late at night with one of the victims you start thinking: how did he get in that position? You're just holding this nozzle, working it around, and you have a lot of time for your mind to wander and think about things. You think about the sailor there and what happened and what that night must have been like."

The turret is no longer just an important Civil War artifact, but a burial place. Even before the discovery of remains, the divers had the feeling that they were working inside a crypt, that they were there with company. Now they know.

Scholley declines the opportunity to go into the turret while the remains are being worked on. The experience of removing bodies from the USS *Cole* is still fresh in her mind. Those sailors had been dead only a few days, and it was a disturbing experience. Even though it was part of her job and she didn't think much about it at the time, those images still haunt her. They come flooding back while she's sitting next to Broadwater, watching Chuck Young excavate around the remains. There's no need for her to go into the turret, she decides. She makes her last dive on the *Monitor* on July 31, helping to place some of the legs of the Spider under the turret.

To other divers, working with the bones is less bothersome than freeing a recently drowned pilot or civilian. These "body jobs," as they refer to them, are a necessary part of their work, and bringing victims back for burial is a necessary and honorable act, but that never makes it easy.

Some of the most accomplished divers are chosen to help free the remains. One of them, master diver Young, has an experience he wishes he could forget. He is given the task of collecting more than twenty separate bones of one of the hands, putting them in a Zip-Loc bag, and placing them in the topside-bound basket. But on the way out of the turret the bag apparently snags on something, and when he reaches the basket most of the bones are gone.

Emery swallows hard and instructs Young to retrace his steps; he does, picking up the bones as he goes. But then, after he reaches the turret, the bones are somehow sucked up by the vacuum device. When he gets to the basket again, most of the bones are gone. Again, he has to report the situation to the dive leaders and archaeologists above. There is a long pause before anyone speaks.

Emery knows the first thing likely to come out of his mouth is not going to be very helpful. He steps out of the shack and takes a couple of deep breaths, then goes back in and puts the headset on again. Fortunately, the bones that were vacuumed up fell into a collection basket, and all but one are recovered.

Colleagues watching Young's encounter with the remains are stunned. "You would never in your wildest dreams think of that happening to someone as meticulous and precise as he is," says Bobbie Scholley. "Not Chuck! That could never happen to him!"

It takes a week to clear the exposed parts of the remains, from the skull down to the pelvis. The leg bones are still wedged under one of the big guns and must wait for later. Divers and archaeologists agree that the remaining bones are protected well enough for their work on the turret to resume, but time is now critical. Scholley's journal entry for July 23 reads: "Continued jetting in Spider legs. Slow progress. CWOs and MDVs [chief warrant officers and master divers] getting restless."

It's looking more and more like a two-year project—with only a year's funding. But Navy divers, it seems clear, don't like to quit. Vern Geyman, an engineer senior chief from the Navy Experimental Dive Unit in Panama City, has a special reason. He has spent hour after hour, saturated with helium, painstakingly removing sediment from around the bones in the turret. As far as he's concerned, there's no way that he and the other divers will fail to bring up this sailor's resting place. If only for themselves, he decides, after finding their fallen compatriot, they're going to get this done. Anything less is out of the question.

Geyman, 40, is known as a worker bee, capable of toiling hour after hour in the deep ocean. Now is his chance to see what he can do with the Spider's stuck legs. It's daunting at first. There are eight legs on the device that are supposed to grip the turret for the lift to the barge. The legs have been prevented from doing so because sea conditions dictated that the Spider be lowered before the excavation around the turret was complete.

Now the legs have to be gradually lowered one at a time. Using high-powered suction tools, Geyman hollows out the area under one leg, then scrambles around to another, then another and another, and the twenty-ton lifter slowly settles. Three legs are especially difficult, and he has to use the hydroblaster to break up concreted debris that is in the way. He decides to try air-lift devices, pumplike tools that blast air out of one end while creating suction at the other. He places them under two of the legs, with a suction hose under the third, then operates all three legs at once. Slowly the steel legs inch down, and Geyman scrambles to the top of the Spider and activates the hydraulic jacks that shove the legs against the remaining sand and sediment until they slide under the turret.

His shift goes on and on and on. The Navy tries to limit saturation shifts to four hours, knowing that divers become fatigued if they work longer. Geyman is pushing six hours, but the dive officers realize that, as usual, he isn't slowing down. His reason is simple: "When you're doing something you love, you don't get tired."

When the Spider is down and locked, elation settles over the barge. Until this breakthrough, not even the optimistic Cavey has thought the lift would be possible. But settling for delay is not acceptable to Geyman and the other divers. The long-dead sailor has spurred them on. Now that Geyman has gotten the job done, Cavey allows himself to think, "This thing's coming up; it's in the bag."

Scholley is elated and allows a hint of optimism to creep into her journal: "Finished jetting in all 8 legs of Spider. GREAT PROGRESS."

EMERY IS at last ready to leave and has the recovered remains packed on ice and placed in a metal suitcase, ready for the trip to Honolulu. This is a solemn moment. "You're not only dealing with a piece of history but a sailor who revered his country," he says as he waits for the crew boat to arrive.

Lori Yost, the school teacher-reservist from Pennsylvania, is also scheduled to depart. She says that while she was diving, she couldn't help thinking about the sailor trapped there, wondering what had gone through his mind at the last moment. "He's one of us down there. If that were my great-great-grandfather, I would want him buried back with his family."

At 10:00 A.M. on August 4 the crew boat *Emmanuel* pulls up beside the barge with a deep-throated growl. Accompanied by a cooler and a black case, Emery transfers to the boat. Yost carries the yellow Igloo cooler bearing a hand-lettered warning: "Do not drink. Possible human remains."

Stenciled on the bulkhead of the crew boat are the words "God with us."

SEVENTEEN

SEND YOUR BOATS!

By 8:00 P.M. on December 30, 1862, the wind was still freshening and the barometer had plunged—the leading edge of the cold front was approaching. It would not take long for some of the Monitor crew to realize that if their iron vessel went down and they ended up in the water, there would be no floating debris to reach for—no masts, no spars, nothing.

Francis Butts, a landsman from Providence, Rhode Island, was having trouble standing as the shock of plunging into waves "would sometimes take us off our feet." He noticed something else that was disturbing: water was pouring into the ship's coal bunkers as waves swept over the deck. If the coal got wet, experience from the *Monitor*'s hair-raising first Atlantic voyage showed, the power of the main engine would slacken, reducing the blowers' ability to create the draft that helped the coal burn. If the blowers failed, the engine room would fill with toxic fumes. Butts could not help noticing the acidic smell of wet-burning coal. Assistant engineer Robinson Hands reported to Commander Bankhead that the coal was too wet to keep up steam. The pressure, which normally ran at eighty pounds, had fallen to twenty.

There are conflicting accounts about when the water began to rise. Bankhead said he gave the order to start one of the auxiliary pumps at about 7:30 P.M. Engineer Joseph Watters said the captain told him between 8:00 and 9:00 P.M. to examine the pumps and have them ready. Fireman George Geer said it was after 9:00 P.M. when Watters told him to have the large steam pump ready, running a hose from the pump to the bilge.

Geer went to look at the bilge and saw that the ship was taking on water faster than the pumps could discharge it, so he hurried to the top of the tower and reported this to the captain. "He told me to go down and start the big steam pump. I did so, and the pump threw a stream as large as your body and for about an hour the water did not gain nor did we gain on it much."

But that stalemate would soon end. It wasn't long before Watters returned to the engine room and found an inch of water over the floor. Watters must have had a sickening realization that fate had dealt him a losing hand. He had been transferred to the *Monitor* on December 29, the day she was to leave Hampton Roads. The previous chief engineer had carelessly stepped on one of the pumps and badly bruised his leg. Watters spent his first day on his new ship heading out to sea, his second trying to keep it from sinking beneath him.

There was more going on than leaks under the turret, the crew realized. Water, lots of it, was also entering between the upper and lower hulls. Because the ship was mostly submerged, much of the vessel knifed through the waves, which broke right over the deck. But the whole ship also rose with each new wave, crashing down into the succeeding trough. The next wave, Keeler noted, "would strike her under her heavy armour with a report like thunder and a violence that threatened to tear apart the thin sheet iron bottom and the heavy armour which it supported."

Keeler and others huddled on top of the turret, wide-eyed as their vessel slid down wave after wave, plunging her bow beneath the water and leaving them "isolated in a sea of hissing, seething foam extending as far as we could see around us. Then as she rose slowly and sullenly under the accumulated weight of waters, the foam pouring in broad sheets off the iron deck, a wave would roll over the bow and strike the pilot house with a force that would send the water in torrents on to the top of the turret, where our little company had gathered."

Bankhead observed that "when she rose to the swell, the flat under surface of the projecting armor would come down with great force, causing a considerable shock to the vessel and turret, thereby loosening still more the packing around its base." Bankhead realized, too, that the *Monitor* had sprung a leak somewhere in the forward part where the hull joined the armor, "and that it was caused by the heavy shocks received as she came down upon the sea."

By now the seas were rising rapidly. The vessel plunged heavily into the troughs, repeatedly submerging the pilothouse and causing water to gush into the blower pipes. The waves that leaped to the top of the turret flowed down through the roof grates into the decks below.

Captain Trenchard on board the *Rhode Island* noticed at the same time that "the wind freshened hauling more to the southward, and attended with rainy and squally weather."

Meanwhile, five miles east, the *Passaic* was also getting hammered. "From 8 P.M. to Midnight, frequent squalls, with rain," the ironclad's log noted. "Ship leaking badly. All hands employed at bailing water, as before, and throwing over shot. Threw overboard 340 32-lb. shot." Along with scrap iron also flung into the sea, the ship was lightened by more than ten tons. Still, water in the engine room was gaining and was within four inches of the fires. "Twenty minutes more at the same rate of increase," estimated Percival Drayton, the captain of the *Passaic*, "would have put them out, when nothing could have saved the vessel from sinking."

Drayton made what was surely a lifesaving decision. At midnight, as the wind picked up to severe gale force, throwing giant waves at the bow of the ship, the log of the *Passaic* shows an abrupt change in course, from southwest to northeast. Drayton had directed the *State of Georgia*, the *Passaic*'s tow ship, to turn around and head north. Other accounts say the ship was towed backward, but this is contradicted by the ship's surviving logs and the report of the tow ship. They were getting out of there. There was no way Drayton could signal his counterpart on the *Monitor*. By now they were out of sight of each other.

It would be a harrowing and exhausting night for the *Passaic*, with men constantly bailing and throwing more shot overboard. Even so, water rose to within two inches of the grates. By 4:00 A.M., after the pumps were fixed, the water in the engine room began to recede. Then, just as the sea settled down a bit, the wind veered abruptly and began to howl out of the north, and the temperature dropped precipitously. The cold front had passed.

At 2:00 P.M. on New Year's Day, at about Nags Head, the *State of Georgia* and the *Passaic* turned back to the south and at last arrived at Beaufort shortly after dark. Before turning in for the night, Captain Drayton wrote to his senior officer that in his opinion, the upper armor projections in the Monitor-class ships "render[ed] them totally unfit for the sea."

There seems to have been no attempt on board the heavily laden *Monitor* to throw shot or any other heavy objects overboard, even though the enormous weight of ammunition and coal in the belly of the ship added to the danger of sinking. The weight also increased the possibility, every time the ironclad rose and slammed into the waves, that the upper and lower hulls would separate. There is no record, either, of discussions about reversing course.

One clue to Bankhead's thinking may be found in an admiring report from Commander John B. Marchand, on an earlier occasion, that the "daredevil Bankhead" had taken his boat into hostile waters near Charleston to locate a Confederate steamer, whereas in the same incident the commander of another gunboat had hesitated. That other commander was none other than Percival Drayton of the *Passaic*, who was then and there taking extraordinary measures to keep his ship from sinking.

Bankhead was also tight-fisted about government property; he once criticized a superior officer for wasting "tons of shot and shell" in one engagement, at great expense to the government. These munitions were "literally thrown away and produced no effect whatever (except noise)," he wrote to his friend Gustavus Fox, the assistant secretary of the navy.

BY 9:00 P.M. on December 30, conditions aboard the *Monitor* had become alarming. The *Monitor* and the *Rhode Island* were making six knots, breakneck speed considering that they were plowing directly into heavy seas and winds up to twenty-seven knots, possibly gusting even higher. It was not quite a gale, but it was powerful enough to make things God-awful for everyone trapped in the belly of that iron ship.

If the sailors had feared that their ship might become their coffin during the battle nine months earlier, the same thought surely dawned on them now. To add to their misery, just then a squall came barreling through.

The last fix on the Cape Hatteras Light, bearing twenty miles northwest, had been made at 8:45 P.M. The watch officer on the *Rhode Island* would have been just barely able to see the light on the horizon— and then apparently the squall erased it from sight.

The wind was relentless, buffeting them heavily over the next five hours while escalating to near-gale force, twenty-eight to thirty-three knots. In such conditions on the open ocean, seas could reach up to eighteen feet, with foam blowing in streaks from cresting wave tops. Beaufort scale notwithstanding, the waves were likely higher than that. The convoy was in relatively shallow water, where wind-generated waves would stand even taller, steepening as they encountered Diamond Shoals. The *Monitor* was in serious trouble.

The 9:00 P.M. log entry for the *Rhode Island*'s says, "the *Monitor* made signal to stop," and the two ships drew close so they could communicate. During the lull, the *Rhode Island*'s captain noted that the smaller ship appeared to "be lying in the trough of the sea, laboring heavily, the sea making a complete breach over her." When they started again about fifteen minutes later they reduced their previous speed by half and, head to wind, "the *Monitor* rode much easier," Trenchard said. But Bankhead could still feel his ship rolling heavily.

On Watters's advice, Bankhead went to his last defense, a centrifugal pump, which could throw off three thousand gallons per minute. From the top of the turret, Butts saw "a stream of water eight inches in diameter spouting up from beneath the waves." That might have been comforting, but it meant the deck of the *Monitor* was completely under water. Furthermore, as it turned out, the pump was quickly overmatched by the amount of water coming in.

Watters soon had all the pumps working, but "later in the evening she began to thump very heavy, which no doubt sprung her somewhere below the water line as the water increased very rapid, notwithstanding the great amount of water discharged by the pumps."

By 10:00 P.M. the water in the engine room had risen so high that the blowers were spitting water. Bankhead was almost out of options.

At 10:30 he ordered the red signal lantern hoisted on the turret mast. He maneuvered close to the *Rhode Island* and shouted across the roaring sea that the situation was hopeless. Keeler's version of the message, shouted through a speaking trumpet, was, "Send your boats immediately. We are sinking." But whether this was understood right away was not clear. "A hoarse unintelligible cry was all that we could get amid the roar of the elements," Keeler remembered.

The *Rhode Island* sailors heard, all right. It was 11:00 P.M., according to the ship's log, when the *Monitor* "made signal of distress. Stopped, hailed her and was informed she was in a sinking condition. Called all hands and cleared away the boats." But calling all hands in the middle of the night and getting boat crews organized and boats lowered over the side into choppy seas can't be done quickly.

"It was nearly eleven o'clock when I was aroused by one of the messenger boys, who told me all the officers were wanted immediately," Ensign William Rodgers remembered. He raced to the deck, where Captain Trenchard gave orders to put the boats over, but there was much confusion and delay as boat crews were rounded up. Some positions had to be filled with volunteers. The seas were running, and lowering boats and oarsmen into the water from the pitching deck, unhooking tackles, and clearing away from the ship would take skill and nerve.

Meanwhile, because the ships were then close to each other, the *Rhode Island*'s crew threw over lines for the *Monitor* sailors to catch and use to hoist themselves on board. But the vessels were rolling so dangerously that it was almost suicidal to try. One account, published January 6, 1863, in the *New York Herald* and in an identical version three weeks later in *Harper's Weekly*, held that "five or six of the crew of the *Monitor* seized the ropes hanging from the side of the *Rhode Island*, and started to climb up her side; but only three reached there. The others were apparently struck by the *Monitor*, when they fell, crushed to death or perished in the sea."

With the ships tossing side by side in the water, the sagging, heavy towline became a problem, interfering with the *Monitor*'s ability to keep its engines—and thus the pumps—running. Bankhead called for volunteers to sever it. It was a difficult decision. Without the towline, the ships were in danger of separating, but Bankhead decided it must be done and called for volunteers to cut it.

"I was pretty sure I was going down anyhow," Master Louis Stodder would relate, "so I decided a minute or two wouldn't make much difference. Picking up a hatchet, I made my way forward, holding on to the rail, followed by two men." According to Butts, the men were boatswain's mate John Stocking and quarter gunner James Fenwick. Fenwick was the Scottish immigrant who had gone home to Boston on furlough two months before, gotten married, and left his new wife pregnant. Now, as they stepped forward, a wave rolled over the deck and swept Fenwick and Stocking to their deaths. Stodder was knocked down but hung onto the rail, struggled to his feet, and hacked through the hawser.

This might have temporarily solved one problem, but it immediately created another. With the *Rhode Island* and the *Monitor* close together, crews from both ships shared a terrifying realization. If the wooden *Rhode Island* rammed into the sharp-sided, iron-armored *Monitor*, it was quite possible that the armor would splinter her sides at the waterline and both ships would be lost. At one point the vessels actually touched.

Trenchard's immediate reaction was to order the *Rhode Island* to steam forward. But now a new catastrophe threatened. The severed hawser was apparently too heavy to recover in the violent seas. At least the logbooks and accounts make no mention of attempting to retrieve it. And now, as the *Rhode Island*'s paddle wheel churned, the hawser became entangled in it. The *Rhode Island* was left without power and at the mercy of the seas.

None of the official reports discuss this calamity. It must have been too embarrassing to put on the record. But junior officers on the *Rhode Island* would later criticize Bankhead for endangering both ships by having the towline cut. "Every seafaring man knows that the safest place for the *Monitor* that night was astern of and under our lee," wrote Ensign Rodgers. Furthermore, he added, "we could have easily held her there, in that position, head to the wind and sea with our ship under easy steam, had the *Monitor*'s people not cut the hawser and thereby cast themselves adrift."

On board the sinking ironclad, desperate men still waited for the rescue boat. Signal rockets were fired off again and again, and these were answered by the escort, but there was no sign of boats. "Words cannot depict the agony of those moments as our little company gathered on the top of the turret, stood with a mass of iron sinking beneath them, gazing through the dim light, with an anxiety amounting almost to agony," Keeler related. "Seconds lengthened into hours & minutes into years." Butts said some of the men wanted to fire on the *Rhode Island* to get their escort's attention.

The men reportedly did not openly panic, but fear surely had the run of the ship. Seeing fellow sailors swept overboard, watching the seas rise, feeling the sluggish response of the vessel—all of this was taking its toll. Master's mate Peter Williams suggested bailing, and a party was organized. Some stood in the engine room, water up to their waists, as they bailed, but probably every one of them knew it was hopeless. For one thing, it was impossible to carry buckets of water from down below and hand them up the ladder to the top of the turret—the only exit—without spilling much of the water. At least, some felt, it kept the men occupied.

At last, after what seemed an eternity, two boats were spotted, appearing on the crest of the huge seas, then disappearing into their troughs as the oarsmen fought to keep them from being swamped. It was exhausting work and, considering what they were up against, flatout courageous. And maybe something else. In that "wild sea," surgeon Weeks felt, "it was almost madness."

EIGHTEEN

YOUR CALL, COMMANDER

THE NAVY anticipated that the turret recovery would take place in late July and even requested that a helicopter be ready to photograph the event. But that date has come and gone. Now the drop-dead day in early August, when funding runs out, is approaching.

After spending several days on the barge earlier in the summer, I'm fortunate to be able to return for the lift. The Navy and NOAA have allowed a pool of print and photojournalists to spend time on the barge, and Steve Earley, a photographer from my newspaper, *The Virginian-Pilot*, and I are among those chosen. This media attention adds to the tension Scholley is under, and at first she opposes it. During past lifts the practice has been to escort a boatload of journalists out for the event itself, but the guest boat would stand off hundreds of yards from the recovery vessel until the exercise was safely over and the retrieved object was on deck. Then we'd be invited on board for brief interviews. But we argued that the turret recovery, involving a national treasure and millions of dollars in public funds, is too important for such stage-managed coverage. Two days before the expected recovery, we get word that we'll be allowed on the barge.

For the Navy and NOAA it's a double-edged sword. The coverage will heighten public awareness of the operation and, if everything goes well, make divers and archaeologists into media stars—if only briefly. But failure, especially failure involving serious accidents, will mean scrutiny that is up close and possibly embarrassing. It also adds to

safety concerns. It's like having reporters running around a construction site without safety training or hard hats. Last, it means sending
public affairs officers to accompany us, to make sure we stay out of
the way and to schedule interviews. But government officials know
that in practice this discipline breaks down and they have to rely on
simple good judgment.

Scholley receives word on Thursday, August 1, that up to eight journalists will be ferried out to witness the lift. This is all she needs. Divers
are still rigging the guns inside the turret, securing the roof, and excavating under the Spider's legs. They are trying to decide how to deal
with the parts of the human remains that were impossible to remove.
The senior divers are pressing for recovery on Saturday. Now she has
to worry about running the operation, focusing on critical issues involving the lift, and doing it all with the media looking over her shoulder. Her journal that day reflects this unwanted pressure: "Very stress-
ful day!"

We drive down to Hatteras Friday night, expecting to go out to the
barge the next morning. Saturday morning looks doubtful, with three-
to four-foot seas and fifteen-knot winds, but on Saturday afternoon, we
step on board the crew boat *Emmanuel* and head out to the barge, expecting to witness the lift the next morning. We go immediately to a
briefing, where Scholley explains the dangers of the operation and
lets us know, in case we don't already, that this is a military operation
and orders will be followed. If they aren't, we'll be off the barge faster
than our heads can spin. "Having said that," she adds with a tight
smile, "Welcome."

THIS IS how they plan to raise the turret: lower a specially built lifting platform and place it near the turret, then lift the turret just
enough to move it over and set it down on the platform, securing it
with the help of stabbing guides. The guides are spearlike probes on
two sides of the platform that will be mated to bell-shaped receptors
on corresponding legs of the Spider as the turret is lowered. Though
it sounds simple, it is anything but; two hundred tons of turret, cannon, and all the rest will be bobbing up and down as the barge rocks
in the ocean swells. The divers and crane operator will have to pre-

cisely line up the probes and stabbing guides before the platform can be locked in place.

Those several minutes—when the turret and its contents are off the ocean bottom and in motion—are when the invitation to catastrophe will be strongest, when the roof might collapse, and, with it, the entire recovery.

Navy policy on salvage jobs is to plan the best you can but be ready with fixes when obstacles spring up. They always do. The divers have on hand all manner of steel beams and girders and clamps, cables and chains, even wooden blocks for shoring and padding—a whole locker of equipment that amounts to a giant tool bag. Now that the team finds the roof is intact, the question is how to brace it before putting the enormous weight of the turret's contents on it. The divers spend ten days at this task. First they dig down through the newly exposed roof hatches, then tunnel under the turret with high-pressure hoses and slide box beams and angle irons underneath, securing them to the Spider's legs with lifting straps.

But master diver Jim Mariano has found, when locking one of the feet of the Spider, that pieces of the turret's iron plates are starting to slip. New measures have to be taken.

The night before the lift is to take place, Broadwater and Johnston meet with the dive leaders, who say they're ready.

"No, we aren't," says Johnston. At first there's dead silence. Johnston meets the eyes of the others in the room and gets the feeling that several of them would like to kill him.

If Chris Murray, the head of Navy divers and the driving force behind the recovery, were not at the bottom of the ocean, working on getting the turret ready, he might do just that. Strangulation is the method that comes to mind as he learns of the latest delay through his headset. To say that Murray is frustrated in his self-imposed exile is to describe only part of his mood. Exhausted from fighting the current, he finds talking difficult. Under pressure in the helium environment of the bell and chamber, he is either freezing or boiling. That might be bearable for people who don't have to make decisions, but much of the weight of the mission is still on his shoulders, even at the bottom of the ocean. The plan was for him to help with the rigging and then come up just before the lift. But to be down on the bottom and know things are ready to go while people above are thinking of more "busy-work," as he calls it, is infuriating. Furthermore, having to convey his frustration in a Donald Duck voice is killing him.

He can understand that if the turret comes up in pieces the archaeologists are responsible for damaging a national treasure. But he knows that the Navy is responsible too. He's spent two saturation dives down there with the *Monitor* and twenty-six surface-supply dives; he's crawled under the wreck, tunneled beneath it, scampered over it. He knows it inside and out. But he can't convey his opinions topside to Johnston and Broadwater. Ironically, he himself gave the assurance that the divers would treat orders from the archaeologists as though they were orders from him, and now he's having to stomach his own words.

Spinning his wheels at forty fathoms below the waves and believing that the NOAA people are inventing more reasons for delay, he's in a stew. He should be helping Bobbie Scholley—she's up there fighting those guys by herself.

Johnston sticks to his guns. He doesn't care what the go-go Navy types think. Here's the reason: On October 25, 1861, *Monitor* designer John Ericsson described to one of the navy commodores how the roof could be opened and the guns removed for placement on another vessel. The top of the turret, he wrote, rested on an iron band bolted to the inside. "The weight alone keeps the top or roof down, so that it may at any time be lifted up or removed," he explained, adding that a crane could do the job in a couple of hours. "Guns therefore may be put in and exchanged with very little trouble."

It is as clear as clear can be. The top of the turret—now the bottom because it is upside down—was not designed to take much of a load, certainly not tons of coal, mud, and cannon, not to mention artifacts and human remains. They now have a box beam and angle irons holding the center, but Johnston still isn't satisfied with the outside supports.

Scholley handles it coolly. Unlike Murray, her predecessor at MDSU TWO, Scholley doesn't lead by doing. She loves to dive and is superb at it, but she would not have selected herself to be in the water when the turret came up. "She doesn't have anything to prove," says Scott Heineman, her command master chief. "Her enjoyment is seeing that everything gets done, and it seems like she's not doing anything: 'This is what I want; this is the final goal. Go out there and execute.' "

OK, master divers, she tells the senior leaders, take a look at this and come up with a plan.

True to form, they look at it not as a problem but as a challenge. What they do is to take sheet iron that had been stacked on deck and slice it with a cutting torch into several fishhook shapes, each with a gap that would grip and hold the roof plates.

How's this? they ask. That ought to do it, Johnston replies, his fears finally at rest. Or at least as much as they can be.

The hooks are lowered to the sat divers and secured with straps. Murray still feels it's busywork, but he has no choice; he has to go along, even though he suspects some of the hooks will fall off during the recovery. The problem is that, at $65,000 a day just for operations, the funding is running out. They had about forty-five days, beginning June 21. They can't tell for sure and have to look at spreadsheets every day to judge where the funds are going and how fast. One thing they do know is that there are just a few days left. If bad weather sets in and they have to suspend operations, the funds will be gone before they can go back to work. The ever-optimistic Murray believes it won't be a huge problem to find the right federal pocket, but positioned at the bottom of the ocean in a diving bell with his helium-strained voice squeaking—and exhausted from the work—he'll never be able to effectively plead with the Navy and NOAA for additional time.

Scholley is plainly worried and gets on the headset with Murray. "Are we going to have enough money?" she asks.

Murray tries to reassure her that the money will be there if need be, but the constraint of being in saturation while all this is going on is getting to him.

Scholley can sense it. "You know, this is silly," she says. "Let's start bringing you up, just in case we need to fight the money battles."

Murray doesn't argue, even though it will now be too late for him to be on deck when the turret comes up. That's a shame. He's invested much of his career making all this possible. Instead, he'll have to spend the next three days in decompression, watching it all through a thick plastic window. But at least he'll be close by, and if they have to come up with a contingency plan, his help will be invaluable.

They need his leadership, too, Scholley realizes. Once they got the Spider down and the weather started going against them, she and Broadwater realized they desperately needed Murray's advice. They'd look at each other and ask, "Do we take the risk or do we wait?"

They decide to do both, as it turns out.

SUNDAY'S WAKE-UP call is at 3:30 A.M. By 4:00 it is already clear what kind of day it is going to be. The wind is blowing and the barge is rocking. Clouds stand off in the east, with a streak of pink on the horizon. A waning moon still hangs in the west.

Emerging from the first meeting of the morning, Broadwater looks grim. "Right now the current on the bottom is just too strong," he tells me. "The ROV can't fight the current, which means we can't put divers on the bottom. All we can do is plan a hold and watch conditions for a few hours." But then he smiles sleepily. He realizes that at least he'll be able to sit down for breakfast, the first time he's been able to do that since coming out here almost six weeks ago.

But breakfast is hardly relaxing. There are disturbing reports of near gale force winds arriving in the next day or two, probably by Tuesday. They meet again—Broadwater, Johnston, Scholley, Cavey, the master divers, the engineers, and the barge operators—and decide to see if a lift is possible later in the day. They begin shifting the barge, slackening and tightening the cables on each of the four corners to minimize the barge's roll in the sea swells. Now the seas and the wind are directly on the bow.

Nearly forty days of this operation and an approaching deadline have taken a toll on everyone, especially on Bobbie Scholley. Her green eyes and drawn face show the strain. Even so, she manages a half smile. "We're going to go one step at a time and then stop and evaluate," she says.

The divers suit up. The giant crane that has lain dormant across the length of the barge comes to life. Looking ahead, once the turret has been secured to the lifting platform, the crane arm will have to rise almost vertically, lift the turret out of the water, and swing it over to the deck; and if the barge rocks, so will the crane. If the crane rocks, the turret will sway. If the turret sways, no one will be safe—not the divers, not the archaeologists, not the crew, not the journalists. At this point, the recovery seems impossible.

One tentative step is taken—picking up the lifting frame, with all sixteen of its straps, and setting it down on a steel beam suspended over the water. Then there's a long pause.

The master divers and warrant officers all push for Scholley to go ahead with the lift. Again and again they say, "Let's go for it; we can do it." It's the old go-go spirit of the Navy salvage crew, a spirit she shares and yet has to hold in check.

She goes to Broadwater and asks what he thinks. "It's your decision," she reminds him.

"Yes, and it's your responsibility to tell me whether you're ready," he replies.

There's only a second's pause. "We're ready," she says.

BUT AS the morning slips by it becomes clear that sea conditions are not going to cooperate. The pressure on Broadwater and Scholley continues. The voice he's heard in his ear for months —the one warning him against going ahead when conditions are not right and destroying what amounts to a national treasure—has not ceased. And conditions, although close, are not quite right. Scholley knows that too. Although she's in charge of successfully landing the turret on deck, her biggest responsibility is the safety of everyone on the barge, including her divers—regardless of how hard they're pressing her. And now, with time running out, it seems that the entire U.S. Navy, the national media, and history itself have come along for a ride on her shoulders.

For years before the summer of 2002, the Navy treated the *Monitor* operation as just another salvage project. Now there is intense interest from senior ranks. On Sunday the strain nearly reaches the bursting point. Press conferences are scheduled. A Navy helicopter is poised to lift off and record the event. Several VIPs, including John Hightower, president of the Mariners' Museum, and Admiral Jay M. Cohen, chief of naval research, have descended on Hatteras and are getting ready to come out to see the lift. The admiral has to leave that afternoon.

Hightower is in his tenth year as museum president and is preparing to launch plans for a $30 million *Monitor* Center—due to open in 2007—that will showcase hundreds of artifacts from the ironclad, but most especially its turret. The Mariners' is official custodian of *Monitor* artifacts, and this is to be Hightower's legacy.

The Mariners' Museum, founded in 1935 by art collector and philanthropist Archer Huntington and his wife, sculptor Anna Hyatt Huntington, is one of the world's great maritime museums, with a vast collection of ship models and marine art. Along with its 35,000 artifacts and reproductions and 600,000 photographs, there are exquisite figureheads, lovingly preserved small craft, and rare nautical instruments. An impressive nautical library now includes original letters of *Monitor* sailors. You could spend days at the museum without seeing it all, and then happily wear yourself out rambling around the beautiful five-mile nature trail circling the lake. The museum is a gem, but except for a mid-1990s exhibition on the *Titanic*, it has not gotten the attention it deserves.

Until now, perhaps. When it became clear that the museum would play host to dozens of *Monitor* artifacts, including the propeller, engine, and turret, the museum responded the only way it responsibly could. It took a gamble. As official repository for *Monitor* artifacts, it had to be ready to both care for them and display them to the public. That meant launching a major fund-raising campaign, even before the first major pieces were recovered. Federal, state, and local sources would contribute $20 million, with another $10 million coming from private donors. Among the plans are a sculptural replica of the ship and a full-scale re-creation of its below-deck quarters.

The Monitor Center will tell the story from the perspectives of both the *Monitor* and the *Virginia*. The museum already owns the wheel from the *Merrimack/Virginia*, dating to about 1856, thanks to a gift from the Tredegar Company, the short-lived successor to the iron works that rolled the plates for converting the frigate. The museum also owns an assortment of other *Virginia* artifacts, including original drawings by which the conversion took place. The collections will shed light on the ironclads and their battle and add a new dimension to public understanding of the Civil War and the sea. The center, Hightower hopes, will surely bring waves of tourists and Civil War buffs. And might they not then be drawn to the rest of the museum's fabulous collection?

Hightower, 68, a former director of the Museum of Modern Art as well as the South Street Seaport Museum, is close to retirement, but this project is too exciting for him to step down now. "Oh, my God, it's a dream come true," he tells me. "And what a fabulous way to go out! I'm still hanging on for dear life until we get over the threshold of opening day, March 9, 2007."

Even though Hightower knows the recovery has to be done with great care, he is biting his nails. There is so much momentum and attention on the recovery effort that if the divers don't get the turret off the sea floor then and there, the balloon that has been getting bigger and bigger will burst and take much of the excitement away from the moment. It's like an incredible novel, he thinks; you can hardly wait for the denouement. A lot will be lost if the recovery is postponed even one more year.

Back in Newport News, an 86,000-gallon conservation tank, fourteen feet tall and thirty-two feet wide, has been built just for the turret by apprentices at Northrop Grumman Newport News Shipbuilding as a gift to the museum. The museum's conservation area, already accommodating the ship's propeller and engine and close to one thousand other artifacts, is rapidly turning into one of the largest such facilities in the world. It has long been assumed that the turret will be its star attraction

Among the potential losses from not recovering the turret now is the media attention that would help drive congressional approval of $10 million for the new center and later funding for conservation. But Hightower knows the risks of a botched recovery and would never add to the pressure on Scholley.

Neither would Admiral Cohen. By telephone from Hatteras, Cohen asks Scholley how she's doing out there. Scholley answers that she's had better days. "It's the weather," she adds, trying to sound optimistic even while biting her lip. There really isn't anyone she can turn to for advice.

He tells her not to worry about his presence or that of anyone else on the beach but to use her own judgment about what's best and safest. "It's your call, commander," she remembers him saying.

That's exactly what she needs: she knows better than anyone what the situation is. Whatever the call, they'll respect her judgment. It's a relief, but it doesn't take away the pressure. She hates to disappoint the brass and the media and everyone else, but there's no way they can safely make the lift today. The admiral and the museum president feel they can wait no longer and depart.

LATE SUNDAY afternoon, divers linger at their stations, restless as waves continue to crash against the barge. "I don't know if this is going to happen today," master diver Mariano tells them, "I don't know if this is going to happen tomorrow. But when this is over, the whole world is going to want to be a Navy deep-sea diver—and you guys are going to be able to say you were there."

Scholley seriously considers making the attempt Sunday night. It would mean a loss of media coverage, not a small consideration. The story will surely be sent around the world. The Navy and NOAA public affairs people have worked for months getting ready for the big day. But the mission calls for bringing the turret up safely. Public attention will just have to take a back seat.

The dilemma vanishes, however, when a camera lowered on the divers' stage shows an underwater blizzard of sediment caused by powerful currents: Sunday night is out of the question, and with a storm expected on Tuesday, Monday is the only choice.

Sunday night, a lot of weary people meet in the communications center overlooking the barge. The National Weather Service is predicting that the Gulf Stream could see fifteen-foot seas and thirty-knot winds by Tuesday. The Manson Gulf people say there's no way they can make the lift in such conditions. It would damage the boom and maybe even endanger the barge and everyone on it. The divers agree that it would be too dangerous. And there's a further dilemma: if they pick up the turret and attach it to the lifting platform and then have to cancel, they'll have to leave the turret on the bottom with the huge Spider wrapped around it. Hovering in the room is an ominous sense of failure.

"We'll have to make tough calls each step of the way," Scholley tells the crew. And then she makes the toughest call she's had to make so far. Cavey calls it a "crucial, crucial, crucial decision."

Even if the weather calms, the barge crew says, the seas will be coming at the barge from the wrong direction. The NOAA weather prediction calls for the waves to be from the southwest Monday morning. Unless the seas hit them on the nose, the operation won't be safe. The barge needs to be repositioned, and not just by tweaking the cables this time. It will need a thirty-degree turn, and they'll have to use the tugboat to move the anchors. It will be difficult and dangerous.

The eight 20,000-pound anchors are splayed out in a sunburst pattern from the four corners of the barge. At the top of each anchor is a crown, or eyehook, with a cable running to a buoy at the surface. The tug crew will have to grab each cable, secure it to a winch, and raise the corresponding anchor, dropping it where the satellite positioning system indicates it must go. Then the big Detroit diesel engines on board the barge will haul on the anchor until it sets. Eight times this needs to be done, over several hours at night, in rough seas.

What if something goes wrong? Scholley asks Cavey and the barge crew. "What if we part a wire or just can't get the barge back in the right location because of the current or wind?" Then it would be all over. Without the right position for the barge, they'll lose the opportunity to lift the turret. But what are the other choices?

Then, too, they've been out here for forty days with pretty much the same team, and Greg "Big G" Clavelle has shown a masterful touch with those anchors, almost a sixth sense about exactly where they should be positioned in relationship to the barge, Scholley feels. The same goes for Cavey, who has an almost uncanny perception of the multidimensional space they're working in: the ocean bottom, the water column, and the ocean surface. She has a gut feeling about these men. After seeing them do phenomenal things all this time, she just has to trust they can do it.

It's now down to the wire. If they don't try something, then all this planning, all this tension, all these hopes go out the window. If they try and it goes wrong, well, that's too awful to contemplate.

Let's try it, she says, try it and at least preserve the chance to go for the recovery on Monday—if the seas will just lie down for a few hours.

Jason Niny, the twenty-nine-year-old field engineer from Manson Gulf, adds one note of caution. "Once you pull the trigger, you've got to go," Niny tells the group. "Once we say let's go, there's no stopping in midstream."

It takes hours as the tug and its crew move from one anchor to another in a late-night waltz with the seas and currents and tonnage. It's far from certain that all will go well.

Scholley, needing reassurance, collars Scott Heineman, her own personal anchor. "Master diver, you've just got to sit and listen to me as I talk this out." She goes over it all, the dangers, the pressures, the weather, the fast-disappearing window. He knows it isn't his job to tell her what to do; she's covered all the bases. But Heineman's big, exuberant personality exudes moral support. "Commander," he finally says, "you've got to do what you feel is right." It is, after all, just that simple.

At a late-night meeting, the mission leaders assign places for the next day. Broadwater will monitor the lift from the sat shack, Johnston and Scholley from the surface-supply station. Broadwater asks Johnston how he feels, and Johnston, knowing that his boss will feel comfortable if he is comfortable, answers as candidly as he can: "I'm 90 percent confident. We've done everything possible to get this thing up and on the platform."

With the barge being repositioned to minimize the effect of the swells, Scholley knows she's done all she can. She knows, too, that there's likely to be only one slim chance. "It's now or who knows when," she says.

That night Cavey writes in his journal, "Anticipate recovery to begin at 0400 tomorrow. Weather does not currently support operations. Day shift: strong currents on the bottom. ROV unable to hold station."

Scholley can't sleep. Late at night she stands at the bow and stares at waves crashing against the barge. "Don't make the wrong decision," she tells herself. If anything goes wrong, she realizes, she's likely to go down in history as "the lady who finally broke the *Monitor*'s turret."

View of the barge *Wotan* at sunrise. (Steve Earley)

Tenders shove stage and divers out over water. (Steve Earley)

Captain Don Liberatore guides the submersible *Johnson Sea Link II* as it approaches the *Monitor*'s turret. A Navy diver can be seen at work. (Steve Earley)

Commander Bobbie Scholley prepares to dive. (Steve Earley)

Jeff Johnston indicates the weakest part of the turret as John Broadwater (left) and Rick Cavey look on. (Steve Earley)

Saturation diver Jeremy Mullis uses hydroblaster to cut away armor belt. (U.S. Navy Photo by Eric Tilford)

Diver videos turret after armor belt is removed. (U.S. Navy Photo by Eric Tilford)

Tenders lead diver from stage after returning to barge. (U.S. Navy Photo by Eric Tilford)

Divers David Keener (left) and Brad Flemming undergo decompression.
(U.S. Navy Photo by Chadwick Vann)

Diver Lori Yost helps escort remains.
(Steve Earley)

Captain Chris Murray is
"unhatted" after dive.
(U.S. Navy Photo by
Eric Lippmann)

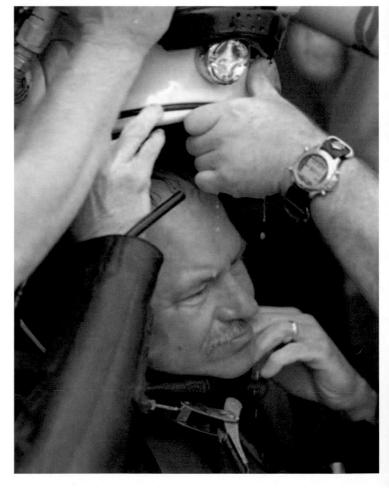

Bell containing saturation divers returns to surface after twelve-hour shift. (Steve Earley)

Broadwater and Scholley just before lift. (Steve Earley)

The turret emerges after fourteen decades at the bottom of the ocean. (Steve Earley)

Crew rejoice as the turret appears. (Steve Earley)

NINETEEN

PANORAMA OF HORROR

As HE stood on the tower watching the rescue boats approach, paymaster William Keeler suddenly embraced the notion that there was time to go below. He was meticulous about his books and ledgers and stringent about spending government money. Losing his records was more than he could bear. He plunged down the ladder to the bottom of the turret, scrambled around the guns, found the hatch, and lowered himself. As he did so he stumbled and fell to the floor of the berth deck below.

In that open room where the crew slept there was a single dim lantern swinging back and forth with the motion of the ship, affording barely enough light to cut through the darkness. The room was filled with steam, heat, and the acrid smell of wet coal. "I passed across this deck, down into the ward room, where I found the water nearly to my waist and swashing from side to side with the roll of the ship, and groped my way through the narrow crooked passage into my state room. It was a darkness that could be felt. The hot, stifling, murky atmosphere pervaded every corner."

Through the darkened passage he went. He reached his little stateroom and managed to gather up the books and papers he felt must be saved. He was about to lug them back up to the tower but realized he'd have to carry them while making a dash across the wave-swept deck and into a tippy, crowded rescue boat. Reluctantly, he set them down. He would have to reconstruct all this later.

Paymasters were charged with keeping careful records of everything from clothing allowances to grog consumption to funds advanced against pay. Trying to remember what each person owed must have been the accounting equivalent of hell. Keeler's reconstructed "Final Pay Receipt and Muster Roll for the United States Steamer *Monitor*," now in the National Archives, shows why. Later, he would somehow remember, for example, that Captain Worden, who was injured in the battle with the *Virginia*, had never paid back part of an advance. "Therefore, I debit him $311.83," Keeler was to write in flowing cursive in a ledger book large enough to cover a desktop. As for himself, the books showed that the Navy owed him, after deductions, $650.94 after 198 days on board.

Although Keeler had given up on rescuing his records from the bowels of the *Monitor*, he wasn't finished yet. He reached for his watch, which was hanging on a nail in his stateroom, and jammed it in his pocket. In doing so he discovered the keys to his safe and decided, even though fear was rising in his throat, that he would try to save the money in the safe. It was, after all, government money, and he, diligent public servant, was responsible for it. The safe was completely submerged, and Keeler had to root around in the black water in hopes of finding the keyhole. He tried several times without success, then looked up through the deck light and realized that waves were dashing back and forth above his head. It dawned on him that time was running out and that if he didn't get out of there quickly he'd be trapped inside a sinking ship.

"My feelings at this time it is impossible to describe, when I reflected that I was nearly at the farthest extremity of the vessel from its only outlet and this outlet liable to be completely obstructed at any moment by a rush of panic stricken men, and the vessel itself momentarily expected to give the final plunge."

Keeler had to wade through deepening water along the crooked stateroom passageway and into the wardroom, where tables and chairs were now surging violently with the sloshing water, threatening to break his bones. He mounted the steps to the berth deck, his heart thudding, stumbled to the ladder, and climbed to the turret. Clawing his way past gun tackle, shot, sponges, and rammers that had broken

William Keeler, *Monitor* paymaster. (Mariners' Museum)

loose, he hurried to the top of the turret. What he witnessed was chaos.

Mountains of water rushed across the deck and foamed along the sides. The rescue boats were pitching and tossing. The wind was howling, officers were shouting orders, and men were crying out as waves threw them into the darkness. Beside him on the turret stood others who seemed paralyzed by fear. The whole scene was lit by the glare of the blue signal lamps of the *Rhode Island*. In Keeler's words, it was a "panorama of horror."

A lifeboat pulled alongside, its crew fighting to keep it from slamming into the iron ship. Crew from the *Monitor* hesitated at first, then dropped from the turret as waves ran across the deck and slammed into them. Some lost their footing and were swept overboard, others grabbed safety lines and fought their way toward the boat, leaping into the water. Some were hauled aboard; others were lost.

Now an even greater danger approached: the *Rhode Island*. Powerless because of the towline-fouled paddle wheel, the big wooden ship veered drunkenly toward the *Monitor*, where the men were getting into the launch. "Keep off! Keep off!" someone cried as the big ship approached, towering over them.

What followed was an explosion of cracking wood as the *Rhode Island*'s starboard quarter slammed into the rescue boat, crunching it against the iron side of the *Monitor.* Thwarts, oars, and splinters flew into the air. Sailors leaped onto the *Monitor*'s deck to escape being crushed. Others grasped lines hanging from the *Rhode Island*'s side and pulled themselves up.

Now the *Rhode Island* bore down on the *Monitor,* and the realization dawned that they could all be lost. "Death stared us in the face," Grenville Weeks recalled. But the larger ship merely grazed the *Monitor* and drifted off to leeward.

The lifeboat was still afloat, though its starboard gunwale was crushed, and after hesitating, men began to get back on board.

Meanwhile, according to the *Herald* account, "Several of the crew and some of the officers also found a watery grave about this time, by being washed overboard. It was death to stand on the deck without having a firm hold, and even then the danger was very great. One by one the gallant fellows disappeared from the deck and were seen no more."

Bankhead gave the order to abandon ship. "It is madness to remain here longer," Weeks quoted him as saying. "Let each man save himself."

Realizing he might end up in the water, Keeler stripped off some of his heavy clothing, possibly including his boots, and made for the ladder to the deck, but the ladder was crowded with men too frightened to move. He grabbed a rope hanging from an awning stanchion and slid to the deck, where a wave knocked him down and swept him overboard. As he resurfaced, some thirty feet from the boat, another wave picked him up and threw him against the *Monitor*'s side. He reached for a lifeline stanchion and, with adrenaline pumping, clambered back aboard, made his way along the lifeline, and collapsed into the leaky lifeboat.

Weeks was next. Just as he attempted to jump into the lifeboat, it lurched away. He leaped, smashing into the boat and landing half in the water. The sailors hauled him in and they were off, crew and survivors stuffing their pea jackets into the holes in the boat, bailing for their lives. Although damaged the rescue launch was seaworthy, albeit barely. But still the seas were chaotic. Most of the time, all that the men in the boat could see were walls of water coming at them, blasting them in the face.

A second lifeboat, commanded by master's mate Rodney Browne, had just set out from the *Rhode Island* with a crew of fourteen. The captain, he said, had "thought it impossible to live in such a sea," but Browne, "an old whale-man," as he called himself, was not to be denied. The waves were so chaotic that the oarsmen frequently had to swing the boat around to meet them head on. In the confusion, they almost crashed into the first lifeboat, overloaded and already damaged. As surgeon Weeks reached out to fend it off, his hand was crushed between the boats and his shoulder dislocated.

Somehow the returning oarsmen negotiated what was now a half mile of heavy seas to the weather quarter of the paddlewheel steamer. But their problems were far from over. As the boat and ship rose on the waves, several of the survivors grasped lines and pulled themselves aboard. Keeler, who had also injured his hand, had to wait until a line with a loop at the end could be passed down. He squirmed into the loop, passing it over his head and under his arms, and the deck crew pulled the exhausted paymaster to safety. Weeks also was hauled aboard and was taken below, where his counterpart, the surgeon on the *Rhode Island*, amputated his crushed fingers.

Ensign William Rodgers skippered the third rescue boat, a much smaller one that could carry only seven passengers. "I got clear of the ship and started for the *Monitor*, which lay quite a distance to the windward of us. The sea was running quite high, and it seemed at times as if our boat would end over." As Rodgers and his crew neared the *Monitor*, one of his men said he heard someone call for help. As a wave rose up, they saw a man's head on its crest and pulled frantically for him. When they reached him and hauled him into the boat, more dead than alive, they realized it was master's mate Peter Williams. Now, with their unexpected extra crew member, they approached the *Monitor*.

"The appearance of the iron-clad at this time was truly appalling," Rodgers related. "She lay in the trough of the sea, and the waves were making a complete breach over her decks."

Meanwhile, the *Rhode Island*, its great paddle wheel still fouled by the cut hawser, continued to drift away from the sinking *Monitor*. By the time a fireman steeled his courage, scrambled into the paddle box, and hacked through the tangled hawser, the distance between the ships over tumultuous seas grew almost impossibly wide.

Commander Bankhead ordered the *Monitor*'s engineer to stop the ship's main engine and use all available steam for the pumps. Ericsson's great cast-iron screw propeller made a last feeble turn and stopped.

Now, with the vessel dangerously beam-on to the rolling waves—rendering a rescue by lifeboat impossible—there was only one way to turn her head back to the seas. Bankhead ordered the anchor let go "and all the chain given her." Then he asked Francis Butts to go below and see what the situation was in the wardroom. The landsman went forward and saw water gushing in through the hawse pipe. Dropping the anchor had torn away the packing in this eight-inch opening.

In the wardroom, the water was two feet high and rising. As Butts passed through he noticed Samuel Lewis, an assistant engineer and one of the youngest men on board, so miserably sick in his bunk that he couldn't get up. Crossing the berth deck, Butts saw George Frederickson, the young acting master's mate from Denmark, hand his pocket watch to another sailor. "Here, this is yours," Butts remembered Frederickson's saying. "I may be lost."

On board the doomed vessel, some had not yet heard any orders to abandon ship and were still bailing. George Geer was one of fifteen sailors still below. "I stayed by the pump until the water was up to my knees and the cylinders to the pumping engines were under water and stopped," he would write to his brother. "She was so full of water and rolled and pitched so bad I was fearful she would roll under and forget to come up again." At about 11:00 P.M., Geer noted, the water rose very fast, and "I was satisfied it was all up with her."

TWENTY

ALL STATIONS, ALL STATIONS

L ONG BEFORE dawn on Monday, August 5, 2002, a waning crescent moon squints at the barge as it rocks gently on southwesterly swells. Chased by unseen predators, flying fish erupt from the surface and catch the lights from the barge as they glide over the water. Except for the hum of generators, all is quiet.

Up in the tower overlooking the barge, master chief Larry Fahey stares at a computer screen showing the remnants of Tropical Storm Bertha dumping heavy rains across portions of Mississippi and Louisiana. "They're getting hammered," he says, shaking his head. Right now, off Hatteras, conditions aren't bad: wind out of the southeast, ten to fifteen knots, seas three to four feet. But this is bound to change. The low-pressure trough that spawned Bertha in the Gulf sprawled across Florida into the Atlantic and has now given birth to a second disturbance.

As divers and archaeologists fumble for their alarm clocks, a tropical depression begins taking shape off the Georgia–South Carolina coast and moving north. The weather disturbance doesn't yet have a name, but it will: Tropical Storm Cristobal, packing winds up to forty-five miles an hour. The National Hurricane Center is already tracking it. If there is a window for the recovery, it will be alarmingly brief.

Rick Cavey crawls out of the sack, shaking off cobwebs from late-night meetings and lack of sleep. The first thing he notices is that for now the swells have decreased and the wind has calmed. Also, he remembers, the barge has been shifted, and the seas should be hitting them on the nose. It's now or never, he feels. All the planning, all the work, all the hopes that he, the divers, scientists, and engineers have shared have come down to this one chance. He knows that Broadwater and Scholley want it badly too, but the huge responsibility each carries makes them hesitate. He decides to make the strongest case he can.

"Ma'am," he says, meeting Scholley in the predawn darkness near the dive station, "I'm going to start trying to lift the turret now. If you want to stop me, you'll have to shoot." She checks for the smile in his eyes and finds only steely determination.

Scholley stifles a laugh. She wants this, probably more than Cavey does, but he doesn't have the responsibility she has. She tells him he's welcome to take his enthusiasm to the all-important meeting they're about to have.

Inside the cramped NOAA shack on the deck level, the chief players in the mission cradle coffee cups as they gather. Things don't look good. Even though the ocean surface looks calm, the current down below is strong—too strong for the ROV to operate. If they do go forward, they will be able to see only by the jerky images sent back from cameras on divers' helmets.

The consensus swings toward postponing the lift. But given how far they've come, this is almost unthinkable. Postpone until when? They're out of time and nearly out of funds, and horrible weather is approaching. This is probably their last chance, but they cannot, must not, be pressured by that.

It's tense in that narrow office. Everyone in the room shares the burden of roles that must be played out flawlessly and within a narrowing window. No one, not the Navy or NOAA or Phoenix or Manson Gulf, wants to do it wrong. At the same time, no one wants to pull the plug—not yet. "I hate to say this," Scholley says. "but we're pushing the envelope with these winds and seas—we're pushing it big time."

There is one cautious approach left, however.

Scholley makes a quick trip to the sat shack, running up the stairs, and gets on the two-way with Keith Nelson, who is down in the bell, suspended over the wreck. The chief boatswain's mate is a powerful diver, an indefatigable man whom some consider a "water hog." Every bit of that might be needed now. It's his job to attach eight 135-pound shackles from the lifting straps to the eyehooks on the Spider.

Nelson's supervisor that morning is master diver Bryon Van Horn. "Nelly knows how to manipulate his body in the water to apply the greatest amount of force," Van Horn says. "He can do things other strong guys can't do."

"Chief," Scholley, says, "You're the guy who's been down there. What do you think?" Nelson is not one to express doubts before trying. "Commander, I can do this," he says in his high-pitched, helium-saturated voice. "Just put me in the water. I guarantee I can get those shackles hooked up."

That's what she needs to know.

"John," she reports to Broadwater. "Chief Nelson's been down there a week. He really knows what's happening, and he's very confident."

Broadwater is full of misgivings, but here is a straw he can grasp, if only to prolong what seems to be inevitable—scrubbing the mission. There is a way to proceed, he realizes, while preserving the option to back down: one cautious step at a time.

"Let's really concentrate on how long every step's going to take," Broadwater says. "And all you master divers—you've done this before. If at any time when we're going through this sequence you feel uncomfortable about what your divers are being asked to do, man, shout it out."

Scholley is first to emerge from the long meeting. "We're going to take the first step real slow," she tells me. "Once we get the sat diver in the water and see what the current is like down there, then we'll know."

Broadwater walks up and stands beside her. "I think this is as good as it's going to get for a week, and we don't have a week," he says with a half smile that does nothing to erase the tension that shows in his face.

So here is the window, they all know—a narrow slit in time between that New Year's Eve 140 years ago and tomorrow, when a new storm is due to arrive. And even though there is caution built in to every step, it's clear that this, at last, is a go signal. The barge that had been slumbering through days of setbacks and disappointments is suddenly alive.

As Jeff Johnston walks to the galley for one more cup of coffee, Oren "Bubby" Haydel, the big, bearded crane operator, who is getting ready to go up to his rig, grabs him in a bear hug. "Don't worry," Haydel tells him, "I ain't going to fuck up your turret."

AT ABOUT 6:45 A.M., just as a lavish sun rises over the Atlantic, the crane begins to move, its big hook swinging slightly as the barge rocks. It's an impressive thing to see a 275-foot crane come to life. The divers begin to suit up.

"All right, men, this is what we've been waiting for," Rick Cavey tells them.

"All we need," says Scholley, "is a hoo yah!"

"Hoo yah!" they sing out.

The tension that has reigned for several days of inactivity seems to have been replaced by the sudden jolt of energy from orders given and acknowledged.

On the dive platform, master diver Mariano pumps up his divers like a high school coach. "Either Neptune's going to kick our ass or we're going to kick his," he says. "Somebody's got to lose and somebody's got to win, and I ain't losin' today. Get in the water; go to work; come on home."

Chief petty officer Steve Janek, who had been part of the *Monitor* expeditions from the start, wanted a chance to do something besides run the dives from the edge of the barge. He volunteered for what seemed an easy job: descend to the lifting frame that was suspended just below the surface and cut free the lifting straps and shackles—now tied in bundles—that are to be lowered and attached to the Spider. Instead of going down on a stage, with heavy weights and boots, though, he walks to water's edge wearing flippers.

Chief petty officer Mike Lutz, running the dive, barks out the order. "Step out like you mean it!" And as divers do, Janek takes a giant step into the void and plunges into the water.

He's immediately greeted by current that's far too strong to operate in, but, wielding a knife, he frees the straps from their bundles one at a time, heart pumping and lungs straining. In the surface-supply shack, the dive officers listen to their friend's heavy breathing with concern on their faces.

The crane is maneuvered into position so the assembly can be lowered. It sways slightly as the barge rocks in the current. After several minutes, Janek pops to the surface, "It's ripping down there, man!" he says, panting, as tenders remove his helmet.

"There's no way you can move around down there," he says, puffing like a wrestler. "It felt like you had six invisible people pushing against you the whole time."

This is bad news. Divers will not be able to function, at least not near the surface. They'll have to lower the spreader assembly to saturation divers on the bottom who have been preparing to attach it to the turret. The big crane, with Bubby at the levers, picks the lifting device off the steel beam and begins letting it down.

In spite of his ordeal, Janek is pumped up. "The visibility is awesome! I could see the whole rig!"

John Broadwater almost does a cheer. "Step one done, man!" he says.

"Step one!" Janek replies. "Hoo yah!"

But step two, as well as quite a few others, may be even harder. Rick Cavey is drinking a cup of water. "It's bad," he says. "We've worked in these conditions before, but divers become pretty ineffective at two knots. It's one to two now." That being said, he nevertheless strides straight to the landing spot on deck and draws a large bull's-eye where he wants the turret to be set down. Workers have just finished clearing it off, using torches to burn away trash and metal junk.

The divers, as they are apt to be, are more optimistic than the archaeologists. When he sees what Janek went through, Johnston concludes that there is almost no chance this will be the day. It's hugely frustrating; Mother Nature tapping them on the shoulder and saying they're not going to do anything, not today and certainly not tomorrow. They can't fight it. Current like this comes up out here all the time and stays for days. Scholley is encouraged that at least Broadwater has not called a halt to the mission. At the same time, he is impressed that she is willing to try, and allows himself to hang on to that thread of hope.

Down at 240 feet, conditions are slightly better, at least for now. When Nelson drops down from the bell, the current isn't too bad, at least no worse than he's seen before.

The lifting frame, with all eight straps and shackles, is slowly lowered. It's Nelson's job to attach each of the shackles to the eyehooks on top of the Spider's legs. As it descends, the frame is at first only dimly visible. But as it comes into sight, all he can see is a big jumble of straps. In the short period since Janek cut them free, the current has turned the straps into spaghetti, an almost impossible tangle. The ends of the straps, with those heavy shackles attached, are flapping like ribbons on a maypole. Some are caught up in the spreader assembly. It was a mistake, the dive leaders realize, freeing the straps before lowering them. Now they'll have to untangle the mess on the bottom.

When Nelson puts his helmet camera on the mess, Cavey shakes his head. They'll have to remove the whole lift assembly from the water and see if it can be untangled on deck, he thinks, but that means somehow lowering it again without fouling the spreaders. He asks Nelson if he thinks he can untangle the straps on the bottom.

"Won't know until I try," replies the ever-optimistic Nelson.

Nelson has to climb up into the Spider's rigging, where the current is stronger, and then, clinging to the assembly with one hand, attempt to untangle the straps. He works at it for over two hours, laboriously untangling one strap and then another. Once or twice one of the big shackles, which he's slung over his shoulder, bangs against his chest. But he's not about to cry out in pain. The less they know about his aches and pains the better, he thinks. One of the 135-pound shackles slips out of his hands and tumbles to the bottom.

Down in the surface-supply van, Bobbie Scholley and Scott Heineman watch the monitors as they relay images from Nelson's camera. As Nelson climbs up one of the straps, his camera shows some of the other straps tangled in a huge knot. "Oh, man, Jesus Christ, that's a mess," mutters Heineman. "This is not going to happen. We're going to lose the whole thing."

But Nelson keeps working at it, untwisting the straps like a giant's string puzzle, one strap and then the next, grunting, talking to himself. His raspy breaths fill the sat shack. "You're fighting me all the way!" he scolds one of the straps.

Slowly, slowly, the knot unwinds, and Heineman crows with delight. "A little marlinspike seamanship at two hundred feet!" he says.

It's about 10:00 A.M. when Nelson gets the last strap untangled. This feat alone is a huge morale booster. People on board begin to think the lift just might happen. There is the slightest sparkle in people's eyes, a lightness in their steps.

But now begins an even more arduous job, hooking the shackles to the Spider: all eight of them, flapping and flying in the growing current. It entails guessing which ones go to which eyehook, swimming with them, sometimes inching along the crossbeams on the Spider to the corresponding location. At first they are dangling about twenty feet off the turret, so Nelson has to call up top to have the crane repositioned.

Up in the sat shack, a crowd has gathered. Master diver Bryon van Horn and dive officer Rusty Deen relay instructions from Rick Cavey. Manson Gulf's Gene Wells, known to everyone as Little G—not to be confused with Big G Clavelle—purrs into his headset to Bubby up in the crane. Sitting on a stool, his face a roadmap of apprehension, is John Broadwater. I've wedged in beside him, thankful that no one kicks me out. These are the archaeologist's times of crisis, and right now none of this looks good. "It's kind of scary," he allows.

What is gnawing at him is the prospect that Nelson will be able to hook up some of the straps, but then the weather will turn worse. If the weather sours, he'll have to go back and disconnect everything. It would be a disaster to have the big crane flying, unable to let go as a storm approaches and, down below, straps with heavy shackles whipping in the current. That's what the Manson crew meant when they warned that once the recovery started it would have to go all the way. It is not a good feeling to start down the road and not be able to get off.

But so far so good.

Nelson begins with the up-current eyehook, so that once he gets the strap and shackle secured they won't swing back and become tangled again. He has to walk the strap across the Spider's beam, fighting the current all the way. As he does so, the strap slackens until the shackle is dangling inside the turret. He picks up the shackle and, straddling the framework, crawls to the other side.

"Nelly," says Cavey, "if he swings the crane a little to the right, will that help you?" "Yeah," comes the reply.

As the strap slowly swings his way, Nelson keeps up a steady chatter. "Come on! Come on! Come on!" he urges the shackles. "Whenever Chief Nelson's in the water, there's another diver down there," explains Van Horn. "He's talking to his buddy."

All the while a barracuda is hanging out at Nelson's depth to escape the stronger current above, and now it seems to be hovering right at his shoulder. Nelson turns and points at the creature. "Are you looking at me?" he squawks in his Chipmunk voice. "You better get your ass out of here!" As the barracuda skulks off, the crowd in the shack above, so tense a moment before, erupts with laughter.

Now a new sound makes its way through the microphone in Nelson's helmet to the loudspeakers in the sat shack: when the first of eight shackles is slammed home around one of the Spider's eyehooks it makes a resounding *Clink!* Then Nelson wrestles the eight-inch pin into place.

"That's one," he rasps.

As he moves from shackle to shackle on the claw structure, Nelson realizes he's getting tired, but he's not letting on. He doesn't want to give up, and he damn sure doesn't want someone relieving him. Everybody had talked him up: he was the one who could do it; he was the workhorse who could manhandle the heavy shackles into place. This job, at least at this minute, is his or no one's.

By 10:45 A.M., five shackles are in place. Cavey begins announcing each one over the barge loudspeakers, and each time a cheer goes up.

"When we get all eight, we'll be ready to lift," says a tentatively smiling Broadwater.

"All stations, all stations, six shackles!" Cavey announces.

Now the crane has to move again.

"All right, Bubby," Little G says, "I want you to come down on three."

"Fast or slow?" the crane operator asks.

"Fast is good. Hold it up. That's it!"

Nelson snaps number seven in place. Again the announcement and again the cheers.

In all the confusion of the straps, Nelson realizes he has hooked the wrong one to one of the eyehooks. He takes a couple of deep breaths and unshackles it. By this time the current has picked up quite a bit, and when the shackle unsnaps, it seems to explode from the violence of the current, flying off and striking him on the shoulder. The force of the water drags him across the top of the turret, slamming him into the struts as he goes. He locks his legs around one of the beams, crawls back to the corner where he needs to go, and now can't reach the eyehook. He has the shackle in one hand and the pin in the other, with the strap and current and umbilical holding him back. He drops the pin into the turret and has to scramble down and retrieve it. Minutes later, pin back in hand, Nelson finally gets the shackle to succumb.

There's just one more to go.

The eighth shackle proves the hardest of all. "Swing left just a little bit," Little G calls up to Bubby. "Quick! Quick! Quick!"

Cavey says, "Come up a little bit, swing left, and come back down." Nelson leaps up and grabs the shackle.

"He's got it," someone else yells.

"OK, stand by," says Cavey.

"Boom it up easy," Little G says.

At that moment Broadwater's cell phone chirps. It's one of his bosses at NOAA. "We're getting hooked up," Broadwater says. "I think we're going to make it."

There's a long pause as Nelson struggles with the shackle. It's crowded in the shack, some people standing sideways to take up less space. "Maybe we should order pizza," Broadwater says. "Maybe we should all leave so we can make room for the media," says Rusty Deen.

Suddenly there's a familiar sound down below, another clink. "That's it!" Nelson squawks.

"All stations, all stations, all eight shackles are on the Spider!" Cavey announces.

It's 11:15 A.M. The roar that goes up this time is full of joy. It has taken Nelson two hours and forty-five minutes to untangle the straps and secure the shackles.

Nelson's performance will be remembered, as will his nonstop chatter. "He used all seven of the words you can't say on TV in one sentence," Cavey marvels to Scholley when the two meet again near the dive station.

Up until the moment when the last shackle clinked into place, it was not clear that the turret would be coming up. Now everyone knows it's a go. The moment of truth has arrived—for the turret, for the Navy, for history, for all of their careers.

NELSON PROMISED his wife he wouldn't be in the water when the turret came off the bottom. When two hundred or more tons of iron and steel begins to move, even underwater, there's no stopping it, and he does not want to be anywhere near. But he is there, fascinated, watching. He can tell, however, by the direction of the current, and by the way the straps tend when tension is applied, which way the massive plumb bob will move. He climbs up onto the *Monitor*'s armor belt, where he can get a good look—and can jump if he has to.

Up top, the mood is cautiously optimistic. "John," Bobbie Scholley says to Broadwater, "do we have permission to lift?"

Broadwater, who has been waiting—and dreading—this moment for ten years, doesn't hesitate. It's on his shoulders. Failure would be more than a national misfortune, and a very public one at that. It would be a personal disgrace.

"Let's go," he says.

TWENTY-ONE

INTO THE ABYSS

THE ACTIONS of the men in the engine room were nothing short of heroic. They knew their ship was going down. They also knew that the longer they could keep the boilers going, the better chance their shipmates had of surviving. The last bit of engine power was going to the pumps. They watched as the ash pits slowly filled with water and the blowers that produced the draft began to spit water.

"At midnight the water reached our fires and extinguished them," engineer Joseph Watters related; "all hopes of saving her was then given up." Still, he and Robinson Hands, second assistant engineer, remained at their posts in the engine room "until driven out by the gas and flames." It is hard to believe that anyone was still in that room. The seawater hitting the fire grates could have caused an explosion of scalding water and steam. But there they remained, almost to the last.

And then there was only one way out, through the berth deck, up the stairs and through the hatch, up the ladder to the top of the turret, then down again to the chaos of the pounding sea and the rolling, pitching deck. George Geer scrambled to the top of the turret and found fellow crew were abandoning ship. One lifeboat was already gone. A second was taking on survivors. A third was approaching. "I can tell you," he would relate to his brother, "it looked rather serious to attempt to get in the boat but I knew I might as well be drowned trying to reach the boat as to go down in the *Monitor*, so I jumped off the tower and made for the boat. A wave struck me and washed me across the deck, I caught a ridge rope, but somebody side of me was swept overboard and drowned. I started again as soon as the wave had passed over and this time reached the boat and was saved."

Watters crawled up through the turret, let himself down to the deck, and succeeded in getting in one of the boats just as it was shoving off. He had served on the *Monitor* just two days.

Francis Butts was next. He occupied the turret all alone, passing buckets from below to men on top. "As I raised my last bucket to the upper hatchway no one was there to take it. I scrambled up the ladder and found that we below had been deserted." Butts shouted to those in the berth deck to forget about bailing.

Butts wanted no part of a sinking ship. He made a line fast to one of the turret stanchions and let himself down. The moment he landed, a wave swept him across the deck, and the only thing that kept him from going over was a brace on top of the smokestack. He hung on as the wave tried to suck him into the sea, leaving him dangling as it rushed by. He dropped to the deck and grabbed a lifeline just as another wave broke, lifting him feet upward but still clinging. As the wave receded, he made a run for the lifeboat. "Now or lost," he told himself as he jumped on board.

Still, a handful of men watched from the top of the tower. After seeing waves crash across the deck and carry sailors to their deaths, after seeing men like Keeler and Geer and Butts nearly lose their lives, it is no wonder they were terrified. It's doubtful that many of them could swim. Bankhead, who had been holding the painter to the last rescue boat while oarsmen frantically fought to keep it from smashing into the ship's iron sides, shouted to them to get in the boat, but they seemed "stupefied by fear," he concluded, and wouldn't or couldn't move. It could have meant death either way, but the place they clung to might have postponed that sentence a little longer.

The author of the account in the *New York Herald*, who clearly interviewed survivors, mentions "six or eight" men still clinging to the top of the turret. "They were told to come down and try to reach the boat, but neither the entreaties of their comrades nor the orders of their officers had any effect on them. The poor fellows had seen their comrades one by one washed over and drowned in the attempt to

John P. Bankhead, captain of the *Monitor*. (Mariners' Museum)

reach the boats; and believing that there was no chance of being saved, even if they reached the boat, they preferred to remain there and linger a few moments more than to come down and meet certain death."

Commander Bankhead was not keen on sharing their fate. He made a dash to his cabin for his coat and his jewel box, then headed for the last rescue boat. As he was about to get in, Richard Anjier, an English-born quartermaster who had enlisted in New York, clambered

The *Monitor* lost in a storm off Cape Hatteras. (Mariners' Museum)

down from the wheel. When Bankhead ordered him to get in the boat, Anjier replied, "No, sir; not till you go." Both men got on board.

"Feeling that I had done everything in my power to save the vessel and crew," Bankhead said, "I jumped into the already deeply laden boat and left the *Monitor*, whose heavy, sluggish motion gave evidence that she could float but a short time longer."

But were there still men waiting on deck to get into a boat? Butts claimed that as soon as Bankhead took his place on board, Lieutenant Dana Greene yelled, "Cut the painter! Cut the painter!"

A later newspaper story in the *Herald* on January 13—written from the perspective of Rodney Browne, skipper of the second lifeboat—says that about twelve officers and men got into his boat while "those on board the *Monitor* held on to her" and that Browne "was obliged to cut adrift in order to save those he already had taken on board."

It is true that several survivors remembered these events differently. They agreed that their captain did all he could to save his men before getting in the boat. Bankhead, Weeks declared, "begged them to come down," but the men seemed "paralyzed by fear." It is also true that a lifeboat already filled beyond capacity simply cannot take on more passengers. But this account seems to indicate that there were more than just scared men who refused to leave the turret, but others who held on to the last boat while it filled up and were left behind.

The lifeboat got away, but the rescued and rescuers were a long way from safety. They now had the daunting task of reaching the still-powerless *Rhode Island,* which by now had drifted some two miles off. When the little boat reached the ship, it crashed again and again against its wooden sides. The boat would rise on a swell as the *Rhode Island* fell into its trough, making a leap from one to the other treacherous. From bow to stern of the towering ship, this dance continued. Butts and ensign Norman Attwater caught a pair of ropes and leaped for the rail, only to miss it and hang dangling in midair. No one seemed to notice. While they were suspended above the waves, Attwater lost his grip. "Oh God," he cried out and fell into the waves. He never rose to the surface.

Butts lost his grip too, but instead of falling into the sea, he crashed back into the lifeboat, startling the other passengers. At last he wriggled inside the loop of a rescue line and was pulled to safety.

Rodney Browne wasn't done. He had promised those left behind that he would return. But his oarsmen were exhausted, and seven of the fourteen men had clambered back on board the *Rhode Island.* Would those remaining make one more pull for the sinking vessel? If you're going, we're with you, they said, and off they went. Trenchard ordered him to stop. The *Rhode Island*'s paddle wheel was working again, and his plan was, as soon as the lifeboats were clear, to steam over to where the *Monitor* was last seen. But Browne either misunderstood this order, didn't hear it in the howling storm, or simply disobeyed. The distance had grown and the seas were dangerously choppy, but Browne was going to get there if he could.

Grenville Weeks, by now minus several fingers on his damaged hand, stood at the rail with others and stared out into the night, barely able to pick out the red lantern on the *Monitor*'s mast. "A hundred times we thought it was gone forever, —a hundred times it reappeared."

From the rail of the *Rhode Island,* the *Monitor*'s light seemed to sparkle as choppy waves momentarily blocked it from view. But then, just before 2:00 A.M., as the moon dipped below the clouds, the light disappeared.

Louis Stodder, who had survived the ordeal of cutting the hawser, lamented that suddenly "she sank and we saw her no more."

Browne also saw the flickering light, but with wind and sea against it, the lifeboat made little progress. He was within a quarter mile of the light when he saw it gradually settle in the water and disappear. When he reached the spot where the *Monitor* had gone down, all Browne could see was an eddy, the last trace of the little ship. He remained near the spot in case any survivors were in the water. "We pulled around, as near as we could estimate, the place where we supposed she had sunk but no sign of anyone could we find although one of my crew was positive he heard someone call." It was probably the howling wind.

A light rain was falling as they started back. But their long night was far from over. Now that the *Monitor*'s lights had vanished, those on the *Rhode Island* could no longer see where the rescuers were, frantically search though they might. "We had looked, most anxiously for the whale boat," Weeks related, but they saw no sign of it. "We knew it had reached the *Monitor,* but whether swamped by the waves or drawn in as the *Monitor* went down, we could not tell." The *Rhode Island* hoisted its boats and steamed off looking for them—but in the wrong direction.

Browne was aghast. "We started for the *Rhode Island,* but before long we found that she was steaming away from us, throwing up rockets and burning blue lights—leaving us behind."

The paddle wheeler spent the night and much of the next day looking for Browne and his crew, as well as survivors from the *Monitor,* but they found no one. Finally they gave up and headed for Beaufort.

Cold, wet, and desperately sore, their hands blistered and bleeding, Browne and his men rowed through the night against the still raging sea, heading northwest in a constant battle to keep from being shoved out of the shipping lanes by the Gulf Stream. They made a drag of the mast to keep the boat's head into the waves, praying that daylight would give them a chance. By dawn's light they spotted something unusual, a small black boat rising and falling in the seas, with a handful of men on board, then they lost sight of the vessel as they continued their fight for survival.

By midmorning they saw a schooner to leeward, sailing close-hauled, and rowed frantically toward her. They stretched their coats between boathooks and oars to act as sails for added power. The schooner, *A. Colby*, out of Bucksport, Maine, was on her way to Fernandina, Florida, with a load of bricks for an army installation that had passed from Confederate to Union hands the previous March. At last Browne and his crew were safe.

THE *MONITOR*'s last roll may have been sudden and violent. Seawater gushing into the turret quickly filled the engine room space where all the heavy machinery lay, causing the ship to dive stern-first toward the bottom. Then the heavy armor and turret on top heeled the ship to starboard as she fell into the dark abyss. A chest of silver-plated dinnerware, a copper teakettle, lamp chimneys, and a container of spare parts tumbled through the deck hatch into the turret. Other unsecured items floated toward the aft portions of the hull.

The now-upside-down ship struck the hard, sandy bottom stern first. The blow probably dislodged the turret and sent it crashing to the seabed; then the *Monitor*'s deck settled on top of the cylinder, leaving a portion exposed. The ship was still heavily loaded with coal, and apparently one of its coal scuttles, a circular hatch, ended up just above the turret and, either then or soon after, dropped several tons of coal on top of the guns and whoever was in that space. Silt later completed the job of turning the turret into a tomb.

TWENTY-TWO

WE *CANNOT* FAIL

A T 1:00 P.M. on Monday on board the *Wotan*, the drum on the big red crane begins to whine, and gently, ever so gently, the turret rises off the bottom, creating suction as it does and generating a cloud of silt that completely shrouds it. "The bird's in the air," Cavey announces.

But there is no celebration yet. Visibility is near zero. The turret looks like a giant tea bag. It bobs a little, then settles down as it makes the barge list. From where he's standing on the wreck, Keith Nelson can tell which way the cloud of silt is moving, but he can't see whether the turret's top has held. Neither can the anxious topside viewers, no matter how hard they squint at the monitors. "God, let the roof hold," Johnston keeps saying to himself.

There's an agonizing pause while the current carries the silt cloud away. And then they know. "The roof is intact!" Nelson rasps from the bottom of the sea.

Up above, among those glued to the video monitors, there's a surge of relief. But one last crucial step remains. Nelson, near exhaustion after his seven-hour aerobic workout, must now follow the turret as it swings over to the lifting platform and secure it to the platform.

This is engineer Jim Kelly's moment of truth. He had fought for the way the turret and platform would be joined—and feared he might lose his job over it. The Spider is equipped with two stabbing guides, one on each side, that have to be lined up with bell-like receptors on

206

the platform and lowered precisely onto them. Then shackles have to be hooked up. But now the turret, all 220 tons of it, begins bouncing up and down as swells jostle the barge.

Kelly had assured Broadwater that once the first stabbing guide was set, a diver would be able to rotate the turret until the other guide lined up. That was hard to believe at first—an individual diver man-handling something that heavy. But it could be done as long as the turret wasn't moving in the opposite direction. Then, no one could stop it.

Kelly also assured Broadwater that once the platform and the Spi-der were mated the turret was home free, that it would not only land on deck but make it all the way to the Mariners' Museum. But not without this last step, and Mother Nature is having her say.

Broadwater watches in agony as the turret plunges downward and misses the stabbing guide. What he fears now is that the turret, bounc-ing wildly, will descend again and the sharp guide will stab through the roof and damage the cannons or the other precious contents. Or it could miss and bend the stabbing guide, making it impossible for the guide and receptor to mate. Broadwater looks at Cavey. Cavey knows the archaeologist wants to step in and stop the operation. But Cavey has already calculated that if they missed the first time, the turret would move away from the guide and swing clear of it. Broadwater resists the urge to interfere; the turret does clear the guide. And Cavey thinks, "He trusts me; this is going to work."

Nelson watches as the turret bounces up and down, six to eight feet each time, actually striking the ocean bottom a couple of times. Each time it rises, suction tugs at him, threatening to pull him and his life-sustaining umbilical underneath. What if he is sucked under and can't get out when the turret comes down again? It would crush him.

Broadwater watches the bouncing too. Each time the turret de-scends, several multiples of weight, like the g-force of gravity, are ex-erted on the vulnerable roof of the turret. There are about eighty tons of cannons, gun carriages, coal, and silt inside. As the turret falls and then stops its plunge, the contents want to keep going. This is torture, watching and waiting and feeling helpless. Once the turret is picked up, it has to be set down. It can't be left dangling in the water. And of course, after landing on the lifting platform, it still has to be raised up to the barge.

At one point Nelson's umbilical becomes wrapped around the large stabbing guide. He untangles it, then manages to wrestle the guide over the receptor just as the turret comes down, and they mate. One of the guides is now on, and the only thing left to do is get the other in place. But he can't see anything and is still afraid of being squashed. He gets down on all fours and tries to crawl over to the other side. Then a big swell on the surface rocks the barge, and the turret rises again, pulling the stabbing guide out of its receptor.

Topside, everyone groans. They'll have to put another diver in the water, they decide, this time a sprint diver.

Nelson isn't happy. He has almost single-handedly hooked up the turret and guided it onto the platform. He has been in the water something like six hours and fifty minutes, without so much as a sip of water or a morsel of food. But he wants to complete this, to swing over to the other side and secure the other stabbing guide.

Bryon Van Horn, supervising the operation in the sat shack, thinks it is too dangerous for Nelson to try this by himself and tells him they are going to send a sprint diver down to help. "Your job is to watch your side and make sure it stays in place," he tells the protesting Nelson.

"Master diver," Cavey calls out to Jim Mariano, "how long will it take you to hat your divers? "Fifteen minutes," comes the reply.

Mariano turns to his divers and tenders. "Mount up!" he barks.

Chief petty officer Brad Flemming is sitting at the dive station when the call comes. He's the red diver. Next to him, at the green diver station, sits chief petty officer Ken Riendeau, also one of the most experienced surface-supply divers on the barge. After their dive brief, Flemming glances over at Riendeau.

"No matter how bad the current is, Kenny, we've got to do this," Flemming says. "On descent, don't say anything; just roll with it."

Riendeau nods.

The minute the stage begins its descent through the water column, the divers know it's going to be rough. It looks like a blizzard, with sediment and sand blowing horizontally. Normally, visibility is about one hundred feet—as it was just hours ago—but now it's about five feet, and distorted because of the sediment. Usually there are patches where the sediment acts this way, but this murkiness is uniform from the time they leave the surface until they reach the bottom. It is the strongest current Flemming has ever been in. He tells himself, "Concentrate on what you have to do; there's so little time that you have to do everything right the first time."

But nothing goes right. When he jumps off the platform at the bottom, Flemming gets only about five feet. The current is so strong that the heavy, thick coil of hoses is shoved against the stage and can't be pulled off. Riendeau has to free it and feed it to him. Now clear, the lifeline snakes over to the turret, where it immediately wraps itself around one of the stanchions on top of the turret like a figure eight. This is not good.

Everyone in the control shacks on deck is watching. It is very bad to have your lifelines exposed like that. Because of the rocking motion on the surface, the 200-plus-ton turret is heaving up and down, threatening to crush the umbilical as a truck tire would flatten a snake. Diver safety, they all know well, is the most important part of this mission, and this is ominous.

As he steps off the stage a second time, Flemming is like a kite in the wind. "Got to get down," he thinks, positioning himself head-down at an angle, like a sail, so the current can push him to the bottom. One of the four tires that was attached to the lifting platform—to cushion the turret when it came down—has blown over to where he lands. He grabs it and holds on. Then, keeping as low as he can, he crawls on his stomach to the turret. He can't help thinking how weird this is. The divers normally don't wear flippers. They wear boots and run. Here he is in full dive gear, crawling across the bottom. He can see Nelson but can't talk with him directly, and he can see that the long stabbing guide is again in its receptor. Meanwhile, Riendeau watches from the stage. Because the ROV is out of commission, his job is to train his helmet camera on the scene.

Flemming reaches the turret, pulling himself hand over hand by his umbilical, then grabs the stanchion. The only way he can work to free the umbilical is to turn upside down and ride with the bouncing turret. He gets it free, but when he lands now he is under the turret, moving fast to get away as it comes down. "Oh, my God," he keeps thinking.

He can hear the topside voices. "What's going on?" they keep asking. He only has thirty minutes—forty maximum—to get the job done, and they are already worried.

Flemming grabs a line attached to the turret, expecting to use it to manipulate the turret until the guides are lined up, but as the turret bounces up and down, it frays the line and finally saws it in half. "Great," he thinks. "Now what?"

Scott Heineman, who is on communications, calls down to him. "Brad, there's another tending line, nine o'clock position. See if you can get over there."

Flemming edges around the turret and spots a yellow propylene line suspended from the upside-down bottom—the current top—of the turret, going up and down like a snake in a whirlpool. He times his jump as the massive turret comes down and grabs the line, then rides it up and down like a yo-yo.

Above, the people crowded into the surface-supply shack watch with their mouths open. The current is so bad, they realize, that bubbles from Flemming's mask are streaming out horizontally. Now there's a new problem. The up-and-down motion of the turret is creating suction and producing a cloud of silt that obscures everyone's vision.

Flemming hangs on.

The whole time he's thinking, This has to be done. We cannot fail on this dive. We cannot leave this site without coming back with the turret. It would be not only a failed mission for all the guys who have been out here, but a failed mission for MDSU TWO, a failed mission for Bobbie Scholley, a failed mission for Rick Cavey. And Navy divers around the world would look at it and think, *those MDSU guys.* . . .

As the turret falls again, Flemming drops to the bottom just in time to have the stabbing guide punch him in the ribs. He takes it stoically, unwilling to let topside know he is hurt. As the turret bounces, it keeps slipping out of the one long stabbing guide.

Everyone in the shack groans. They can see it come out like an arrow. Broadwater looks down, barely able to watch.

But suddenly the wild bouncing pauses, and Flemming knows this is the opportunity everyone has been waiting for. Nelson has the large stabbing guide back in the receptor, and it's Flemming's turn to rotate the turret and get the other one lined up.

How am I going to do this, he wonders. I'm 180 pounds and the turret is 200-plus tons. I can't possibly budge this thing. But they are telling me I can, so I'll give it the old college try, dig in my heels if I can, and shove.

The stabbing-guide receptor on the Spider is flared out from the center like a bell, so if the stabbing guide, a long shaft attached to the platform, hits the bell at any point, the flare will guide the shaft into the receptor and the guide will then lock in place. The guide comes down right on the edge of the bell, gouging the steel but not quite engaging.

"Listen, all we have to do is come up just enough so it will move over," Flemming says, puffing from the exertion, staring at the guide so the people up there can see through his camera what he is seeing. He figures there's so much pressure on the inboard side that if the turret is raised slightly and he can shove it just a fraction of an inch, it will rotate itself in.

He says this several times, remembering all the training he's had as a dive supervisor. Listen to your divers; they're your eyes on the bottom. But all he hears from above is, in effect, "We're talking about it."

"They're not listening to me," he thinks.

While Heineman is handling communications with the divers, Jim Mariano is running the dive, and he knows he is pushing Flemming and Riendeau to the edge, and maybe beyond the edge. There's only about sixty seconds of bottom time left. "Come on, come on," he keeps urging.

Up in the tower, Jim Kelly hears all the conversations and knows Flemming is right. "Raise the turret," he pleads, "and it'll move over. He knows he can do it! He knows he can do it!" Yes, a 180-pound diver can move a 220-ton turret in the water, as long as it isn't already moving the opposite way.

At last Flemming hears the call from above: "They're coming up with the turret. Keep his camera on it."

As it rises, as the point of the guide clears the lip of the bell, and as Flemming shoves with all his might, the guide moves inside the flared edge.

"Down! Down! Down!" Flemming yells.

"Down! Down! Down!" Mariano and Cavey and Broadwater and Johnston and Scholley echo. There is a delay, but only a slight one. The crane operator can't see the monitors and has to wait for the call. But he seems to anticipate it and works the levers. The turret drops and seals right in the guides.

It gets quiet in the dive shack, a quiet you can feel, and then they all start shouting. There's no longer any doubt: the turret is coming up.

Up in the tower, master chief Larry Fahey grins at Jim Kelly. "Now you have a line for your obituary."

Down in the dive shack, watching the monitors, Johnston can feel a wave of relief wash over him. "We're getting this sucker today!" he says to himself.

Scott Heineman calls to Flemming: "Red Diver, get back to the stage! Good job, Brad. Awesome."

Flemming looks at Nelson and gives him a salute. Nelson acknowledges with a thumbs-up. Flemming climbs to the top of the Spider, grabs his umbilical, and upside down, hand over hand, pulls himself back. Exhausted, he lets the current push him onto the stage, where he sits as it rises off the bottom.

Scholley, by now wearing a huge grin, gets on the comms and speaks to the divers below. They ask how she's doing. "I'm doing way, way better now," she says, as relieved as she's ever been in her life. "You guys are all right. It's because of you guys I'm going to sleep pretty good tonight. You know that, don't you? Super, super job."

Cavey is grinning, but still shaking his head. "I hope I never see a dive like that again."

THERE IS one more critical underwater job to perform. Steve Hall, a diving medical technician who was in the saturation bell with Nelson, is called over to secure the Spider to the platform with a series of shackles. Now the whole assembly—lifting frame, Spider, turret, and platform—can rise as one.

The last pair of divers drop down to inspect the rigging, making sure everything is in place. There's a long delay as they go through decompression. It would not be safe to raise the turret while divers are in the water or in the recompression chamber. The chamber is next to the dive platform, where it could be crushed by a lethally heavy swinging turret. Normally the divers attach control straps to whatever they're retrieving, but only gravity can control this giant wrecking ball.

At last, the drum on the crane spins as the prize comes off the bottom and rises partway up the water column. There is a long pause as adjustments are made to the lifting apparatus, then the final stage of the lift begins.

An entourage of vessels carrying the media and dignitaries begins arriving, and Navy and television helicopters clatter in the clear afternoon sky. A loggerhead turtle breaks the surface, as though curious about all the commotion, looks around, and dives.

At least a hundred sailors, mostly shirtless, watch from the top of the saturation station two stories above the deck. Everyone else, it seems, crowds onto the dive station. Broadwater gets on the satellite phone with his bosses at NOAA. "We're still keeping our fingers crossed," he says. "There's a little bit of sea movement out here, which means that it's going to take some real skill by the crane operator to set it down gently, but we have a lot of confidence in him, and we think it'll be safely on deck very shortly." He hangs up and then says, to no one in particular, "I'm starting to let myself get a little bit happy here."

The first things to emerge are the Union flag that had been placed on top of the lifting frame, the black lifting straps, and the top of the Spider. And then the turret, orange with rust, encrusted with sea life, full of water, coal, big guns, and fourteen decades of history, rises from the depths.

Again there is silence. The added weight as the turret moves from buoyant sea to thin air causes a few to hold their breath. Then a cheer that can probably be heard all the way to Hampton Roads erupts from the divers and archaeologists, engineers and barge crew. Big Navy divers hug scientists and almost knock them over with high fives. Bobbie Scholley and John Broadwater almost dance for joy, hugging, whooping, and shouting, the pressure of all those days suddenly gone.

Broadwater raises both arms in a victory salute.

Scholley shouts to her divers. "For a bunch of pretty tough Navy divers, there's an awful lot of cheering and hugging going on here," she declares, fighting back tears.

Inside the sat chamber, Chris Murray, still decompressing, first sees the turret on the monitor in the chamber, courtesy of network television, then cranes around to look through the window and see it swinging over to the deck.

As it does, everyone—scientists, divers, and journalists—scrambles for the stairs to the weather deck, knowing that if the barge starts rocking, the turret could wreck the barge and everything on it. But the sea continues to cooperate and keeps the rocking to a minimum, and that huge hunk of history, still gushing water, sails through the afternoon sky fourteen decades after it went down, and lands on deck.

A new round of celebrations begins. Johnston, whose long-gone ancestor was a gunner on the *Virginia,* reaches up to the turret and lovingly places his hand in every dent he can find. "I think this is the most beautiful piece of rust I've seen in my whole life," he says with a lopsided grin. "I can tell you that, no matter where he is, John Ericsson is smiling today."

Rick Cavey strides up to Bobbie Scholley. "Ma'am," he says, "I'd like to present you the *Monitor* turret." She turns to John Broadwater and repeats the line. "John, I'd like to present *you* the *Monitor* turret."

Broadwater can't stop grinning. "It's hard to even put into words," he beams. "I've been looking forward to this for a long time. But here it is. It's in good shape, and we're going to be able to take it back and share it with future generations. This is the ultimate icon of Civil War naval history. This is the ultimate prize."

The prize easily could have slipped away and again been relegated to the bottom. That Navy salvage divers and underwater archaeologists were able to modify their agendas just enough to compromise; that a museum had the vision to bring the pieces home; that an engineering firm and an oil rig company were able to figure out how to make it work; that the money had lasted long enough; and that the weather, however grudgingly, had cooperated is something of a miracle.

The next morning, the leading edge of the approaching storm begins to be felt. Divers drop down to clean up and remove tools and missed artifacts, but conditions below have deteriorated so much that even the strongest are overpowered by the current. Scott Heineman feels as though he's in a white-out, with current so strong that he's quickly exhausted. He has to drag himself along the bottom with his knife.

He retrieves several tools and places them in a basket that is supposed to be lifted to the surface, but he can't find the hook or strap being lowered to him. "Is this going to clock me in the head?" he wonders. This struggle goes on for twenty minutes until he's forced to give up. And now, as he pulls himself to the stage by his umbilical he feels a stab of panic. Unable to take in the oxygen his huge body demands, he's been overbreathing. Feeling closed in, almost claustrophobic, Heineman props himself up on the stage and keeps telling himself to get a grip, to control his breathing, until he finally recovers.

All he's been able to accomplish on the dive, he realizes, is to survive. They will have to leave the tools and lift baskets for another day.

The crew didn't celebrate Monday night. Everyone was exhausted, and besides, Chris Murray was still in the saturation chamber. Tuesday afternoon, as they gather on the helicopter deck to celebrate, the rain begins, and they have to crowd into the galley. They pass out special *Monitor* mission coins. Scholley had ordered them and personally taken them to the bottom, placed them on the turret at 240 feet, then hauled them back on deck and kept them just for this moment. There are toasts and hugs and cheers.

That night, as they attempt to get under way, the tug's propeller gets fouled in the towline and divers have to free it, even as the storm bears down on them. As they cast off one of the anchors, the force of the sea swings the barge around, but the tug brings it into the weather. Waves crash over the sides. It's a fitting end, the turret under tow, in nasty weather, heading back to the place it left all those years ago.

There's one more chore for the archaeologists—to check the condition of the lower part of the skeleton that remains trapped under coal and silt in the turret. When the weather lets up briefly, they zip on their coveralls, gather up picks and trowels, and clamber down through the hatch. They soon realize that when tons of water gushed out of the turret as it rose from the ocean, the contents shifted slightly. Wayne Lusardi, archaeological conservator for the Mariners' Museum, can't believe what he sees.

There's a tibia, or shinbone, angling away from the other bones in a way that suggests a severe break. But when he chips around it, he realizes it's not a broken bone at all but one that is connected to others. There's a rush of excitement as the possibility of this new discovery begins to sink in. Everyone on the team is involved now, on their knees in the muck, chipping around the bones hour after hour. Divers who had been watching from the turret rim begin passing down supplies and water and rigging up lights. Now they are the watchers and the archaeologists are the diggers.

Perpendicular to the leg they find a well-preserved two-bladed pocketknife, four inches long, with brass endcaps and the remains of a wooden panel inlay, lying where it might have rested in a front pocket. Nearby, cemented together in a clump, are a brass key, two copper pennies, and hard rubber buttons. Also possible pocket contents, they agree.

It slowly dawns on them that what they have found is a second complete set of remains, just as intact as the first. Apparently, in the tumult and chaos inside the sinking ship, the second sailor came to rest with his legs bent over the hips of the other. His head and torso are lying flat on the iron grate that served as a roof, and the skull, vertebrae, ribs, and collarbones are stained a deep iron red, almost as though they were part of the turret. The sailor's iron-saturated bones, when they are finally removed, are heavier than those of the companion whose fate he shared.

Lusardi can't help but wonder what else they might find down in the black sediment of the turret. The archaeologists decide to postpone further excavation of the skeletons until the turret can be deposited on land.

Two days later, the barge and all its company clear the Virginia capes. This is a very different cast of characters than the intrepid but wary sailors who, standing on the same turret 140 years before, passed this way, took a bearing on the lighthouse, and stood out to sea. Or that time before, when guns bellowed in the distance and the hot blood of revenge coursed through their veins. But these sailors—a new breed that dwells beneath the waves—have inherited the legacy the *Monitor* passed down, and they all feel it.

This time, as they pass Fort Monroe, modern soldiers let off a twenty-one-gun salute. The divers and archaeologists are close enough to the fort that they can feel the concussions. They get goose bumps as they pass over the scene of the great battle. Crowds gather—as they did on a March day once before—but this time to cheer, at long last, a homecoming.

TWENTY-THREE

PROUD PAPA

THERE IS much pomp and ceremony as the turret-laden barge enters Hampton Roads. Navy and NOAA ships come alongside as escorts. Fireboats send geysers of water into the air as they make their way past the site where the ironclads fought. The divers man the rails, their faces all "sunglasses and smiles," as one reporter puts it. A bugler plays taps. And then, in a two-stage process that includes transferring the turret to a smaller barge, one of the best-known icons of naval history arrives on the shore of the James River and the grounds of the Mariners' Museum. The turret, along with its clinging Spider, is swung lazily onto an eighty-eight-wheel transport, and an honor guard of Civil War reenactors leads the way. A parade of dignitaries and guests follow as the turret moves along the wooded pathway to its new home. Lifting frame and all, it is lowered into the fourteen-foot-high, thirty-two-foot-wide octagonal tank that has been prepared for it, and a sprinkler system is turned on to keep it wet.

Curtiss Peterson watches the arrival of the turret with elation and dread. He has lived through this long process, visited the wreck site as often as many of the others, planned for the arrival, and offered his advice about the turret's safe homecoming. As chief conservator of the museum, this lanky, mustachioed man with a passion for preserving the past now has the responsibility for the care and restoration of the turret, as well as a growing cache of artifacts. "Now it's my problem, and that's pretty terrifying," Peterson says shortly after the turret's arrival. "Iron things left unmaintained turn out to be not iron things for long."

Left at the bottom of the ocean, the turret would have continued to deteriorate, but slowly and gracefully. Once exposed to sunlight and dry air, salt crystals buried in the metal would begin to explode, causing the iron to disintegrate rapidly. Stabilizing the huge artifact will be a phenomenal job. After archaeologists finish sifting through the coal and silt, after the big guns and the gun carriages are removed, the 180 iron plates that were bolted together all those years ago will have to be peeled apart like the layers of an onion. Corrosion from hundreds of bolts has surely spread into the iron sheets. The sheets will have to be preserved separately—bathed for years in an electrolytic bath that leaches out salt crystals—and then reassembled. It will likely take fifteen years. Peterson, sixty-one years old, says he might well be "pushin' up daisies" or "gone fishin' " or "canoe-paddlin' " long before the project is complete.

He is now managing what has suddenly become one of the largest archaeological conservation facilities in the world. There are dozens of *Monitor* parts from previous recoveries, among them the propeller and the engine, all resting in a kind of vast tank farm. Among the nearly one thousand artifacts is Peterson's favorite: a large brass engine register, an instrument that counted the number of revolutions made by the propeller shaft so that engineers would know when it was time for maintenance. The reading shows the engine stopped after 749,088 revolutions. (Perhaps it was reset after the last maintenance, Peterson suggests.) It is exciting that during the early stages of conservation, the word *Monitor* emerged on the face of the register as well as the date: 1862.

Peterson is confident that he and the other conservators at the museum are going to live and breathe, eat and sleep with the artifacts for years to come. "One of the characteristics of this old iron is it's sharp. We'll be using chemicals on it that'll burn you. We're going to be burned, we're going to be cut, and we're going to become intimately familiar with it."

Meanwhile, John Broadwater, Jeff Johnston, and a crew of other museum and NOAA staff members don coveralls and knee pads and descend ladders into what is to be their iron workspace for the next several months. It is damp and cold in there, with the smell of rust, coal, and decaying sea life. Down in the muck one day, his face smeared with coal, Broadwater can't suppress a laugh. His Kentucky friends have been kidding him. "I managed to get an education and avoid the coal mines," he laments, "but now my past has caught up with me."

The turret has become a rich archaeological dig. Every ounce of silt and coal and shell is placed in a bucket, then sent to a crew that sifts through it all. It is dirty, cold, and wet—but fascinating. I get to climb down into the turret that day and observe. Because of the sprinkler that keeps the turret wet, there is always the sound of trickling water, as though we're in a deep cave. Johnston invites me to get down on my knees in the muck and look up at the letters that were engraved on one of the guns when the ship was being repaired in Washington. "We all spend a lot of time on our heads, just looking at it," he says. He points to the largest of the dents made during the battle in Hampton Roads, probably the one that knocked one of the gunners senseless. It's one thing to read about such events in history books, he reflects, but quite another to touch it.

ON A breezy September morning two years later, after all the muck has been cleared and the gun carriages removed, shipyard workers sling padded straps under both of the 17,000-pound Dahlgren cannons. Then, with lots of easy-does-it advice from anxious crew leaders, the Coke-bottle-shaped guns are raised out of the turret and settled into individual tanks. The cast-iron guns had gone soft during their long stay underwater, so the operation is as gentle as a hospital delivery. "I feel like a proud papa," Broadwater beams.

For the first time in all those years, John Ericsson's turret is empty, but it is not hard to imagine the commotion that must have filled that space: twenty members of the gun crew and their officers, firing those guns and gasping the first time a cannonball crashed against their armor, choking in the smoke-filled, stifling enclosure, shouting and answering orders, turning toward an unseen enemy. And then, nine months later, fighting for their lives as their iron coffin slipped beneath the waves.

TWENTY-FOUR

PROUD MAMA

JUNE 29, 2005, was a stormy day, not unlike many experienced off Cape Hatteras. In the crowded equipment building at MDSU TWO at Little Creek Naval Amphibious Base in Norfolk, in the presence of shipmates, family and friends, Captain Bobbie Scholley ended her naval career. There were dozens of officers and divers with whom she had served, but now the most important members of the audience were her two adopted daughters, Sarah and Hannah. She and Frank had flown to China in December and brought the twin sisters to their new home.

Behind where she stood on a temporary platform was a large American flag. Below, to one side, a dive suit topped by a steel and bronze Mark V dive helmet stood like a suit of armor.

Among others in the audience were John Broadwater, manager of the Monitor National Marine Sanctuary, and John Hightower, president of the Mariners' Museum. The museum had begun construction of its new wing, soon to house hundreds of recovered artifacts from the *Monitor* and *Virginia*. At this point, the turret was wrapped in a protective covering to guard against damage during construction. When the Monitor Center opened in 2007, the turret would surely be the star attraction.

Many of Scholley's divers from the *Monitor* expeditions were present, giving her a couple of lusty hoo yahs. Chief Warrant Officer Rick Cavey presented her a shadow box containing memorabilia from her career. Master Diver Jim Mariano served as honor boatswain. One who couldn't attend was Captain Chris Murray, who was in the Mediterranean conducting submarine rescue drills.

The organizers had thoughtfully placed a box of tissues on the speaker's stand, knowing she might have a tearful moment or two. She resisted the urge through a long list of personal remarks about colleagues, but dabbed at a tear as she bade farewell. "I can sleep peacefully at night knowing we have the very best defending our country."

In an exquisitely solemn ceremony, Navy enlisted men and officers saluted as they passed a folded flag from one to another, then finally presented it to Scholley.

Scholley turned to her commanding officer; her wet eyes glistening from the overhead lights. She raised her hand to her forehead in salute.

"Permission to go ashore, sir?" she said.

"Permission granted."

Side boys and a half dozen of her shipmates formed a line. Mariano sounded the traditional navy pipe, and with that, a beaming retiree, accompanied by her husband and daughters, Scholley walked down the aisle into her new life.

TWENTY-FIVE

SECRETS OF THE BONES

INSIDE THE sprawling Hickam Air Force Base in Honolulu—right next to the channel that leads to Pearl Harbor—is a complex of single-story buildings that houses the military's Joint POW/MIA Accounting Command (JPAC). The access drive there goes past a two-story former barracks with walls that still bear the pockmarks of bullets fired from Japanese warplanes on December 7, 1941. The holes have been painted over but not plastered, so the yellowish building looks like a moonscape. At the entrance to the JPAC area is a monument to a forensic team whose helicopter flew into the side of a mountain in Vietnam in April 2001. It is a sobering reminder of the work that is done here.

Up until October 1, 2003, this was the Army's Central Identification Laboratory, Hawaii (CILHI), but it was then merged with Joint Task Force—Full Accounting. It bears a solemn responsibility: finding, identifying, and bringing home for burial thousands of missing U.S. troops. "Until they are home," is the motto of the command.

Although it was not true for earlier eras of military service, men and women today take it as a given that if they are killed on foreign soil their country will do everything possible to find them and bring them back—even if they crash into some mountain, even if they are buried in a shallow jungle grave, even if they tumble to the bottom of the sea. JPAC maintains eighteen search-and-recovery teams of about ten to fourteen people each. They include a forensic anthropologist, a linguist, a medic, a photographer, an explosive ordnance disposal technician, and mortuary affairs specialists.

The teams fly to former combat zones around the world to investigate crash and burial sites. With an estimated 90,000 combatants missing from World Wars I and II, Korea, and Vietnam, it is a never-ending job. Nearly 80,000 of these were from World War II, and most—those who died on beaches or crashed into mountainsides—will never be found. But it is not for want of trying.

This facility houses the largest forensic anthropology laboratory in the world, with a closure rate of about two individuals every week. When this happens, the remains are taken to a mortuary, placed in a coffin with an appropriate uniform and insignia, and escorted home for burial.

JPAC must constantly juggle its cases. The most pressing sometimes involve families with aging parents or siblings who want to know, before they die, that their loved ones have finally been laid to rest. So it is hard to justify spending a lot of time and resources on remains from the Civil War. Surely there are descendants out there, but they were not pressing the military for answers. There was much press coverage of the turret recovery and the discovery of remains, but no one came forward to inquire about any long-lost great-great-granduncles. So the Civil War bones waited.

ERIC EMERY, the forensic archaeologist who escorted the first set of remains to Hawaii, had been back home only one week when he learned that more bones had been found. He said good-bye to his girlfriend and headed back to Virginia. With hammers and chisels, he and the NOAA and museum archaeologists extracted the second set of remains, one bone at a time, marveling at how perfectly preserved the skeleton was. There was no doubt, he realized, that this sailor too had been quickly buried where he lay.

Emery now began chipping away at the mass of coal where he thought the right arm and hand of the first sailor should be, considering how he was lying. So solid were the coal and encrustations that it was like carving the bones out of concrete. It was no less so with the finger bones, which had fallen back between the roof rails. As he chiseled around the bones he found something oddly solid circling the fourth finger of the right hand. He knew right away what it was, and it stopped his breath. It was a thin gold band with a delicate pattern etched on the outside.

The discovery was an archaeologist's treasure and the occasion for a special announcement and press conference. Could it have been a wedding band? Its being on the right hand didn't advance that scenario. Although some Europeans wore wedding rings on the right hand—and many from the crew were immigrants—those whose traditions related to mid-nineteenth-century Britain did not. No one was prepared to exclude the possibility of a wedding band, but it could just as likely have been a family heirloom. Now, if only there were initials. Conservators cleaned the ring, hoping to find them, but there were none. They would have to start from scratch if they hoped to identify either of the men.

The sailors who drowned on New Year's Eve, 1862, made up a small melting pot of Civil War America. There were three black men, former slaves or sons of slaves, who had thrown in their lot with the Union navy only months before their deaths. Robert Cook, a former slave from Gloucester, had enlisted as "first-class boy" at age 18. Robert H. Howard, born in Howard County, Virginia, was thirty-eight when he signed on in Washington as officers' cook. Daniel Moore, born into slavery in Prince William, Virginia, came on board as landsman on November 13 when the ship was anchored off Newport News. He was the sole support of his mother, who was by then living in Washington.

There were nine other enlisted men: William Allen, landsman, born in England, 24; William Bryan, yeoman, born in New York City, 31; William H. Eagan, landsman, born in Ireland, 21; James R. Fenwick, quarter gunner, born in Scotland, 23; Thomas Joice, first-class fireman, born in Ireland, 23; George Littlefield, coal heaver, born in Saco, Maine, 25; Jacob Nicklis, ordinary seaman, born in Buffalo, New York, 21; John Stocking, boatswain's mate, born in Binghamton, New York, 27; and Robert Williams, first-class fireman, born in Wales, 30.

Because their names did not appear on the ship's official muster, less is known about the officers who drowned. They are Norman

Attwater, George Frederickson, Robinson Woollen Hands, and Samuel Lewis.

The two skeletons found in the turret could have been the remains of any one of these sixteen men. The mystery of who they were would not quickly or easily be solved. As he had done with the first set of remains, Emery packed the new skull and bones in a cold, dark, wet container and accompanied them to Hawaii.

THE JPAC laboratory is a place of glass walls. On one of them, leading to the scientific operations, is an etched inscription from a letter President Abraham Lincoln wrote to the mother of a fallen soldier: "I pray that our Heavenly Father may assuage the anguish of your bereavement, and leave you only the cherished memory of the loved and lost, and the solemn pride that must be yours to have laid so costly a sacrifice upon the altar of freedom."

To the right as you enter are the offices of several staff anthropologists. To the left, behind a wall of glass, is a vast room with about twenty tables lined up in neat rows. On every one is a skeleton, or parts of a skeleton, or simply unrelated bone fragments. Investigators wearing plastic gloves move among the tables sifting the bones for clues: age, height, race, evidence of trauma.

Robert Mann, a forensic anthropologist and deputy scientific director of the laboratory, greets me and takes me on a tour of the evidence room, swiping his ID card to gain entrance. Mann is an intense and affable man who has just returned from what he estimates was his seventieth trip to Vietnam. He is able to read the bones of each case as we walk between the aisles, pointing out, for instance, how purplish bones from a mass grave in North Korea have survived in frozen ground while those from warm, acidic soils in Southeast Asia have almost completely disintegrated, leaving just fragments. The remains of combatants killed on land are reasonably intact, but those who died in plane crashes are jumbles of broken bones. Every bone in your body breaks in "rapid deceleration events," he says. And they break symmetrically: left hip, right hip; left collarbone, right collarbone.

One of the tables has a gray skull with fracture lines between pieces of bone. It has been glued together like a three-dimensional jigsaw puzzle. But pieces are missing from the lower right and the upper left: entrance and exit wounds. The soldier had been shot in the head. You could not tell that from a handful of skull fragments, my guide explains, but once you fit them together, the bones tell their story. It is clear that great pains were taken to reconstruct them.

On one side of the room are video cameras arranged so that one can be focused downward on a skull while another looks at a photograph that might have been of the deceased. When the photo is brought up to scale and superimposed over the skull, the eyes and eye sockets are lined up to determine whether they match. If they do, though it isn't definite proof, Mann says, it is "presumptive."

On the left side of the room is a complex of movable space-saver shelves, like a specimen library, where some nine hundred boxes of bones await various stages of investigation. White-coated evidence manager Sardiaa Plaud checks the boxes in and out with a bar code reader. Everything here is, after all, evidence. And every one of the cases is treated as though part of a homicide investigation. Rigid chain-of-custody rules apply.

A new "accession" has just arrived in a Priority Mail package with a return address in Midway City, California. Plaud cuts open the box and removes two small items packed in Styrofoam pellets, then unwraps what appears to be Christmas paper and finds that the packages contain a tooth and a small, spongy part of a bone. Mann identifies it as part of a jawbone. That's it; no note, no explanation. She photographs the pieces, places them in an evidence box, and assigns them an accession number and a bar code.

At Mann's request, Plaud goes back to the stacks and brings out two boxes that are no larger than cardboard file boxes and light enough for both to be carried at the same time. These are the remains of the *Monitor* sailors. The bones are neatly packed in plastic bags, large bones in one, small bones in another, skull in still another. Mann points out how much darker one set of bones is, stained during more than a century of contact with iron, and demonstrates how much heavier the mineralized bones are than the other set. One of the skulls, the white one, seems to have a perfect set of teeth. The iron-stained skull has a detached lower jaw.

Somewhere in these clumps of hard calcium are clues that drive
people like Mann to learn their identities. "These guys are not just two
sailors who died one hundred forty-two years ago; these are two heroes
who are part of history," he says. "I mean real American heroes."

When the *Monitor* skeletons arrived here in late 2002 they were
placed in tubs, with cold water cascading over them eight hours each
day. Over a period of weeks, the salinity content gradually dropped
to the level of tap water, so salt crystals would not expand and destroy
the bones. One of the skeletons, it turns out, was still wearing shoes,
and the foot bones would thus take much longer to separate. The
skeletons were laid out on tables in the lab, and the anthropologists
went to work. The first step in any identification is a biological profile, establishing sex, race, height, and age.

The first characteristic was easy because there were no women on
board, but the identification game is nothing if not exact. Pelvis size
and shape are the obvious clues. The male pelvis is narrow and deep,
the female pelvis wide and shallow. The skulls are also different, the
male tending to have a heavier brow ridge over the eyes, the female a
rounder, smoother brow. There are several other, more subtle differences, including the more graceful shape of the female chin.

Because there were two intact skulls, the races of the two men were
quickly apparent. As Mann puts it, "race is in the face." Whites tend
to have rounded skulls, narrow nasal openings, well-defined nasal
bones, and a bony projection, or nasal spine, at the base of the nose.
Blacks, in comparison, tend to have long skulls, wide circular nasal
openings, small nasal bones, a projecting mid-face, and a small or non-
existent nasal spine. There are differences for Asian skulls too, such as
even smaller nasal bones, "flattish" faces, and an edge-to-edge bite, but
these characteristics were not relevant here. In the absence of skulls,
one other difference, Mann says, lies in the shape of the thigh bones.
Whites' femurs are mildly curved front to back, Asians' femurs are
moderately curved, and blacks' femurs are straight. It was quickly apparent that these men were Caucasian.

It is too soon to guess the identities of the two sailors. Investigations
are incomplete as of this writing, and final reports are a long way from

being written. Genealogical searches have not yet gotten under way. Preliminary findings are just that, and could change.

But it seems fair to match these findings with what is known of those who went down with the *Monitor* and consider who, among others, they might be.

Excluding the black crew members, thirteen out of the sixteen who drowned are left.

The way Mann and his colleagues estimate height is by measuring one of the long, tubular bones of the arm or, preferably, the leg. Since the skeletons were mostly complete, they chose the femur of each. They placed the bone on a wooden measuring device known as an osteometric board—essentially a yardstick marked off in centimeters, with a fixed upright post at one end and, like a shoe-size calibrator, a sliding upright post at the other. They took the length of the femur and plugged it into the appropriate regression formula for a white male. There are several formulas, depending on how old the remains are. For the *Monitor* remains they used a formula based on the stature of white males who died in the early 1950s. That might seem unreliable, because of stature differences between eras, but it yields a point estimate that works for any period and covers the likely stature of the person, within a small plus-or-minus range.

Based on this formula, the investigators estimated the height of the first skeleton at about five feet eight and one-half inches. That was tall for his day, at least a few inches over the average seaman. His companion was within the crew's average range, approximately five feet six and one-half inches.

Now the case turns to age. To determine someone's age at death, forensic investigators examine bones and teeth. Teeth develop and erupt at a predictable rate and age up to eighteen years old, when they essentially stop growing. Other than the observation that one of the individuals had healthier-looking teeth than the other, teeth were not going to yield any age-related information. But the bones would.

Mann says the human skeleton is constantly building and taking away bone—the rate of this "exchange" varies with the person's age. In other words, a child's skeleton builds bone faster than it loses it, so the skeleton grows in length and circumference. "Kind of like a tree," he says, "it grows a lot when it's young and slows down when it's an adult—but continues to adjust itself as long as it's alive." In the human skeleton, this process begins to slow down as we reach adulthood and then reverses itself in the elderly. During the growth phase (from birth to about twenty-one years of age), the bones have "growth caps," at each end. These caps are separated from the shafts of the bones by cartilage, and this is where the bone grows longer. As a child matures, the cartilage separating the growth cap from the rest of the bone turns to bone itself. At this point the skeleton stops growing, but it will continue to add and lose bone until the person dies.

If the subject is an adult in his or her early twenties, the anthropologists turn to degenerative changes in the skeleton. They can see progressive changes in the hips where pubic joints slowly change their architecture from ridges and valleys to a flat surface. In the elderly, these joints become concave and pitted. Elderly people's bones weigh less than those of young adults. The entire skeleton is examined for growth and degenerative changes, each one recorded in notebooks, each one narrowing the age possibilities. Finally, it comes down to experience. The investigators use their judgment based on years of examining the bones of those long departed.

Precise estimates were not possible, but Mann and his boss, Tom Holland, tell me there was about a decade separating the two men and that the taller of the two was the older.

So they were both Caucasian males, one a few inches taller than the other, with about ten years between them. There could be other clues.

EVERYTHING WE do in our lifetimes, especially if it is habitual, is recorded in our bones, Mann and Holland tell me. Repeated motion causes an enlargement in the muscle attachments to bone, and those attachments respond accordingly. A weight lifter—or, in the old navy, a coal heaver—would carry these clues. A pipe smoker would have a groove in his teeth, as would a carpenter or roofer who habitually bit down on nails. There are several markers of occupational stress. If sailors carried heavy packs, there might be grooves in their upper arm bones. A fisherman pulling a line between his teeth or a woman who constantly opened bobby pins by biting them open would wear the marks in the teeth. Disease can also take a toll on a person's skeleton.

Soccer players sometimes develop bony projections on the front surface of their ankles where the bones repeatedly strike the ball. Any repetitive activity that places unnatural stress on a joint may cause the bone to respond to the "insult," either by building bone at that spot—a muscle attachment, for instance—or by taking bone away, leaving a small crater or groove. Some young male soldiers the lab has examined have narrow grooves, or cortical defects, that run parallel to the shaft of the humerus near the shoulder, possibly from carrying heavy packs for long periods. Archers who pull back heavy bows place great stress on their shoulders, sometimes causing a portion of the scapula to separate. This tip of bone will remain separate for the person's entire life.

The University of Tennessee at Knoxville has a facility—where Mann studied—that is officially known as the Anthropology Research Facility. (Students have long called it the Bone Farm.) It now has a collection of nearly four hundred donated skeletons that have been laid out in a field so the students can study how the bones age in similar climatic conditions. The skeletons themselves range in age from birth to 101, and several bear the effects of mortal wounds, from gunshots and stabs to blunt trauma. One thing the bones have yielded is a better understanding of what happens to human bones as they age.

When they begin profiling the individuals, the anthropologists prefer doing their work "in the blind." The less they know about the person's life, the more objective they can be. "We would much rather let the evidence speak for itself than speak for the evidence," says Mann.

In modern times, one way that evidence has spoken for itself has been through dental records and, when there's any doubt, through deoxyribonucleic acid, the genetic signature we all carry with us from our mothers and fathers. DNA helps solve modern crimes and settle paternity disputes. But nuclear DNA, those helical chains residing in the nuclei of cells, doesn't last long in the bones. What does survive, however, even in bones lying for more than a century at the bottom of the sea, is mitochondrial DNA—mtDNA for short.

These tiny organelles are the energy factories that allow cells to function. And by and large they are inherited only from our mothers. They are present in sperm, but only in the tails, which usually fall off when sperm and egg unite. Mark Leney, the DNA expert at the lab, says there are rare cases where a father's DNA has been detected, but the only reliable marker is passed on through the female side of families. The mtDNA is passed on to sons and stops there, but in daughters it keeps going through endless generations. It doesn't have to be a mother-daughter-daughter continuum. You could start with an aunt, a sister, or a grandmother and weave your way through generations of female offspring. After more than a century, this would be challenging for genealogists, but not impossible.

While the *Monitor* skeletons were laid out on the examination tables, the scientists, wearing gowns and gloves and masks so as not to introduce their own DNA to the subjects, took samples from one of the femurs and one of the teeth of each skeleton. They dissolved away the mineral components of the samples, then used an enzyme to slowly digest the protein. What was left was an organic residue that was frozen and sent to a secure evidence locker at the Armed Forces DNA Identification Lab in Rockville, Maryland.

It might take years, but genealogists hired by the Navy will ultimately seek to find female descendants of the sailors. Assuming that they will provide skin or blood samples (in the case of the CSS *Hunley* and its Confederate submarine crew one relative was exhumed from a grave), a match could be made. It is not an exact fingerprint, but it would be considered primary evidence. Then the likely candidates would be matched with the evidence of the bones for a positive identification.

This is the only way JPAC will positively identify the sailors. But the available forensic evidence has already, at least partly, lifted the veil.

OF THE four officers, Attwater is the least likely, especially if landsman Francis Butts was right. The young ensign was last seen clinging to a rope as the men were being rescued from a lifeboat, then losing his grip and falling into the sea. Butts also claimed to have seen Lewis lying in his bunk, so seasick that he was unable to get up before the ship went down. The problem with this is that an account of the sinking was written by someone named Samuel Lewis and published in 1888. Lewis says he shipped under an alias, a practice common among seamen who did not want to be found if they jumped ship. The name he supposedly went by was Peter Truskitt, pretty close to the name of Peter Truscott, a seaman born in Ireland. That Lewis was officially listed among the missing and Truscott among the survivors is a mystery historians have not been able to solve, although a small clue appears on a crew list at the National Archives that appears to have been written many years ago on a manual typewriter. Among the names is George H. Lewis, third assistant engineer, "missing at sea," while Samuel Augee Lewis, also third assistant engineer, is listed as a survivor. The genealogists have another puzzle to solve.

A case could be made for George Frederickson, the twenty-eight-year-old Danish-born ensign from Philadelphia who often stood night watch when the *Monitor* was in Hampton Roads. He was married and the father of two children, a boy and a girl. His full last name is on a spoon that was found in the turret. The same could be said of Robinson Woollen Hands, a third assistant engineer from Maryland who was last seen in the engine room just before water reached the fire grates.

If Frederickson was married, could that ring from the fourth finger on the skeleton's right hand be his? Pension records show that he married Magdalena Hoelst of Philadelphia in 1858 at Olivet Baptist Church and that at the time of his death they had two children, Catherine, 3, and George, 1. His wife received a navy pension of ten dollars a month until her death. Her husband stood five feet five, with typical Scandinavian features: blue eyes, light complexion, brown hair. One problem with Frederickson as a candidate is his slight stature. Another may be the fact that he was an officer.

Most of the evidence found in the turret seems to point to enlisted men, not officers. In the vicinity of the skeletons were a hard-rubber pocket comb, a four-inch, two-bladed pocketknife, and Goodyear buttons with the date 1851 still visible. But there were no brass buttons, the kind officers all wore. Although some stripped off their jackets in the final moments, there was no reason to remove vests, and these too were buttoned with brass. Neither were there remnants of the gold thread that was typically used to sew on officers' shoulder boards. The archaeologists sifted through every inch of sediment in the turret. There was one boot, however, possibly left by an officer, as well as the remains of a woolen coat. Remember, paymaster William Keeler stripped off his heavy clothing before making a dash for the lifeboat.

As the archaeologists and divers reached the feet of the first sailor they realized that the skeleton was still wearing shoes. Brogans, they called them, most likely the footwear of an enlisted man. According to Jeff Johnston, the *Monitor* historian, this evidence excludes officers. Also, I suspect the officers would have been on top of the turret rather than in it when the ship was going down, and would have been thrown into the sea.

This leaves white enlisted men, and we're down to nine.

Butts also identified the two sailors who were swept overboard when they tried to cut the hawser. One was James Fenwick, a quarter gunner from Boston. He got married during a ten-day furlough and left his new bride, Mary, with child. Although something of a brawler, he wrote his letter home with what seemed genuine affection and longing. He was 23 years old and five feet five, a possible match. But the man who wore the ring was older and taller, and it likely wasn't a wedding ring. Although some of his other claims were exaggerated, Butts was probably right.

The other man Butts identified in the same incident was John Stocking, a 27-year-old boatswain's mate from Binghamton, New York. He was five feet eight, which puts him among the tallest of the crew and makes him a possible candidate for Individual One. Butts, however, seemed to be a good friend, calling him "one of the very best types of an American sailor, and my tutor in seamanship." So his memory likely would have been sharp about this man's loss.

That narrows the field to seven.

THERE WERE other clues. Under the left hip of Individual One there was a silver-plated spoon, in a position that, according to an archaeologist's field notes, suggests "placement within left front pocket." The spoon bears the engraved initials J.N.

Jacob Nicklis, a young seaman from Buffalo, New York, who had expressed his fears about the voyage in a letter to his father, perished that night. Records show that he was 21, stood five feet seven and one-half, and had gray eyes, light hair, and a "ruddy" complexion.

On December 28, 1862, just before the *Monitor* left Hampton Roads, the young tailor's son described how he spent Christmas Day. "The first thing in the morning," Nicklis wrote, "I had my place in the captain's boat, and we landed him from one boat to another until noon, when we had a chance to get our dinner, which was a good one. . . . We had chicken stew and then stuffed turkey, mashed potatoes, plum pudding and nice fruit cake with apples for desert." He went on to mention the plans for heading south and his dread of making the passage around Cape Hatteras.

According to an account in the Buffalo News, Nicklis entered the navy when he was only 16. Five years later, on October 13, 1862, he reenlisted in his hometown for a one-year term as ordinary seaman. He went first to New York and Washington and then, on November 7, took his place on board the *Monitor*. The newspaper recounted that three out of the four living descendants of William Nicklis, his father, met to discuss a favorite project: turning over the letters and other memorabilia to the Buffalo Naval and Servicemen's Park. There was no mention in his letter of a wife or children. In an old section of Forest Lawn cemetery, the story added, there is a family obelisk with a plaque that has these words: "Jacob Nicklis, lost on U.S. Steamer *Monitor* Dec. 31, 1862, aged 21 years."

It is true that many other pieces of silverware were scattered throughout the turret, along with a wooden drawer that might have been dumped into the turret from the galley when the ship turned upside down. And there were other initials. A fork and spoon had the initials SAL, probably belonging to Samuel Augee Lewis, the third assistant engineer; a teaspoon bore the letters NKA, matching the name of Ensign Norman Knox Attwater, 35, of New Haven, Connecticut, a descendant of one of the original settlers there. Landsman Butts had written about him losing his grip on a rope passed down to one of the rescue boats. Last, a fork bore the name "G. Frederickson," matching the name of George Frederickson.

The turret contained more than twenty pieces of silverware, all apparently having cascaded down with the silver drawer that fell through the hatch, but it is eerily coincidental that the only ones bearing initials belonged to members of the crew who perished. Could the men have foolishly risked their lives by going back into the galley in the last moments? It isn't very likely, considering the dire situation they were in. Of course, they were the last ones. The rescue boats had left. Perhaps they thought they would eventually be saved and might just as well gather up what few belongings they could.

Then, too, the silver items were very personal to each of the sailors. They were not navy issue, but exclusively theirs. They were small, portable pieces of home, maybe given by Grandma when they went off to sea. When the order to abandon ship was given, what would they try to save?

What would this young sailor have grabbed at the last minute and thrust into his pocket? Could he have known he was going to die and that the spoon would one day identify him and, at last, bring him home?

There are other possibilities for Individual Two, but the age and stature of this young tailor's son from Buffalo, roughly matching the lab estimates, put him high on the list.

There are other possible matches for the two sailors. One would be William Bryan, a yeoman born in New York City. He was five feet seven and one-half, well within the margin of error, and 32 years old. The others were William Allen who, at five feet ten, was the tallest of the lot, but too young at 24 to be Individual One; William Eagan, a 21-year-old Irishman who stood five feet six, a possible Individual Two; Thomas Joice, another Irishman and first-class fireman, but 23 years old and tall, so not a likely match; and George Littlefield, a Maine-born coal heaver and, by profession, a stonecutter who was 25 and stood five feet seven and one-half. The ages and heights don't match the anthropologists' profile.

A photograph of *Monitor* sailors taken by James F. Gibson in July 1862 shows men in dark long-sleeved shirts, many of them sitting, possibly playing cards or checkers. One is reading a letter, one thoughtfully smoking a pipe. Others are standing in the background. On the far right is a tall, powerful-looking man with a walrus mustache, shirtsleeves rolled up, arms crossed, wearing a jaunty hat and looking right at the camera. According to a letter from one of the survivors, this is Robert Williams. Born in Wales, Williams enlisted in New York for a three-year term as a first-class fireman on February 15, 1862.

By March 6, 1862, Williams had been transferred from the receiving ship *North Carolina* to the *Monitor*. The only mention of Williams in any of the shipboard accounts has him standing with another sailor when Captain Worden passed by during the battle of Hampton Roads.

The job of first-class fireman was to keep the fires in the furnaces burning. It was a dirty, nasty job, though not as bad as that of the coal heavers, who had to bring the coal to the furnaces and chop it into pieces, or the second-class fireman, who actually fed and tended the fire. Everyone down there had lungs full of coal dust and almost certainly had the beginnings of black lung disease, not to mention suffering from the noxious fumes. A fireman might also have a touch of rheumatism from the constant damp.

Williams was apparently not married. Pension records, kept on microfilm at the National Archives, show no applications on behalf of anyone by that name. There were no fewer than twenty Robert Williamses in New York in the Census of 1860, and there is no way to identify which one might have been our sailor. The New York City Municipal Archives, in the ornate, yellow marble Surrogate Courthouse near City Hall, don't yield any marriage records for a Robert Williams between 1853 and 1862. The grainy photograph captured Williams with his right hand showing, but there's a dark shadow right where the ring might have been.

What we do know about Williams is that he enlisted for a three-year term in February 1862, just before the *Monitor* sailed. He had hazel eyes and a swarthy complexion, made $30 a month as first-class fireman, and over a period of ten months, according to Keeler's account, spent $12.29 for clothing and received a credit of $6.10 for spirits not drunk. He was 30 years old then, probably 31 at the time of his death, and stood five feet eight and one-half.

This makes him the only member of the crew whose height exactly matches the anthropologists' estimate. It is true that there is normally a margin of error of one and one-half inches on either the high or low side, but here they had the full skeleton, not just the femur, and thus could nail down the height more closely. He was also the right age—about a decade older than Individual Two.

Robert Williams, "Bob" as they called him when he was first found, has to be a top contender for Individual One.

It seems it would be extremely difficult to track down family members for an unmarried Welsh immigrant who perished in the Civil War. Or would it?

Those same New York City marriage records show that hundreds of people named Williams were married in the decade before the Civil War, but one name that stands out during that period is Frank Williams because, under "Nativity of Male," the word "Wales" appears. That isn't surprising, since Williams is a common name in Wales, but none of the other grooms on those lists was born there. The 30-year-old resident of Market Street married 19-year-old Levinia Masters of Newberg, New York. Perhaps he was "Bob's" brother. Perhaps there were sisters whose DNA might lead to a match.

As for Individual Two, it is tempting to conclude that, because of the spoon with his initials and because his age and height matched the identification lab's conclusion about bone characteristics, the man was Jacob Nicklis. Besides, more was known about him because of his letters home, so he is an appealing candidate. The possibility of finding distant relatives would be strong.

But late in 2004, more than two years after they were found in the turret, an intriguing clue emerged from deep within the bones of the two individuals. A preliminary analysis of the stable isotopes found in the bones and teeth of the two individuals, most likely reflecting drinking water and diet, indicated that they matched isotopes found not in the United States but in Europe.

Scientists know, for instance, that oxygen isotope values of bones and teeth often track the isotope composition of surface water or rainfall. Other signatures can be determined by diet, and some bioarchaeologist sleuths go so far as to say that we are what we eat. British investigators say that teeth are archives of childhood exposure to water and food. Incidentally, they note that Britain has recently undergone a detailed survey of rainfall, surface water, and groundwater oxygen isotopes. So it is possible, perhaps, for those studying the bones of Civil

War sailors to quickly match their isotope signatures. The science is still young, and its conclusions are not always accepted. But if the evidence is solid, the remains must be those of immigrants.

It is not known when he came to the United States, but enlistment records show that William H. Eagan was born in Ireland. He had blue eyes, sandy hair, and a fair complexion. He was of medium height for the day, five feet six. On October 6, 1862, at age 21, he enlisted in the navy in New York City, was transferred to the Navy Yard in Washington, and, while the *Monitor* was in that city awaiting repairs, came on board as landsman, the lowest crew rank, earning $12 a month. His navy career was to be exceedingly brief.

If you take Eagan's age and height, as well as his European upbringing, there is a strong possibility that he died that awful midnight in the *Monitor*'s turret.

Without DNA matches, though, it would be risky to positively identify the two sailors and inappropriate even to try. Given the demands on investigators, these mysteries may not be solved for several more years. At some point, though, the cases will bubble to the surface. Even though the military considers the sea a fitting resting place for those who have gone down with their ships, it would be disappointing to those who brought their remains up from the ocean floor if they were not identified and, at last, returned home.

Shortly after the first of the two men was found, chief warrant officer Rick Cavey realized that the mission had gone far beyond removing artifacts. "We're actually pulling an American hero off the bottom," he said. "In my mind, a guy who was in the turret could have been one of the ones who stayed behind to man the pumps or help other people out of the boat, and stand his watch till the last minute. Why else was he still on the boat? He wasn't the first guy off, that's for sure. Was he a hero? That's the way it goes down in my mind. Here's a guy who gave his life for the Union that we're all so proud of now."

HERE'S A scenario, perhaps far-fetched, but perhaps not: In the early morning of December 31, after the ship was lost, Rodney Browne and his seven oarsmen saw something that made no sense. In his report on Browne's rescue, Captain Trenchard of the *Rhode Island* wrote, "He also mentioned seeing a small black boat some distance off, with two or three men in her, seeing her as she rose three times upon the waves and then disappearing." The lost sailors were too busy saving themselves to investigate.

The original specifications for the *Monitor*, dated September 16, 1861, included a kind of stowable lifeboat. "A skeletal frame of metal will be furnished by the contractor," the specs say, "with an India rubber covering which may be put together in case of need, suitable light seats and oars to be furnished."

There is no mention in anyone's account of such a vessel. We know that lifeboats and davits were added when the ship went to Washington for repairs and that the regular lifeboats were transferred to the *Rhode Island* for the ocean passage. But it stands to reason that the components for such a small black rubber boat were on board and that the men knew about them.

The drowning victims were surely inside the turret, not on top of it, when the ship rolled over and went down. Anyone still clinging to the top would have been flung into the sea. Perhaps the men, realizing the last rescue boat would not reach them in time, remembered the stowable lifeboat and scrambled frantically to put it together, and the two men, sailors to the last, were standing in the turret passing up thwarts or oars when the ship went under.

This nudges the story of *Monitor*'s demise toward treacherous shoals, but a long-dismissed legend reasserts itself. Shortly after the sinking, the story goes, villagers combing the beach near Cape Hatteras Light found the bodies of several men, possibly in sailors' uniforms, and federal soldiers carted them off and buried them. The story, too, has long been laid to rest, but we can at least speculate that a few sailors made it to within sight, within a last gasp, of survival, when their boat overturned.

One thing that is now beyond dispute is that two others remained at their posts until nearly the end, perhaps keeping the pumps going as long as they could so their shipmates could get off, perhaps going below in the last minutes to make it possible for some of them to survive, and that they found a resting place in that strange iron ship at the bottom of the sea. They may have been brothers or fathers, and of course they were sons, whose mothers could not have imagined a more desolate end for them, but who might have shared or passed on a microscopic clue that would one day identify them and bring them home.

Connections from past to present and back again run through every walk of life, and no more so than in the military. Soldiers and sailors are, through the depths of time, what Shakespeare—and Stephen Ambrose—called bands of brothers, linked by common ideals and experiences. Bobbie Scholley, Rick Cavey, Chris Murray, and others often spoke of this kinship. The divers who plunge into the sea after lost sailors and civilians, and who now have brought some of their own from the depths of time, have special cause to feel this.

Back in 1862, one of the civilians who cheered the *Monitor* sailors called them "iron hearts." They were ordinary people from ordinary places, from New York's East Side and Hell's Kitchen, from Boston's South Side, all of them volunteers for jobs that no one could have prepared them for. The Monitor Boys, as they called themselves in a letter to their favorite captain, were banded together by something thrust upon them, not once but several times—heroism.

Now they have new brothers, and sisters. Iron hearts all.

1862

USS *Monitor* Crew
William Allen, landsman
Richard Anjier, quartermaster
Norman Knox Attwater, ensign
John Bankhead, fourth and last captain
William Bryan, yeoman
Francis B. Butts, landsman
Siah Carter, former slave who signed on as crew
Robert Cook, first-class boy
John Driscoll, fireman
William H. Eagan, landsman
James R. Fenwick, quarter gunner
George Frederickson, acting master's mate
George Geer, fireman
Samuel Dana Greene, executive officer
Robinson Woollen Hands, third assistant engineer
Robert H. Howard, officers' cook
William M. Jeffers, third captain
Thomas Joice, first-class fireman
William Keeler, paymaster
Samuel Augee Lewis, third assistant engineer
Daniel Logue, surgeon
Daniel Moore, landsman
Jacob Nicklis, seaman
Thomas Selfridge, second captain
Edwin Stanton, secretary of war

Alban Stimers, chief engineer
John Stocking, boatswain's mate
Louis N. Stodder, acting master
Peter Truscott, seaman
Joseph Watters, engineer
Grenville Weeks, surgeon
George White, engineer
Peter Williams, quartermaster
Robert Williams, first-class fireman
John L. Worden, first captain of *Monitor*

OTHERS

Rodney Browne, master's mate on the *Rhode Island*, skipper of rescue boat
Franklin Buchanan, flag officer on the *Virginia*
Cornelius Bushnell, New York industrialist
Richard Curtis, *Virginia* crew
Percival Drayton, captain of the *Passaic*
John Ericsson, inventor of the *Monitor*
Gustavus Fox, assistant secretary of the navy
John Griswold, Bushnell associate
Catesby Jones, executive officer of the *Virginia*
William Kline, seaman on *Virginia*
Abraham Lincoln, president of the United States
Stephen R. Mallory, Confederate secretary of the navy
Isaac Newton, superintendent of ironclad construction
Dinwiddie P. Phillips, *Virginia* surgeon
H. Ashton Ramsey, *Virginia* chief engineer
James Rochelle, crew of CSS *Patrick Henry*
William Rodgers, ensign on *Rhode Island*, skipper of rescue boat
Albert Taylor, ensign on *Rhode Island*, skipper of rescue boat
Stephen D. Trenchard, captain of *Rhode Island*
Henry Van Brunt, captain of *Minnesota*
Gideon Welles, secretary of the Union navy
John Winslow, Bushnell associate
John Taylor Wood, officer on the *Virginia*
John Wool, army general at Hampton Roads

2002

Wade Bingham, senior chief
Brick Bradford, master diver

John Broadwater, manager, *Monitor* National Marine Sanctuary
Rick Cavey, chief warrant officer, dive officer for 2002 project
Greg "Big G" Clavelle, Manson Gulf barge operator
Jay M. Cohen, admiral, chief of naval research
Rusty Deen, saturation dive officer
Harold Edgerton, strobe inventor
Eric Emery, forensic archaeologist
Larry Fahey, master chief
Brad Flemming, chief petty officer, surface-supply diver
Vern Geyman, engineer senior chief, saturation diver
Steve Hall, diving medical technician
Gina Harden, commander
Oren "Bubby" Haydel, Manson Gulf crane operator
Scott Heineman, master diver
John Hightower, president of Mariners' Museum
Tom Holland, scientific director, JPAC
Steve Janek, chief petty officer
Jeff Johnston, NOAA historian
Jim Kelly, chief engineer for Phoenix International
Mark Leney, identification lab DNA expert
Eric Lindberg, engineering manager, Phoenix International
Wayne Lusardi, Mariners' Museum archaeologist
Mike Lutz, chief petty officer
Robert Mann, deputy scientific director, JPAC
Jim Mariano, project master diver
Robert Marx, author and wreck diver
Chris Murray, captain, chief diving officer Naval Sea Systems Command
Keith Nelson, chief boatswain's mate, saturation diver
John Newton, Duke University marine superintendent
Jason Niny, Manson Gulf field engineer
Curtiss Peterson, chief conservator, Mariners' Museum
Sardiaa Plaud, evidence manager, JPAC
Ken Riendeau, chief petty officer
Bill Robertson, commander of MDSU TWO
Barbara "Bobbie" Scholley, tactical commander of Navy diving operations
    on the *Wotan*
Karen Shake, commander
Bryon Van Horn, saturation master diver
Gordon Watts, marine archaeologist
Gene "Little G" Wells, Manson Gulf barge operator
Lori Yost, lieutenant commander
Chuck Young, saturation master diver

ACKNOWLEDGMENTS

W HEN I began researching this book I saw it as two simple stories of loss and recovery. What I did not yet appreciate was the wonderful complexity of the human dramas that played out on both stages, the present and the past. For this I have many, many people to thank.

First of all, my editors at *The Virginian-Pilot* allowed me to spend much of 2002 covering this story and gave it the kind of space and attention it deserved. Editor Kay Addis believed in the story and then made this book possible by granting me a leave of absence. Maria Carrillo, a superb narrative editor, championed and helped shape a series of articles that ultimately led to this book, and then she did me the ultimate favor of reading this book and offered countless suggestions for making it better. Tom Holden never flinched at my requests for time and then, often on deadline, helped give breaking stories the urgency they deserved.

At first I assumed it would be difficult to explore the human dimension of what was, after all, a military operation. But of course it wasn't a war the Navy divers were engaged in but the recovery of a unique part of their history and, ultimately, the bones of fellow sailors. Even so, it took a lot of trust for people like Bobbie Scholley, Chris Murray, Rick Cavey, Jim Mariano, Scott Heineman, and dozens of others to share their stories, their hopes and fears—and even parts of their journals—with me.

It is understandable that officials were reluctant to allow reporters on the barge during the tense days before and during the lift. The platform out on the Atlantic was already crammed with people who had critical jobs to do. Adding a half dozen more might well have compromised the mission and surely added to safety concerns. I'm grateful to the Navy for agreeing to allow a pool of writers and photographers to be there. Mark St. John Erickson of *The Daily Press* and I stationed ourselves at separate places on the barge during the lift so that we were able to cover it from different perspectives, and then we shared our notes with each other and with the Associated Press.

John Broadwater and Jeff Johnston with NOAA were infinitely patient with my requests for interviews and the dozens of follow-up questions as the work progressed. Whether out on the barge, in their offices on the grounds of the Mariners' Museum, or down in the turret while they were sifting through silt and coal and history, they could not have been more generous. John's enthusiasm for the recovery and Jeff's passion for the history it revealed were contagious. Michelle Fox and David Hall helped make this all happen.

The Mariners' Museum is impressive not only for what it collects and displays but for how it invites writers and researchers into its treasures. Curtiss Peterson, the chief conservator, never fails to see the human dimension in the most inanimate pieces of recovered wreckage. John Hightower, the president, shared his hopes and fears for the recovery. Claudia Jew, licensing manager, Anna Holloway, *Monitor* Center curator, and Jeanne Willoz-Egnor, collections manager, were also especially helpful. The staff of the library, including Susan Berg, Lester Weber, Josh Graml, Lynnette Dillabough, Cathy Williamson, and others, could not have been more helpful. And finally, I owe a special thanks to Justin Lyons, director of communications, who always seemed able to open doors. Thanks, too, to curator Joseph M. Judge and staff of the Hampton Roads Naval Museum, and James C. Dixon, NOAA regional navigation manager.

I am indebted to Larry Atkinson, Slover professor of oceanography at Old Dominion University, who patiently helped develop the theory, based on log entries and eyewitness accounts, of how the storm that sank the *Monitor* developed. I also want to thank Scott Stevens and colleagues from the National Climate Data Center for suggesting the cold-front theory in the first place.

Thanks to Dr. Harvey Bercowitz, of Sentara Leigh Hospital Baro-trauma Medicine, for helping me to understand dive medicine. Also, Dr. Robert Leuken, MDSU TWO diving medical officer, Dr. Jennifer Livingood, and Dr. William Spaur, former senior medical officer, Navy Experimental Diving Unit. I can't say enough about the assistance I received from the central identification lab at JPAC in Honolulu. Drs. Robert Mann, Tom Holland, Mark Leney, and Eric Emery allowed me into their facility, explained the Byzantine art of forensic archaeology, and answered countless follow-up questions. Public affairs officer Jerry O'Grady helped make it possible.

Special thanks to John Thornton at Joseph Spieler Literary Agency for recognizing the excitement in this story, to Jonathan Eaton of International Marine for giving it a home and Benjamin McCanna for careful, intelligent copy editing. One of the joys of working on this book was having Peter Nichols, one of my favorite sea story writers, serve as editor.

My wife, Barbara Berguin Clancy, may one day forgive me for my obsessions, nautical and otherwise. My thanks to her, Beth, Corrie, Diane, Buff, Lil, and Bessie.

CHAPTER NOTES

PROLOGUE

My in-person visit to the *Monitor* was made in the Harbor Branch Oceano-graphic Institution's submersible *Johnson Sea Link II*, on June 25, 2002. The sub pilot was Don Liberatore and the historian was Jeff Johnston.

One: NOTHING IN THE HEAVENS ABOVE

For historical background on the *Monitor* and *Virginia*, I relied on William C. Davis, *Duel between the First Ironclads* (Baton Rouge: Louisiana University Press, 1975), Lt. Edward M. Miller, *U.S.S. Monitor, The Ship that Launched a Modern Navy* (Annapolis: Leeward Publications, 1978), and James Tertius deKay, *Monitor* (New York: Walker and Company, 1997). The scene at the launching is from the *New York Herald,* January 31, 1882. Also, Craig L. Symonds, "The Nick of Time: John Ericsson and the USS *Monitor*," Seaport: New York's *History* Magazine, Winter 2003.

For life on board, I consulted David A. Mindell, *War, Technology and Experience aboard the USS* Monitor (Baltimore: Johns Hopkins University Press, 2000). All of Keeler's letters are contained in Robert W. Daly, Ed., *Aboard the USS* Monitor*: 1862, the Letters of Acting Paymaster William Frederick Keeler, U.S. Navy, to his Wife, Anna* (Annapolis: United States Naval Institute, 1964).

All telegrams and dispatches concerning the *Monitor* and *Virginia* can be found in *Official Records of the Union and Confederate Navies in the War of the Rebellion* (hereafter referred to as *Official Records*), North Atlantic Blockading Squadron (Washington: Government Printing Office, 1897). The Mariners' Museum has a set of the *Records* and they are available online at Cornell University's Making of America website, http://cdl.library.cornell.edu/moa/.

For background on John Ericsson, I benefited from the Mariners' Museum website, History and Legacy, "John Ericsson: Life before the *Monitor.*" I found his letter to James Gordon Bennett in the Frank Pierce Collection, New York Public Library Rare Books and Manuscripts Room. The work orders for the *Monitor* have recently been donated to the Mariners' Museum.

I am indebted to the work by historian Irwin W. Berent—*The Crewmen of the USS* Monitor*: A Biographical Directory,* prepared for Underwater Archaeological Unit, Division of Archives and History, North Carolina Department of Cultural Resources, 1982. He unearthed virtually everything known about the enlisted crew, including rank, height, weight, complexion, and eye color, and, if married, whether or not a widow had filed for a pension.

Other sources for this chapter include: Gideon Welles, "The Annals of War: The First Ironclad *Monitor*," available online at www.mariner.org; Cheesebox (Monitor National Marine Sanctuary Activities Report), December 1997; and the Naval Historical Center.

Two: FLOATING CITY

I relied on interviews with Manson Gulf officials and company publications for specifications on the *Wotan.* The scene at the load-on comes from interviews with Rick Cavey and Jim Mariano, and from follow-up e-mails.

The Navy's saturation dive program is described by Captain Chris Murray in www.oceanexplorer.noaa.gov. He and Michael P. Leese wrote about saturation diving history in an August 2002 issue of *Sea Power Magazine.* See also Joseph M. Cocazza Jr., "Naval Force Propels Diving Technology" in *Immersed,* Spring 1998. The preparations for Dive School are outlined on MDSU TWO's website.

I have further reconstructed the scene on the barge through interviews with Jeff Johnston and Bobbie Scholley. Captain Scholley provided excerpts from her journal. Phoenix International engineer Jim Kelly showed me the presentation he developed for the Spider.

Three: STANDING OUT TO SEA

Details of the weather that week are from the "Shipping News" columns of New York Herald, Feb. 28, 1862. A copy of the *Log of U.S. Steam Battery* Monitor is at the Mariners' Museum Library and the National Archives. There are biographical sketches of Worden at the Naval Historical Center, but the most useful is William N. Still Jr., *Ironclad Captains: The Commanding Officers of the USS* Monitor, Marine and Estuarine Management Division, National Oceanic and Atmospheric Administration, Washington, D.C., April 1988. The offer to Worden and his reply are in *Official Records,* as are the desperate orders from Welles and the messages from Worden.

The best description of the *Monitor*'s attempted departure is in Keeler's letter to his wife. There's a much less colorful account in the *Official Records*. Portions of Geer's letters are contained in *The* Monitor *Chronicles*, William Marvel, Ed. (New York: Simon & Shuster, 2000), but the complete collection of the letters is at the Mariners' Museum.

I owe my understanding of conditions in the engine room to Curtiss Peterson, chief conservator of the Museum, and Alan Mitchell, a former Navy engineer and now Monitor Center volunteer docent. The account of the gun trial is in Charles W. MacCord, "Ericsson and his *Monitor*," *North American Review*, Vol. 149 (October 1889).

Four: STRUCTURAL TIME BOMB

The discovery of the wreck is detailed in Gordon P. Watts Jr., "The Location and Identification of the USS *Monitor*," *International Journal of Nautical Archaeology and Underwater Exploration* (1975); Watts, "Exploring the *Monitor*," Archaeological Investigation of the Civil War Ironclad, Philadelphia Maritime Museum, 1988; and John G. Newton and Watts, "The Role of Archival Records in the Search and Discovery of the Wreck of the U.S.S. *Monitor*," National Archives Conference on Naval History, 1974. Also, Robert E. Sheridan, *Iron from the Deep: The Discovery and Recovery of the USS* Monitor (Annapolis: Naval Institute Press, 2004).

John Broadwater's early role and his profile are from numerous interviews. Also helpful in the recovery story was "Discovery & Recovery Chronology" at www.monitorcenter.org and "Remarks" by Philip K. Lundeberg in the May 1985 *Cheesebox*, a newsletter published by NOAA. The story of Project Cheesebox is told by Lt. Miller, one of the midshipmen investigators, in USS *Monitor*.

The profile of Chris Murray is from interviews on board the barge in 2002 and in Alexandria, Virginia, in 2003. I went out to see the propeller on board the salvage ship Kellie Chouest in the summer of 1998—my introduction to the *Monitor* project.

Five: AS DEAD AS MEN EVER WERE

Of the several accounts of the perilous journey from New York to Hampton Roads, the best among them are Greene's letter to his parents, March 14, 1862, at the Mariners' Museum Library; his later article, "In the *Monitor* Turret," in *Century*, March 1885; and Keeler's letter to his wife. Driscoll's account is in Berent's *The Crewmen of the USS* Monitor. The log from the trip is at the Mariners' Museum.

Six: IF THE BUG AIN'T FLYIN'

Descriptions of the barge's arrival and the storms that greeted it are from NOAA Ocean Explorer's "*Monitor* Expedition 2002: Logs." I spent four days on the barge in late June 2002 and did many of the early interviews during my stay.

Seven: DARK MONSTER

I relied on several sources for the battle, including Davis, deKay, and Mindell, also John V. Quarstein, *The Battle of the Ironclads* (Charleston: Arcadia Publishing, 1999), and *Official Records.*

The Anaconda Plan is described in the History and Legacy page of the Mariners' Museum website. Mallory's dispatches to Buchanan and Jefferson Davis, as well as Welles's frantic telegrams are in *Official Records.* The dimensions of the *Merrimack, Congress,* and *Cumberland* are from the Naval Historical Center. The Georgia infantry private who witnessed the commotion of the *Virginia* coming down the river was quoted in the *Daily Press* of Newport News, December 31, 1997. The quotes from the Confederate crew are from "A Midshipman Aboard the *Virginia,*" *Civil War Times Illustrated,* Vol 3, April 1974.

A memoir by Gideon Welles, long after the battles, as well as the recollection of H. Ashton Ramsey, historical papers on the Gosport Navy Yard and the transformation of the *Merrimack* are on the History and Legacy page of the Mariners' Museum website. An article by Lt. John Taylor Wood, "The First Fight of the Ironclads," was in *Century,* March 1885. I found it online at Cornell's Making of America website. Van Brunt's dismay at being protected by the upstart ironclad was overheard by Keeler. The captain's later estimation is in *Official Records.* Worden's letter home was related in *Cheesebox,* February 1987.

Eight: WHEN THINGS GO DOWN

I recreated this sequence by watching dozens of dives, and then, in order to understand all of the steps, I interviewed Master Diver Jim Mariano and Chief Petty Officer Brad Flemming. I watched divers practicing at their base in Virginia Beach in 2004 and, while there, interviewed Commander Robertson—Scholley's replacement as head of MDSU TWO.

There are excellent sources on dive medicine on the Web, including Divers Alert Network, mt.sinai.org, emedicine.com and scubadiving.com. I also interviewed Dr. Robert Leuken, diving medical officer at MDSU TWO, and Dr. Harvey Bercowitz, head of barotrauma medicine at Sentara Leigh Hospital in Norfolk.

For historical background on saturation diving, I relied on Dr. James Vorosmarti Jr.'s "Very Short History of Saturation Diving," *Historical Diving Times*, Winter 1997. The Cousteau quote is from Jacques-Yves Cousteau, *The Silent World* (New York: Harper, 1953).

The quotes from the divers are from interviews on the barge in June, July, and August, 2002. There were follow-up interviews, most of them in person. A few were by telephone.

Nine: SLUGFEST

The most vivid descriptions of the first ironclad battle are contained in letters and diaries of people who had never been in harm's way. These letters, from George Geer, William Keeler, and Dana Greene, as well as a few official accounts, make the *Monitor*'s feat all the more remarkable. The recollections of the *Virginia* crew, many of which are available at www.cssvirginia.org, include Curtis, from a pamphlet at the Southern Historical Society, October 1874; Cline, from the *Richmond News-Leader*, April 1, 1904; Phillips, from the *Southern Bivouac*, March 1887; James Rochelle, letter to Flag Officer John B. Tucker, January 30, 1865. See also, Davis, *Duel between the First Ironclads*. I was greatly assisted by a chart on the battle of Hampton Roads by Robert E. Pratt, with text by John V. Quarstein, Jeff Johnston, and Craig L. Symonds.

Catesby Jones's recollections are rarely quoted, but they can be found in Franklin Buchanan's report on the battles and online at www.cssvirginia.org, a memoir for the Southern Historical Society, October 1874.

Truscott, ever wary of revealing his identity, took the name of Samuel Lewis in a memoir included in *Campfire Sketches and Battlefield Echoes* (Cleveland: N.G. Hamilton & Co., 1888). Stodder's recollections are from "Aboard the USS *Monitor*," *Civil War Times Illustrated*, January 1963.

Fox's congratulations are related in *Official Records*, March 9. The *Times of London* editorial is quoted by deKay. Nathaniel Hawthorne's comment is from a report he wrote for *Atlantic Monthly*, July 1862, "Chiefly about War-Matters, by a Peaceable Man."

Ten: IT'S A MAN'S JOB, MA'AM

This profile incorporates interviews with Scholley, Murray, Cavey, Mariano, Heineman, and Yost, and e-mail exchanges with Perna.

Eleven: EVERLASTING IRON

The telegram to Welles is in *Official Records*, March 9. In Greene's letter to his parents, he continued: "I was captain then of the vessel that had saved New

Port News, Hampton Roads, Fortress Monroe (as Genl. Wool himself said) and perhaps your Northern Ports. I am unable to express the happiness and joy I felt, to think I had served my country and Flag so well, at such an important time."

Hawthorne bestirred himself from his fireside in Concord, Mass., to make the long journey to Hampton Roads. On the way, he toured Civil War battlefields and met with President Lincoln, but his editors at *Harper's Weekly* decided to remove his account of the Lincoln visit because it "lacks reverence," they declared. The writer's challenge that "poets brood upon the theme" was quickly taken up by his friend Melville, as Mindell points out. I found Verne's reference to a "submarine monitor" in *20,000 Leagues Under the Sea* (Annapolis: Naval Institute Press, 1993).

Lincoln's visit to Worden is related by deKay. The fate of the *Galena* is described by Daly in *Aboard the USS* Monitor. Siah Carter's story is told by Berent. Welles's order is in *Official Records*, Vol. 8, December 18, 1862. I found White's letter of August 19 in Monitor *Expedition Log*, August 19, 1999.

Twelve: LUCY'S THE TURRET

Most of the material for this stage of the recovery comes from personal observation out on the *Wotan*. Both the Navy and NOAA were generous in allowing me to make frequent trips to the barge and witness their operations, even when things became tense.

Broadwater's speculations about the recovery were made during a March 2002 interview in his office on the Mariners' Museum grounds in Newport News. These temporary quarters in a cramped, trailer-like structure, were to be replaced in 2005 by a new NOAA headquarters.

Thirteen: ORDERS AT LAST

Fenwick's story is included in *Berent's Biographical Directory*, as is the Buffalo News story about Jacob Nichols. The profile of Bankhead is in Still's *Ironclad Captains*. The numerous dispatches concerning the ship's new deployment are included in *Official Records*. Speculation about the damaged propeller comes from conservators and historians at the Mariners' Museum.

Fourteen: SELF-EXILE AT FORTY FATHOMS

I was onboard the barge through the early struggles with the armor belt, but not when it finally gave way. For those details, as well as the lowering of the Spider, I relied on the *Expedition Logs* and interviews. The rift about the Spider and the lifting platform is based on personal observation, expedition records and interviews with Phoenix International officials, especially Kelly and Lindberg.

Murray, Scholley, and Cavey were helpful in discussing the command conflicts and Murray's unconventional solution.

Fifteen: COLD GREY MANTLE

I obtained copies of the logs from the *Rhode Island, Passaic,* and *State of Georgia* from the National Archives. The official reports on the *Monitor*'s fate from Bankhead, Trenchard, Watters, and Drayton, can be found in *Official Records.* Grenville Weeks wrote "The Last Cruise of the *Monitor,*" *Atlantic Monthly,* March 1863.

Sun and moon cycles are from U.S. Naval Observatory data for Nags Head, North Carolina, December 30, 1862.

My reconstruction of the weather situation was with the generous help of Larry Atkinson, Slover professor of oceanography at Old Dominion University. The calculations were made by consulting ship's log entries about wind direction and speed, air and water temperature, barometer readings, and weather observations, as well as survivor accounts. Scott Stevens, a meteorologist at NOAA, was also helpful.

Keeler's observation about the liquor supply is contained in a letter to Frank H. Pierce, November 15, 1885. I found it in the Frank Piece Collection at the New York Public Library.

The story of Sir Francis Beaufort is from the article "The Beaufort Wind Scale, Or Who Put Wind Speeds in the Admiral's Force Scale?" at NOAA's website (www.crh.noaa.gov/lot/webpage/beaufort/). The history of the Cape Hatteras Light is from the National Park Service, "History of Light." The *New York Herald* account appeared on January 6, 1863.

Sixteen: MICHELANGELOS OF THE DEEP

The story of the discovery and recovery of remains is based on interviews with Bingham, Johnston, Emery, Cavey, Young, Scholley, Murray, Mariano, Lusardi, Geyman, and Yost.

Seventeen: SEND YOUR BOATS!

Francis Butts wrote about his experience in *Century* magazine, December 1885. His account has generally been given less credibility than others. He was a landsman, the lowest rank aboard, and yet he claimed to have played a leadership role, including acting as helmsman. I have avoided using his often-repeated story about stuffing a quarrelsome cat in the muzzle of one of the guns because there is no mention elsewhere of such a shipboard animal. Later examination inside the weapons may prove otherwise.

Watters made an official report to Bankhead, and that became part of the record. I discovered the letter to his wife in the Frank Pierce Collection at the New York Public Library.

Louis Stoddard related his experience in "Captain Louis N. Stoddard as told to Albert Stevens, reporter for *The New York Herald Tribune*," published in *Civil War Times Illustrated*, January 1863. The account of Ensign Rodgers is in Miller, *U.S.S.* Monitor.

Eighteen: YOUR CALL, COMMANDER

I was on board the barge August 3–5, through the turret recovery. As a reporter, I took copious notes of what I saw and heard, but much of the inner drama of the events leading to the lift was revealed in later interviews. Captain Scholley (who received her promotion shortly after the lift) spoke to me in her office at the Earle Naval Weapons Station near Colts Neck, New Jersey, where she was then in charge. There were several subsequent phone conversations and e-mails. Some of Johnston's, Murray's, and Hightower's recollections are also from later interviews.

A copy of Ericsson's letter to Commodore Smith, October 23, 1861, is in the *Monitor* Files at the Hampton Roads Naval Museum library.

Nineteen: PANORAMA OF HORROR

As with his other descriptions, Keeler's amazing account was written to his wife, Anna. Unlike others, who wrote for publication years later, his and Geer's were dashed off as quickly as they could get to paper and pen. Keeler's accounting skills are revealed in "Final Pay Receipts & Muster Roll, United States Steamer *Monitor*," at the National Archives.

I was impressed by the work of the unnamed reporter for the *New York Herald* who apparently later sold or gave his story to *Harper's Weekly*. He was seemingly able to interview most of the key figures in the drama and get the story in his paper by January 6.

Twenty: ALL STATIONS, ALL STATIONS

I was on the barge the day of the lift. The scenes and conversations are from my own reporting, including those in the saturation shack, into which I was able to squeeze. The story of Keith Nelson's account is partly from what I could hear in that crowded room and later interviews with him, Scholley, Johnston, Van Horn, Cavey, and others.

Details about Tropical Storm Cristobal, August 5–8, 2002, are from the National Hurricane Center.

Twenty-one: INTO THE ABYSS

Watters was writing to his wife. In the Weeks account, there is no way he could have heard what Bankhead said since at the time he was already aboard the *Rhode Island,* but he may have heard Bankhead discuss his actions later. It isn't clear when an actual order to abandon ship was made, since many were still in the engine room while rescue boats were taking crew off.

Browne's account appeared in the *New York Herald* on January 13, 1863. The reporter apparently had an exclusive interview with the rescue boat skipper after he and his crew were themselves rescued. Part of Browne's story is detailed in "Sequel to the Story, The Loss of the *Monitor,*" by D. Rodney Browne, ZC File, Division of Naval History, Washington, D.C. Trenchard's report on Browne's rescue is in *Official Records,* January 10, 1863.

The conclusion that sailors were trapped inside the turret as the ship suddenly rolled is based on my interview with Eric Emery, who studied the position of the skeletons. The theory of how the ship sank was developed by Watts and others in their explanation of how the ship struck the bottom and how the turret became dislodged.

Twenty-two: WE *CANNOT* FAIL

These scenes are all from personal observations on board and later interviews with Broadwater, Scholley, Johnston, Nelson, Flemming, Heineman, Cavey, Mariano, Kelly, and others.

The other newspaper reporter in the pool was Mark Erickson of *The Daily Press* in Newport News. I was stationed in the sat shack during preparations for the lift while he was in the surface-supply van. We shared some notes with each other and with the Associated Press, so a few of the quotes attributed to the divers are from him. I was also greatly informed by his later series of stories.

Twenty-three: PROUD PAPA

I have re-created the arrival scene from press accounts, including one by Matthew Jones of *The Virginian-Pilot.* I interviewed Peterson shortly after the turret's arrival. After the skeletons were removed, I was able to climb down into the turret and watch Broadwater, Johnston, and Lusardi as they dug through the coal and silt residue. I returned two years later when the cannons were removed.

Twenty-four: PROUD MAMA

I went to Captain Scholley's retirement ceremony on June 29, 2005.

Twenty-Five: SECRETS OF THE BONES

I went to the JPAC lab in Honolulu in April 2004. I had a tour of the facility and interviews with Mann, Holland, Emery, and Leney. Mann kindly answered numerous follow-up questions. Earl Swift, a reporter at the *Virginian-Pilot*, wrote *Where They Lay: Searching for America's Lost Soldiers* (Boston: Houghton-Mifflin, 2003), which follows a JPAC team in Laos. It contains an excellent explanation of mitochondrial DNA.

Judy Rudoe at the Decorative Arts department of the British Museum answered my questions about right- and left-hand wedding band traditions. Again, I used Berent's work as basic source on crew members, adding what I found at the National Archives. A distant family member, for instance, wrote to the Archives in 1981 to say that John Stocking, one of the crew, was a nom de plume for Wells Wentz. I went to the New York City Municipal Archives in search of marriage records pertaining to some of the enlisted sailors. There are files with some additional material on crew members at the Mariners' Museum library.

Other sources on forensic anthropology included Peggy Thomas, *Talking Bones: The Science of Forensic Anthropology* (New York: Facts on File, 1995). To help understand isotope analysis, I found discussions online by Kathryn Hoppe, Department of Geological and Environmental Science, Stanford University, and by Andrew Millard, et al., University of Durham.

INDEX

Numbers in bold refer to pages with illustrations

DATE	ISSUED TO

Ethel K. Smith Library
Wingate University
Wingate, NC 28174-0219